P9-CKA-396

Completing the Food Chain

Edited by Paula M. Hirschoff

and Neil G. Kotler

Completing the Food Chain

Strategies for Combating Hunger and Malnutrition

Papers and Proceedings of a Colloquium Organized by the Smithsonian Institution

Smithsonian Institution Press
Washington and London

Printed in the United States of America.

Carla M. Borden, *Editor*

The paper in this publication meets the requirements of the American National Standard for Permanence of Paper for Printed Materials Z39.48-1984.

Volumes in this series are based on annual colloquia organized at the Smithsonian Institution, in cooperation with the Kraft General Foods Foundation and the Winrock International Institute for Agricultural Research.

Previously published:

Science, Ethics, and Food, edited by Brian W. J. LeMay (Washington, D.C.: Smithsonian Institution Press, 1988).

Library of Congress Cataloging-in-Publication Data
Completing the food chain : strategies for combating hunger and malnutrition : papers and proceedings of a colloquium organized by the Smithsonian Institution / edited by Paula M. Hirschoff and Neil G. Kotler.
p. cm.
ISBN 0-87474-561-6 (Smithsonian)
ISBN 971-104-209-6 (IRRI)
1. Food supply—Congresses.
2. Food supply—Government policy—Congresses.
3. Agriculture—Congresses.
4. Agriculture and state—Congresses.
5. Agricultural assistance—Congresses.
6. Food relief—Congresses.
I. Hirschoff, Paula M.
II. Kotler, Neil G., 1941.
III. Smithsonian Institution.
HD9000.5.C627 1989
363.8′8—dc20 89-6168
CIP

Contents

List of Tables and Figures

Tables

Figures

Foreword

Robert McC. Adams
Secretary, Smithsonian Institution, Washington, D.C., United States

Among the thorniest problems confronting the world community today is the problem of food shortages and diet deficits. Attention to increasing food production is a critical factor in banishing global hunger and malnutrition. Experience has shown, however, that no single output alone can cope with the mounting challenge of feeding humankind. Rather, what is needed is a comprehensive, coherent set of strategies targeted to each and every link in the complex food chain, and their careful and synergistic orchestration.

Ample food production in itself is not enough. Rot and spoilage diminish the food supply, even though the knowledge and technology to safely store and transport food exist. Endemic diet deficiencies and health disorders demand solutions, especially since medical technologies and a growing body of knowledge of nutrient requirements and a healthy diet presently exist. Agricultural research has spurred manyfold crop and animal yields, yet the skewed distribution of scientific and technological capabilities worldwide robs the areas of the world most in need of scientific and technical wherewithal of the ability to develop their agriculture to the fullest. Political and economic factors, too, are prominent, as millions of people lack the income and other resources with which to command their fair share of food. The best techniques and resources in the world cannot overcome the ruinous effects of public policies that shortchange food supply, or reward urban populations or better-off classes at the expense of the poor.

No single body of knowledge and field of specialization alone is sufficient to unlock the will and provide the direction to overcome hunger and malnutrition. No firm formulas developed in the industrialized nations can satisfy the ecological, cultural, and social diversities that characterize the world's regions. On the other hand, new combinations of knowledge and the interrelatedness of cross-disciplinary and multisectorial efforts carry within themselves the potential for designing broad-gauged strategies for feeding and providing nourishment to the peoples of the world.

That the colloquium brings together leaders in agriculture and food science from every corner of the world and from every major discipline and sector that bears on the world food supply is particularly noteworthy, as is the fact that all of the participants have worked extensively in diverse nations and regions of the world, especially in the Third World. Generating new forms of knowledge and cooperative research lies at the heart of this international colloquium, as does its unique vantage point of recognizing that the individual consumer of food is both the starting point and the end point of food and diet self-sufficiency. The Smithsonian is proud to convene this colloquium, "Completing the Food Chain."

Acknowledgments

This book is an outgrowth of a world food colloquium convened on October 4–5, 1988, at the Smithsonian Institution in Washington, D.C. The colloquium and this volume of papers and proceedings form the second in a series of programs on international agriculture and food policy and on the means of alleviating hunger and malnutrition in the world. The first colloquium, convened on October 6–7, 1987, resulted in publication of a volume entitled *Science, Ethics, and Food* (Smithsonian Institution Press, 1988). A third colloquium, entitled "Global Sharing of Agricultural and Food Innovation and Development," with accompanying volume is planned for October 1989.

Each program was planned in conjunction with the awarding of the General Foods World Food Prize. Sponsored by the General Foods Fund, Inc., the prize is awarded to an individual of any discipline anywhere in the world who in the judgment of the selection committee has contributed profoundly to increasing the global food supply in terms of quantity, quality, or availability. The prize laureate in 1987 was Dr. M. S. Swaminathan of New Delhi, India, an architect of India's Green Revolution. The prize laureate in 1988 was Dr. Robert F. Chandler, Jr., founding director of the International Rice Research Institute in the Philippines and director of the Asian Vegetable Research and Development Center in Taiwan, who helped spearhead the Green Revolution in Asia.

Both the awarding of the World Food Prize and the convening of a world food colloquium at the Smithsonian Institution embody a common purpose: to expand knowledge of the applications of science, research, and technology in feeding the world's population; to enable scientists and policy leaders from many nations to exchange ideas and insights; and to honor leaders in food policy, agriculture, and nutrition science who have worked tirelessly to generate an ample supply of wholesome food in the world.

The colloquium "Completing the Food Chain" was organized at the Smithsonian Institution by Dr. Neil G. Kotler of the Office of Interdisciplinary Studies and Cheryl B. LaBerge of the Office of Conference Services.

Dr. Nevin S. Scrimshaw, institute professor emeritus of the Massachusetts Institute of Technology and director of the Food and Nutrition Programme of United Nations University, generously provided counsel and assistance in planning the colloquium.

Dr. John W. Mellor, director of the International Food Policy Research Institute (IFPRI) in Washington, D.C., offered substantial advice in planning the colloquium and graciously convened at IFPRI an important roundtable discussion, the proceedings of which are reproduced in this volume. In addition, Dr. Mellor generously agreed to write an introduction to this volume.

The colloquium benefited from the guidance of Dr. Robert S. Hoffmann, assistant secretary for research, and of Dr. David Challinor, former assistant secretary for research, and the special oversight and experience of Dr. Wilton S. Dillon, director of the Office of Interdisciplinary Studies, all of the Smithsonian Institution.

Edward S. Williams, administrator of the General Foods World Food Prize, at the Winrock International Institute for Agricultural Development in Morrilton, Arkansas, provided substantial assistance in coordinating the colloquium and the World Food Prize award ceremonies. Edith Yalong of the IFPRI staff always has been generous in assisting in the colloquium arrangements. Robert Bordonaro and Laurie Goldberg of IFPRI provided excellent support services. Stephany F. Knight coordinated the World Food Prize reception and ceremony at the National Museum of Natural History. Teresa Johnson and John W. Franklin of the Office of Interdisciplinary Studies helped facilitate the program.

Acknowledgment is made of the high-quality work of Catherine M. Morris, assistant manager of the Smithsonian's Office of Staff, Volunteer, and Intern Services, and of Vivian B. Morris, a Smithsonian volunteer, in transcribing the colloquium proceedings for publication. Elaine Sullivan, a vice president of Editorial Experts, Inc., in Alexandria, Virginia, supervised the preparation of the manuscript. Jeanne M. Sexton of the Smithsonian Institution Press provided substantial assistance in preparing the materials for publication.

Carla M. Borden, senior program specialist in the Office of Interdisciplinary Studies, worked closely and tirelessly with the editors and the publisher of this volume and served as copyeditor of the manuscript.

Her careful overseeing of the manuscript development is gratefully acknowledged.

The Office of Disease Prevention and Health Promotion, Office of the Assistant Secretary for Health, U.S. Department of Health and Human Services, and the Agricultural Research Service, U.S. Department of Agriculture, facilitated publication of this volume with their support.

Acknowledgments would not be complete without expressing deep appreciation to the General Foods Fund, Inc., and to A. S. Clausi, chairman of the Council of Advisors of the General Foods World Food Prize, for their generous support on behalf of the world food colloquium and the resulting publications. Their assistance in so many ways has made these events possible.

Introduction

John W. Mellor
Director, International Food Policy Research Institute, Washington, D.C., United States

The General Foods World Food Prize is a grand recognition of the critical role of food in determining the state of health, sense of well-being, and livelihood of peoples everywhere. Roughly a quarter of the world's people, however, hardly recognize food's importance; being blessed with its abundance, they take it for granted. But for the three-quarters of the world's population living in developing countries, its importance strikes them daily; and for the one billion people with grossly inadequate diets, the need for decent food is deeply felt.

Uncertainty of food supply brings a terrible urgency to daily life: not just the immediate impact on physical and mental health, but also the indirect effects on income, purchasing power, and livelihood. In developing countries, even those people who enjoy an ample food supply because their incomes are more than enough to buy the essentials of life may find that income greatly diminished as a result of a drop in food production. Decline in food production noticeably diminishes income; its effects ripple throughout the economy, resulting in reduced demand for luxury agricultural commodities like livestock products, fruits, and vegetables, or for nonagricultural products like rickshaw rides and textiles. This reduction in demand for labor-intensive goods and services, in turn, will sharply reduce the employment and purchasing power of large numbers of poor people.

The award of the 1988 General Foods World Food Prize to Bob Chandler is testimony to the critical importance of improved agricultural technology in completing the food chain. In most parts of the world, land is a limited resource, as it soon will become throughout the world.

We cannot forever increase the supply of food by just bringing additional land into production. As country after country grows beyond its land frontier, each must rely on increasing the productivity of the existing land. This was the case in India a few decades ago and in Bangladesh even earlier, while in Thailand this may not be the case for another decade or so. Similarly, some African countries are simply running out of usable land, while others will not run out for another decade or so. Indeed, we are already discovering in many parts of the world that the trend toward increased annual crop production to meet minimum subsistence needs is occurring on land that simply cannot sustain it indefinitely. This land can be restored and returned to uses that are sustainable only if we increase production on better, less fragile lands, and that depends on improvements in agricultural technology and productivity.

In all of these processes, Bob Chandler, the International Rice Research Institute (IRRI), of which he was the founding director, and the entire system of international and national agricultural research institutes have been major factors. They have already brought us a Green Revolution in Asia and can in the future produce further sustainable increases in agricultural production.

Completing the Food Chain

This colloquium volume emphasizes in paper after paper that technology is central to completing the food chain, but it certainly is not a sufficient condition. Even more remains to be done.

Nevin Scrimshaw forcefully argues that developing an ample world supply of food that meets the dietary needs of people depends on improvements in every link along the food chain—research, training, and technology, food storage and distribution, nutrition and public health, rural income, employment, and food policy. Other colloquium papers examine the food chain across different regions and conclude that strategies to improve the food supply will vary from one region to another. The papers also highlight the fact that there are many different disciplines and areas of knowledge, research, and enlightenment that significantly affect the advances that can be made in completing the food chain. Yet the cataloging of the elements of the food chain is not sufficient; analysis of each element and their interactions also has to be accomplished.

How can we make progress in the face of such complexity? How can development occur? How can we complete the food chain? First, we must recognize the reality. Countries that have successfully completed the food chain—the industrialized countries—have highly complex societies and economies. The work of vast numbers of people educated in countless institutions developed over decades is coordinated by a complex mix of human planning and market forces, each of which brings constant readjustments through continuous interactions.

Second, we need to bring some order to the food policy and development process. We must recognize, as Nevin Scrimshaw has told us, the major links in the food chain. Third, we must recognize the need for a massive expansion and reorganization of human capital. We must continue to have large numbers of people at all levels of education, particularly higher education, to help us understand these problems in their diverse and varying forms and to work toward solutions. The appropriate institutions must then be created to organize people for effective action. One of the more difficult roles a government can play is deciding what complementary functions are best kept as public ones and how they may best be coordinated with private activities. Achieving a sound balance between the thoughtful hand and the unseen hand is itself an important part in closing the food chain. Perhaps no one can understand completely the food chain as a whole and how to close the various links. What we must understand, however, is that some people must cut across those links while relying on markets to carry out a critical role.

Fourth, while recognizing the myriad tasks to be performed, it must be kept in mind that at any one point in time and space there may be specific links in the chain that are missing or particularly weak. We should then concentrate our efforts on these, on the assumption that other links in the food chain will remain intact—a diagnostic task of identifying what to emphasize and when. Governments cannot concentrate on everything at once. They can, however, maintain many things at once. That is an important distinction.

The Relation between Production and Distribution

There is at present particular confusion about the relation between production of food and distribution of food. Some say that lack of food in the hands of the poor of the world is due to insufficient production; others, that if you divide the total supply of food in the world by the total number of people, the result will show that an adequate diet does exist for all, and so the problem is not one of production but of distribution. In fact, a term has been coined to deal with the distributional problem—namely, "food entitlement." This assumes that people need food but lack the claim and entitlement to it, because they lack the necessary purchasing power.

What we need to face up to, however, is that all the food in the world is not going to be evenly distributed at any foreseeable time. Dealing with the problem purely through redistribution would mean, first of all, massive reductions in food consumption in the high-income countries of the world—eliminating the bulk of livestock consumption, for example—so that grain could be distributed to the poor in other parts of the world. Second, the poor would be placed on a permanent dole if they were to receive food solely through redistribution. Third, the quantity to be redistributed would increase every year with increasing population. That is not a workable solution.

The core point is that the bulk of the poor reside in the rural areas of low-income countries. If we are to make them self-reliant, we must find a way to enable them to generate adequate income through their own efforts and work, so that they can purchase the food they need. We find that in those rural areas we cannot increase the incomes of the massive numbers of people—frequently half of the population in low-income countries, amounting to at least a quarter of the world population—without increasing food production. Stepped-up food production would increase the supply available, which, if not purchased at existing prices, will result in declines in prices and, therefore, in a smaller share of the income of the very poor that is spent on food. The effect of this is to increase the incomes of the very poor who, after all, spend most of their income on food.

But far more important is that in many areas of the world relatively well-off people sell much of the food that they produce and use the proceeds to buy other goods and services that are quite labor intensive in their production. This creates employment for the landless and small farmers that, in turn, gives them the purchasing power to feed themselves. Thus, the purchasing power for some people comes from the production of food by other people. We find that in the developing countries of Asia peasant farmers spend 40 percent of their increments in income on locally produced nonagricultural goods and services, and another 20 percent on agricultural commodities that are labor intensive, rather than land intensive. Where the distribution of land is reasonably broad, this process works exceedingly well.

Thus we cannot separate the production issue from the distribution issue—which brings us back to Bob Chandler's achievements, the miracle of high-yielding rice varieties, IRRI, and agricultural research. The process begins with technological change that raises production within a limited set of resources. The purchasing power this generates creates the demand for goods and services that the poor are able to produce, thereby providing them the income and entitlement with which to purchase food. It is truly a food chain; food production and food distribution are parts of that chain.

The Need for Research

We need a wide range of research programs if the food chain is to be completed. To find answers, questions have to be properly defined. We need to know who the poor are and where they are located, so that we can identify the kinds of technology that are necessary for agriculture, how that technology can be adapted, to what extent inputs are needed, how they are to be provided, and to what extent infrastructure such as roads and power plants is needed for the technologies to work. We must know the extent to which capital for growth can be generated domestically, and how much must come from other sources. And we need to know how much foreign aid is necessary if we are to save ourselves several years in completing the food chain to benefit the billion people of the world who are hungry. Thus, some trained people must do research in the agricultural sciences, developing input supply systems and adequate price policies for governments to effectuate. Others must raise the difficult economic, social, and anthropological questions that have to be answered in this process.

Eliminating Hunger

It is time to talk about accelerating the completion of the food chain. We now know broadly what needs to be done. That is clear from the colloquium and the succession of General Foods World Food prizes that have been awarded. We, of course, lack many details and perhaps even a consensus about what we know, so that appropriate action may at times seem unclear.

But we need to recognize some simple facts about who and where the world's poor are. Some 700 million people lack sufficient energy intake to maintain activity at a level of 40 percent higher than their basic metabolic rate—the basic amount of energy to sit up and stand occasionally. Roughly half of these 700 million are in South Asia. Another quarter of them are in subsaharan Africa, and 10 percent of them are in China. The remaining 15–20 percent live in Latin America, North Africa and the Middle East, and Southeast Asia.

Most important, the bulk of the world's poor live in the poorer countries. There is a severe resource constraint to closing the food chain for those people through the processes of growth and distribution. Those developing countries that have been raising their income relatively rapidly over the last few decades have been reducing the number of people in dismal poverty quite rapidly. The numbers of the poor, however, are increasing in the very poorest countries. It is hypocritical for people in rich countries to deplore such poverty without recognizing that resource transfers can save ten or fifteen years in the process of eliminating hunger.

It is particularly important to note that roughly on the order of one-third of those poor people live within reach of high-potential agricultural land in the poor countries. In other words, we can complete the food chain through technological change in agriculture, infrastructure investment, and in the other processes that accompanied the Green Revolution. We simply have to bring more resources to bear in those areas if we want to make rapid progress. We could, in a relatively short period of time, five to fifteen years, eliminate poverty for at least 250 million of the poor who live in the high-potential areas in the very poor countries.

Why are we not doing that? Is the reason that we do not care? Do we really believe that there is a major form of poverty that cannot be dealt with relatively easily? Do we not believe that in very poor countries there is a scarcity of resources for dealing with these problems? I think that ten or fifteen years ago, we did not have enough knowledge to adequately address these questions. As a result, foreign assistance efforts were not effectively carried out as a means of reducing the poverty level. And this has left us a bit jaded and cynical about future prospects. But the knowledge base for recognizing the processes for eliminating poverty is now ample and sound, and this calls for concerted action.

The problem is more difficult with respect to the few hundred million poor who live in the middle-income developing countries. These countries have experienced rapid growth, are doubling their per capita incomes within ten to fifteen years, and are thereby rapidly bringing down poverty levels. Their poverty, however, tends to be concentrated in rural areas with lower agricultural potential, while much of the poverty in the high-potential areas has been eliminated. It is difficult for these countries to keep their growth rate sufficiently high to reduce poverty and at the same time place substantial resources in the poorest areas. There is thus a place for foreign assistance in this context.

We have learned at the colloquium that completing the food chain involves the functioning of many interlocking components in a complex process. Several disciplines must be brought to bear on this process, and it is also evident that solutions will vary from place to place. But we know where the priorities must lie, even if we cannot do everything at once.

It is time that we pursued the hope our understanding offers.

Readings

Lele, U., and J. W. Mellor. 1981. "Technological Change, Distributive Bias, and Labor Transfer in a Two-Sector Economy." *Oxford Economic Papers* 33, no. 3 (November):426–41.

Mellor, J. W. 1986. "Agriculture on the Road to Industrialization." In *Development Strategies Reconsidered,* ed. J. P. Lewis and V. Kallab. New Brunswick, N.J.: Transaction Books for the Overseas Development Council, 67–89.

———. 1976. *The New Economics of Growth.* Ithaca: Cornell University Press.

———. 1966. *The Economics of Agricultural Development.* Ithaca: Cornell University Press.

Mellor, J. W., and R. Ahmed, eds. 1988. *Agricultural Price Policy for Developing Countries.* Baltimore: Johns Hopkins University Press.

Mellor, J. W., C. L. Delgado, and M. J. Blackie, eds. 1987. *Accelerating Food Production in Sub-Saharan Africa.* Baltimore: Johns Hopkins University Press.

Mellor, J. W., and G. Desai, eds. 1985. *Agricultural Change and Rural Poverty.* Baltimore: Johns Hopkins University Press.

CHAPTER 1

Completing the Food Chain

From Production to Consumption

Nevin S. Scrimshaw
Institute Professor Emeritus, Massachusetts Institute of Technology, Cambridge, Massachusetts, United States

We live in a world in which the developing countries have more malnourished people than ever before, while most industrialized countries stock huge surpluses of food—a world in which social inequity is the root cause of most hunger.

We live in a world in which countries that have the least food lose up to 40 percent of grain crops and more than 50 percent of fruits and vegetables to rodents, insects, mold, and spoilage. Yet such losses are largely prevented in the industrialized countries.

We live in a world in which most people know little or nothing of the principles of good nutrition, even though reliable information about food and nutrient requirements for good health is widely available.

We live in a world in which iodine and iron deficiencies affect a third to a half of developing-country populations with adverse consequences for morbidity, cognitive development, and work performance. Yet fortification of salt can cheaply and effectively prevent these deficiencies.

We live in a world in which many children still go blind from avitaminosis A, even though green and yellow vegetables or an inexpensive vitamin A capsule can prevent this blindness.

We live in a world in which agricultural research has increased crop and animal yields beyond the wildest dreams of fifty years ago, and biotechnology is certain to bring further improvements. Yet most developing countries lag far behind in the application of these technologies, and the gap in these countries between the yields of the most advanced farmers and the poorer ones is often still greater.

We live in a world in which famines still occur even when national food supplies are adequate because, for basically political reasons, some population subgroups lack the capacity to produce or purchase food. This is the case even when famines are precipitated by drought or other disasters, such as war and civil disturbances.

We live in a world in which inexorable population pressures have led to the loss of most forests on the Asian subcontinent and are resulting in the rapid destruction of the world's remaining tropical forests in Latin America and Africa, with serious effects on climate and loss of species. Similar pressures, along with the lack of responsible land management, have led to increasing desertification in the Sahel and the loss of topsoil in many other regions.

In this kind of world, there are no simple or direct cause-and-effect relationships between food production and hunger.

Clearly, agricultural research is important to developing countries, and agricultural extension efforts should be intensified, but there is no assurance that their benefits will reach the poor.

Clearly, more attention must be focused on field and harvesting losses and postharvest food conservation, storage, and distribution, but this will not ensure consumption of the food that is saved.

Clearly, nutrition and health education is required to give people the knowledge to make wise food choices, yet this will not give them the land to raise food or the money to purchase it.

Clearly, policies and programs are required to help the poor acquire food through increased employment, better wages, and, for the most vulnerable, appropriate entitlements, yet the success of such efforts depends on adequate food production and wise food choices.

These examples should be sufficient to make the point that achieving food security and overcoming world hunger require the shared knowledge and cooperative work of a variety of disciplines and professions, including agriculture, health, nutrition, social science, public policy, administration, and management. Every step in the food chain requires attention if hunger and malnutrition are to be banished and if the food system is to become environmentally sustainable (see table 1–1).

This colloquium will emphasize the need to accelerate agricultural

Table 1–1.

Actions to Prevent Hunger and Malnutrition

Maintain Food Production	Improve Food Utilization
Reduce Food Losses	Improve International Policies
Improve Access to Food	Provide for Natural Disasters

research, to take full advantage of the contributions of biotechnology, to avert preharvest food losses, and to ensure postharvest food conservation, storage, and distribution. It will emphasize the need for nutrition and health education and for policies that give poor people a chance to acquire food through employment opportunities, better wages, and appropriate entitlement programs. The colloquium will recommend actions to improve access to food and food utilization and to strengthen international food policies and disaster relief programs. All of these issues will be examined from both regional and disciplinary perspectives. The conquest of world hunger and malnutrition, it should be evident, depends primarily on the synergism of multidisciplinary efforts within each country.

Maintenance of Food Production

The first essential element is to ensure that food production keeps pace with demand (see table 1–2). Agricultural research that merely increases productivity and adds to surpluses in North America and Europe will not solve world food problems. Research is needed that is applicable to food production in developing countries. It must take into account constraints on the availability of land and water, local inputs to production and/or foreign exchange for food purchase, environmental factors, and national food preferences. It should also take account of the traditional roles of women in agriculture.

Words are not adequate to convey the vital role of Green Revolution technologies in improving human life throughout the world. The development of higher-yielding maize and wheat varieties by George Harrar, Edward Welhausen, Norman Borlaug, and other researchers at the Rockefeller Foundation Agricultural Research Center (CIMMYT) in Chapingo, Mexico, initiated what is now referred to as the Green Revolution. No single development has been more significant than the early

Table 1–2.

The Essentials of Food Production

Agricultural Research and Extension	Adequate Prices to Farmers
Application of Biotechnology	Improved Rural Social Justice
Sustainable Agricultural Systems	Supportive Trade Policies
Rural Credit and Accessible Inputs	

success of the International Rice Research Institute (IRRI) under the leadership of Robert F. Chandler, Jr. Rice is the staple cereal for a large segment of the world's population; in Asia it is the labor-intensive crop of small farmers. Dr. M. S. Swaminathan, the General Foods World Food Prize laureate last year, not only led the adaptation and successful introduction in India of Green Revolution strategies from Mexico, but also continued and expanded Chandler's pioneering work on rice at IRRI. The resulting yield increases not only assured enough of these cereals for Asia's huge population, but also have brought the benefits of increased income to rural households.

The achievements of CIMMYT and IRRI have led to subsequent achievements by the eleven other institutes that comprise the Consultative Group on International Agricultural Research (CGIAR) network and the Asian Vegetable Research and Development Center (AVRDC) in Taiwan, also created by Chandler. These institutes collaborate and provide technical support to regional and national agricultural research institutions in all regions of the world. Support of this research must continue to receive high priority.

It is fashionable in some circles to focus on what the Green Revolution technologies have not accomplished. But these deficiencies reflect national social and political factors, not the potential of the Green Revolution technologies and agricultural research to improve yields and the well-being of farmers.[1] Green Revolution cereal technologies in the 1960s rapidly increased yields in Mexico. For a brief period, Mexico was self-sufficient in wheat and corn. However, failure to check one of the world's highest rates of population growth, combined with national policies that have deprived small farmers of the benefits of agricultural extension, credit, and fair prices for their crops, have resulted once again in a rapid rise in food imports.[2] Policies of the Sistema Alimentaria Mexicana (SAM) temporarily reversed this trend in 1981–82, but the government that took office in 1983 failed to continue them.[3]

Green Revolution technologies in India facilitated production gains that accompanied agricultural policy changes in the 1960s. This resulted in a short time in grain reserves of 20 million tons; by 1988, reserves totaled 309 million tons. However, these large reserves have not eliminated either poverty or hunger.

A recent study by Mahabub Hossain[4] for IFPRI on the Green Revolution's impact in Bangladesh concluded that for villages where nearly three-fifths of the cropped land was planted with modern varieties of rice, agricultural income was about 40 percent higher and total household income 29 percent higher than in villages where less than one-tenth of the area was planted with modern varieties. An estimated 32 percent of the population in the better developed villages was still living in poverty, only 10 percent less than in the underdeveloped villages.

In Asian countries with greater social equity, such as China, Korea, and Taiwan, the rice technologies pioneered by IRRI have helped eradicate the extremes of rural poverty. This has not occurred in the Philippines, despite the fact that higher-yielding rice cultivars originated there, because of widespread rural poverty, tiny plots, and limited technical knowledge.[5] These examples make clear that agricultural research achievements need to be matched by government policy achievements. On the other hand, without the benefits of agricultural research, policymakers in developing countries for the most part will not be able to devise measures that will feed their growing populations.

Advances in biotechnology and genetic engineering are reducing the time needed to develop improved plant cultivars. Moreover, the technological possibilities of aquaculture are already providing added food supplies in some developing countries.

Agricultural systems result in enormous quantities of cellulosic, starchy, and fruit and vegetable residues[6] that can be used to produce further residues that can be treated with microorganisms to yield products suitable for animal feeding and, in some cases, single-cell protein for animal and human feeding. In addition, great amounts of animal and human waste could be much more effectively used than at present for the production of energy and fertilizer.

Significant, sustained agricultural improvement requires a national leadership that not only is committed to agricultural development but also has the understanding to make wise policy decisions.[7] Unfortunately, policy decisions in developing countries that are based on short-term political goals often have disastrous long-term consequences for agriculture. Examples include artificially low prices for farm products to please the more politically powerful urban populations, discrimination in favor of cash crops to obtain foreign exchange, counterproductive taxation policies, and trade policies that negatively affect national food production.

A great deal of attention has been paid to the role of agricultural price policies in food production. John W. Mellor and R. Ahmed have documented the profound effect of agricultural prices on growth, equity, and stability throughout a developing economy.[8] They noted the frequency with which governments have intervened with policies that grossly distort prices.

Governments must not only avoid policies that discourage food production, but they also must act positively to enable small farmers to obtain the agricultural inputs needed to utilize Green Revolution technologies, gain access to good extension services, and store and sell their crops advantageously. Governments must also adopt trade policies that avoid damage to domestic agricultural production. Foreign credit and foreign aid cannot significantly affect food security and development if domestic policies result in a misallocation of resources.[9]

Sound policies must be based on the conviction and commitment of national governments. External advisers and international lending agencies cannot effectively impose policies, and their advice is not always in the best interests of the country. In fact, individual experts or teams of advisers have had remarkably little influence on national policies. There is no substitute for knowledge and understanding on the part of individuals and institutions within every country. Indigenous agents can evaluate exogenous advice and influences on the basis of intimate knowledge of local physical, biological, and social factors. Moreover, until a country develops this capability, its political leaders are unlikely to acquire the knowledge and motivation needed to promote sound agricultural and social development.

Reduction of Food Losses

Measures to reduce food losses represent another major element of strategies to increase food production and consumption (see table 1–3). In some areas of developing countries rats consume half of the cereal crops in the field before harvest. In West Africa and the Near East, swarms of locusts can eat as much as 80,000 tons of plants in a single day.[10] Some of the largest preharvest losses result from plant and animal diseases that could be controlled by resistant varieties or by pesticides.

Food losses also occur because of inappropriate methods of harvesting and processing crops.[11] In many tropical countries, mold and spoilage, resulting from poor handling, lack of marketing, and inappropriate storage facilities, destroy huge quantities of fruit and vegetables. Moreover, anyone who looks at a handful of chaff from a traditional Asian village rice mill will recognize that as much as 10 percent of the edible rice kernel is unnecessarily lost to human nutrition. Additional losses in harvesting, drying, transportation, and storage are more difficult to ascertain. However, cumulative physical losses can amount to as much as 40 percent and are accompanied by a deterioration in quality.[12] Because of poor home and village storage, more than a quarter of the corn and wheat can be lost to rodents and insects.

Agricultural policies that waste energy, despoil tropical forests, and diminish productivity through soil depletion, erosion, salination, and desertification must be replaced by sustainable agricultural practices. It is time to view the earth as a closed system. Satellites are now capable of collecting data on the earth as a whole, and new supercomputers and information systems can store and process large sets of data and run complex coupled models of the earth's subsystems. This information should be made available to improve land and water utilization. The microcomputer's capacity to store, analyze, retrieve, and exchange infor-

Table 1–3.

The Essentials of Food Loss Reduction

More Efficient Milling of Grains
Protection from Rodents and Insects
Handling and Storage to Reduce Spoilage

mation to help solve national food and nutrition problems must be more fully utilized in all developing countries.

It is well known that oilseed meals fed to nonruminant animals, such as poultry and swine, have about 7 percent efficiency of conversion compared to an estimated 70 percent if the same protein is consumed directly. Although Western countries use soy mainly for animal feeding, in Asia it has long been a major source of protein in human diets. Asian methods of preparing soy, such as tofu and tempeh, are becoming common in other countries, and soy concentrates and isolates are now widely used in processed foods. Groundnuts, sesame, and sunflower meals, prepared in both traditional and modern ways, can also be palatable and nutritious substitutes for animal protein in human diets.

World food supplies would be grossly inadequate if the rest of the world consumed animal protein at the same rate as the advanced countries. Moreover, these levels are neither necessary nor desirable for good health. Meat consumption in many industrialized countries is declining for health reasons. In developing countries, however, meat consumption can be expected to rise as purchasing power grows.

Animal protein supplies in developing countries can be increased by developing sustainable agricultural systems, such as bioregenerative communities; utilizing microbiology to convert agricultural wastes for animal feeding; establishing more multitrophic production systems on land and in the water; and exploiting ranches where native fauna live on their natural food sources. The meat produced on such ranches does not threaten health as does the fat of domestic animals, because wild animal fat has a favorable ratio of polyunsaturated to saturated fatty acids.

Improved Access to Food

The concept of improving access to food has a double meaning: not only facilitating the distribution and marketing of foods but also increasing the ability of poor households to acquire food (see table 1–4). Particular-

Table 1–4.

The Essentials to Improving Access to Food

Efficient Distribution and Marketing	Entitlement Programs for the Most Vulnerable
Policies to Increase Employment and Improve Wages	Equitable Access to Agricultural Land

ly important are measures to help landless agricultural laborers acquire or gain access to land to raise food for their families. Some countries need land reform to decrease the concentration of good agricultural land, much of it inefficiently used or left idle in the hands of a few extended families, as is the case in Guatemala and El Salvador.[13]

The potential of urban gardens to supplement the food supply of poor families is consistently underestimated,[14] yet growing urban populations in most developing countries cannot be expected to produce a significant percentage of their own food. For them, the capacity to acquire food depends on purchasing power, which is closely related to employment opportunities, a major concern to any government.

In many countries, food prices are unnecessarily high because of the proportion of food costs attributable to middlemen, particularly during seasonal shortages. One of the achievements of the Companía Nacional de Subsistencias Populares (CONASUPO) in Mexico has been to make food available to the poor year-round at fair prices and to provide competition that keeps retail prices down. On the Asian subcontinent, "fair price" shops serve a similar purpose, but for a smaller range of commodities.[15] At an absolute minimum, every developing country should aim to improve its food distribution and marketing system to ensure that food prices are not unnecessarily high.

However, fair or even subsidized food prices will not prevent hunger and malnutrition if people are too poor to purchase food. Every country needs some kind of social safety net to keep people from going hungry. Local resources, administrative capacities, and external assistance determine what form this support takes in a given country. Food stamps probably provide the most effective targeting but require a level of administrative and other resources that often is not available in most developing countries.[16] However, a number of countries have found alternative methods of targeting needy populations to increase the cost effectiveness of programs using limited national resources.

It is evident that continued rapid population growth in food-short countries will further decrease agricultural land per capita and increase the magnitude of the effort required to meet food needs. Efforts to slow this growth without improvements in social equity have generally failed, as in Egypt, India, and Mexico. On the other hand, family planning efforts have been much more successful in China, Korea, Singapore, Taiwan, Costa Rica, Cuba, and other countries that have improved health services, education, and income distribution. There can be no relaxation of the crusade to stabilize the world's population.

Improvement of Food Utilization

Measures to improve food utilization include meeting nutrient requirements (not just food-energy needs), processing to preserve nutritional value, fortifying selected staple foods, nutrition education to improve food choices, health education, and measures to reduce infectious disease (see table 1–5).

There is a mistaken notion among some nutritionists, which has generated confusion among economists and plant breeders, that if dietary energy needs are supplied, requirements for protein and other essential nutrients will also be met. This notion, however, does not take into account the constraints on food selection that exist in some developing countries. It is true that traditional diets in most developing countries meet adult protein needs when foods are consumed in sufficient quantity to meet normal energy needs. But this is true only when populations can afford these diets in sufficient quantities.

The 1985 report on Energy and Protein Requirements issued by the Food and Agriculture Organization (FAO), the World Health Organization (WHO), and the United Nations University (UNU)[17] analyzed new data, much of it from investigations sponsored by UNU of the amount of protein needed for nitrogen balance.[18] The research demonstrated that adult protein requirements were about one-third higher than had been assumed during the preceding twelve years—a partial explanation of the origins of the myth mentioned above. However, the most important explanation is the failure to recognize that a significant proportion of

Table 1–5.

The Essentials to Improving Food Utilization

Meeting All Nutrient Requirements	Nutrition Education to Improve Food Choices
Immunization against Preventable Disease	Processing to Preserve Nutritional Value
Health Education to Reduce Infectious Disease	Fortification of Selected Staple Foods

developing country populations cannot afford their "traditional" diets. Instead, economic circumstances force them to depend almost entirely on a cereal, root, or tuber staple.

To be adequate, diets based on such a staple must be complemented by a better, and usually more costly, protein source. In northern Latin America, where the staple is maize, a rise in the price of beans can be devastating. In Southeast Asia, where the staple is rice, an adequate diet for the poor usually depends on the availability of soy. On the Asian subcontinent, where wheat or sorghum is the staple cereal, legumes are critical to an adequate diet for much of the population.

However, the quantity and quality of protein in the usual diet cannot be taken for granted in certain other circumstances, even when energy needs are met. One example is the widespread practice of giving low-protein starchy gruels to weanlings, especially when they have symptoms of infection. As a matter of fact, the frequent infections characteristic of preschool children in developing countries make an increased percentage of protein calories necessary for repletion and catch-up growth.

There is another significant reason why a diet may be deficient in protein, even when the ratio of protein to calories appears to be adequate. When people do not consume enough food because they are sick or poor, they can adapt to a lower energy intake over time by reducing their physical activity. However, there is no comparable physiological mechanism for adapting to a low-protein intake. On the contrary, diarrheal and other infections that are common under these conditions are likely to increase the need for protein and can even precipitate clinical protein deficiency.

Moreover, human beings do not live by dietary energy and protein alone, but require a variety of vitamins and minerals as well. For example, even when both energy and protein are adequate, a lack of iron can impair cognition, resistance to infection, work capacity, and productivity. A lack of vitamin A reduces resistance to infection and causes a drying and then softening of the cornea that results in blindness. Iodine deficiency during pregnancy causes a range of disorders in the child, from cretinous dwarfism to mild degrees of cognitive and hearing impairment. Other long-banished nutritional deficiency diseases, such as scurvy and pellagra, are reappearing under the extreme conditions experienced by refugees in Africa.

Meeting food needs, therefore, involves meeting requirements for all essential nutrients. A diet that is deficient in one or more nutrients is wasteful. The work of the Asian Vegetable Research and Development Center is particularly important because vegetables improve the nutritional adequacy of diets that are based on a cereal or tuber staple. Chandler's work at AVRDC on breeding heat-tolerant vegetables for the tropics is another major contribution he has made to food security in developing countries.[19]

The most obvious solution to obtaining an adequate diet is to improve the individual's capability to acquire food and to make wise choices among available foods with the help of nutrition education. Other measures can help to promote the optimum utilization of food, such as methods of storing and processing that preserve or even enhance its nutritional value. Moreover, nutrient content can be improved during processing by such methods as fortifying cereal flours with B vitamins, iron, and calcium, adding iodine and iron to salt, adding vitamin A to sugar during the refining process, and treating milk with ultraviolet rays to enhance its vitamin D activity.

Among the low-income populations of developing countries, infectious disease is a major factor in precipitating malnutrition.[20] Particularly for preschool children, the high morbidity from diarrheal and respiratory diseases and from the common communicable diseases of childhood has multiple adverse effects on nutrition. These include the metabolic loss of nutrients in the urine as a stress response, reduction in the absorption of food nutrients when the gastrointestinal tract is involved, internal diversion and sequestering of nutrients as part of the body's resistance mechanisms, and reduced food intake.

For this reason, children whose diet is borderline in protein may develop kwashiorkor as the consequence of repeated episodes of infection. Similarly, infections can precipitate a corresponding clinical deficiency in diets lacking in vitamin A or any other specific nutrient. In individuals with iron deficiency, anemia can occur as the result of blood loss due to hookworm disease or schistosomiasis, and to the sequestering of iron from hemolyzed red blood cells in malaria, despite a dietary intake of iron that would otherwise be adequate.

The issue is complicated by the fact that even relatively mild degrees of specific nutritional deficiencies reduce resistance to most infections and increase their prevalence and severity. The relationship is synergistic in the sense that the combined impact of malnutrition and infection is greater than the effect of either alone. For this reason, measures to reduce infection or its consequences, such as immunization, control of parasitic diseases, improved environmental sanitation and personal hygiene, and oral rehydration for diarrheal cases, result in improved food utilization and reduced malnutrition.

When the primary cause of malnutrition is absolute poverty, nutrition education can accomplish little. Even modest improvements in household income do not always lead to improved nutrition, because additional funds may be spent on prestige foods of lower nutritional value or on consumer items.[21] In the latter circumstances, nutrition education can contribute to better utilization of available food supplies. It is now evident from many studies that dietary habits can be modified when people perceive such change as advantageous to them.

Food processing procedures that favor nutrient conservation can have a significant effect. When Great Britain suffered from food shortages during World War II, the nutritional status of the population actually improved, primarily because of the use of less refined flour in making bread, which resulted in higher protein and vitamin B content.

Improvement of International Policies

In past decades it was fashionable to attribute a lack of development, including food shortages, to colonialism and neocolonialism. However, this so-called dependency thesis can no longer account for the differences among developing countries.[22] I have argued that the primary responsibility for hunger and malnutrition lies with national policies rather than external factors, although it is clear that the latter can help or hinder the development process. For example, U.S. eagerness to make agricultural surpluses available at concessionary prices has, in some instances, discouraged the application of adequate national policies and resources to the agricultural sector. India's situation in the 1950s is an example.

Internal agricultural subsidies and food import restrictions of the industrialized countries narrow the market options of developing countries.[23] When OPEC succeeded in more than doubling oil prices in 1973, the cost of fuel for irrigation pumps became prohibitive for many farmers in India, and the sharp rise in the cost of nitrogen fertilizer markedly curtailed its use. The oil shock shattered the development plans of many developing countries throughout the world.

For the poorest and most debt-ridden countries, the economic adjustment policies of the International Monetary Fund limit national policy choices and often result in decisions that reduce social services and increase poverty. So alarming was this trend that the United Nations Subcommittee on Nutrition (SCN) held a special symposium during its 1986 meeting at the United Nations University headquarters in Tokyo. Led by the United Nations International Children's Emergency Fund (UNICEF) and WHO, SCN launched an effort to promote "adjustment policies with a human face." The World Bank and regional development banks significantly influence the way in which national resources are used. If the projects they support turn out badly, as happens far more often than anyone cares to admit, they hinder rather than assist the efforts of developing countries to help themselves. There is far too little objective evaluation of the impact of intervention programs designed to improve food and nutrition in developing countries, despite the hundreds of millions of dollars that these programs cost.

The evaluation that is being done is generally either process evaluation or the subjective conclusions of an individual consultant or consultant team. In recent years, a joint program of UNU and UNICEF has successfully helped anthropologists in twenty-six developing countries to determine the impact of nutrition and primary health care programs. By spending several days with individual households employing participant observation and structured but open-ended surveys, an experienced evaluator can usually determine not only whether a program is having positive effects on the health of household members, but also why a given program is being accepted or rejected.

This kind of information is not obtained from conventional surveys, no matter how extensive and costly they are. Several agencies are using an approach known as Rapid Assessment Procedures (RAP) to evaluate health and nutrition programs, food-for-work programs, reforestation projects, and other types of intervention.[24] With an investment of $5,000 to $20,000 and two to six weeks of time, this evaluation technique can make a major contribution to judging and improving the effectiveness of intervention programs designed to raise the food and nutrition status of developing countries.

Provision for Natural Disasters

While in general I accept Amaryta Sen's concept that famines in modern times are due fundamentally to lack of entitlements,[25] national governments and external agencies can do a great deal to mitigate their effects, regardless of the precipitating cause. To prepare for a possible famine, food reserves should be stored, plans developed to mobilize transport, and civil servants trained in disaster relief. However, the very circumstances that make countries susceptible to famine often prevent them from responding appropriately to the threat of food shortage. Elaborate early warning systems sponsored by international assistance agencies are of little help if the warnings are not properly heeded.

Because natural and man-made disasters will continue to strike populations that lack the resources to cope, most developing countries will require international assistance in such circumstances. Floods, earthquakes, droughts, and the influx of refugees from war or civil disturbance reinforce the need for agencies that can respond quickly and appropriately. This is not the case at the present time. Assistance has often been poorly coordinated and sometimes inappropriate or useless. Some aid agencies have competed rather than cooperated with each other.

India, with its vast experience and a well-developed civil service, does an excellent job of handling relief when famine threatens. Its achievement in feeding nearly fifteen million refugees from west Bangladesh in 1976 was without parallel.[26] However, few countries have this managerial capacity. Relief agencies must adjust their policies to this reality.

A major proposal for a system of food reserves was generated at the 1974 World Food Conference in Rome. At that time world food supplies had dropped to only twenty-eight days of supply, it was estimated, and were judged to be vulnerable to unforeseen events. However, the industrialized countries were unwilling to bear the cost of such a system. The conference, however, did call attention to the urgency of world food problems and established the World Food Council as a continuing forum in which population and food issues could be brought to the attention of governments.

It is noteworthy that the North American drought that reduced wheat, maize, and soybean production by up to one-third in 1988 caused little global concern and little fluctuation in food prices. The reason, of course, was the large stores of food. Food reserves have helped India cope with frequent regional famines. Each country has to determine and strive to achieve the appropriate size of its food reserves.[27]

Need for Multidisciplinary, Multisectorial Actions

Researchers in individual disciplines are essential to the advances required to maintain adequate food supplies, reduce disease, and protect and improve the environment. They must be part of strong institutions and be able to work in multidisciplinary teams. It is particularly important for developing countries to build the capability to deal with their own problems without having to depend on expatriate experts and consultants.

High priority, therefore, must be given to institution-building, and both internal and external resources must be committed to this purpose. Strengthening an institution involves human resource development in all of the disciplines necessary for accomplishing its mission. For example, building an agricultural university or agricultural research station requires training in a variety of agricultural specialties and also the relevant social sciences. Schools of public health and the national health services require health science professionals, nutritionists, anthropologists, sociologists, economists, and political scientists.

Specialists in various disciplines, unless they work in a stimulating multidisciplinary environment, may overlook issues in related fields that have important bearing on their work. The challenge is to create institutions that are more than a collection of separate subunits. The present reward structure in most professions overwhelmingly favors disciplinary performance and even penalizes interdisciplinary collaboration. Because most specialists in developing countries are forced to deal with the complex problems of the real world, they must have the support of institutions with an applied orientation and the opportunity to participate in multidisciplinary problem-oriented research teams.

The single, most important permanent contribution to the prevention of hunger, I am convinced, is support for advanced multidisciplinary and applied training of research scientists in agricultural and health sciences and in related social sciences. They are needed so that developing countries can deal with their unique food and nutrition problems. This kind of training has been the major focus of the UNU fellowship program. International and bilateral assistance agencies invest far too little in the development of human resources. However, without supportive government policies, it is difficult to develop good institutions of higher education and research in agriculture, health, and related sciences.

There is often little that external agencies can do to ensure sound national policies. But such agencies can support policies and governments that contribute to improved food supplies and better nutrition. Conversely, international funding agencies and other institutions involved in development assistance should withhold support from policies that exacerbate hunger and malnutrition. This has special cogency in the present decade when many developing countries are being forced to adopt economic adjustment policies that adversely affect the most vulnerable segments of their populations.

Conclusion

There are no simple or direct cause-and-effect relationships between food production and hunger. Moreover, hunger is not limited to a deficiency of calories; the food consumed must also be adequate to prevent nutrient deficiencies. Agricultural research and extension efforts in the developing countries should be greatly expanded, and more attention should be given to reduction of field food losses resulting from deficiencies in postharvest food conservation, storage, and distribution. Nutrition and health education to enable people to make wise food choices is also important.

None of these measures will be sufficient, however, unless everyone has the ability to acquire necessary food, either by producing or gathering it or by obtaining the resources to purchase it. For most developing countries, this means more equitable land tenure policies, greater availability of rural credit for agricultural inputs, fairer agricultural purchase and trade policies, and increased resources devoted to the agricultural sector. Poor households that are not in the food production sector will require policies and programs that enable them to acquire food through increased employment, better wages, and appropriate entitlement programs.

Attention must be focused on every step in the food chain in order to banish hunger and malnutrition as public health and social problems and to achieve food security that is environmentally sustainable. Developing countries need strong institutions that facilitate cooperation among the agriculture, health, social, and policy sciences, and public administration disciplines and professions. Their leaders need a realistic understanding of and commitment to the welfare of all sectors of society. Human policy failings are the ultimate cause of hunger as a social problem, and appropriate policy decisions can prevent it in every country, regardless of the environmental, economic, or demographic constraints.

Notes

1. C. C. de Vries, "Increasing Crop Yields—Relative Potential of Specific Crops by Regions and/or Country," in *Man, Food, and Nutrition,* ed. M. Recheigl, Jr. (Cleveland: CRC Press, 1973).

2. E. J. Welhausen, "The Agriculture of Mexico," in *Food and Agriculture* (San Francisco: W. H. Freeman, 1976).

3. A. N. Blanc Andrade, "SAM's Cost and Impact on Production," in *Food Policy in Mexico: The Search for Self-Sufficiency,* ed. J. E. Austin and G. Esteva (Ithaca and London: Cornell University Press, 1987).

4. M. Hossain, *Nature and Impact of the Green Revolution in Bangladesh,* Working Papers on Food Subsidies no. 4 (Washington, D.C.: International Food Policy Research Institute, 1988).

5. G. T. Castillo, "The Farmer Revisited: Toward a Return to the Food Problem," in *Proceedings—The World Food Conference of 1976* (Ames: Iowa State University Press, 1976).

6. United Nations University, *Bioconversion of Organic Residues for Rural Communities,* Food and Nutrition Bulletin supplement no. 2 (Tokyo: UNU, 1979), 176. National Academy of Sciences, *Food, Fuel, and Fertilizer from Organic Wastes* (Washington, D.C.: NAS, 1981).

7. C. R. Wharton, "The Role of the Professional in Feeding Mankind: The Political Dimension," in *Proceedings—The World Food Conference of 1976* (Ames: Iowa State University Press, 1976). N. S. Scrimshaw and L. Taylor, *Food in Economic Development* (San Francisco: W. H. Freeman, 1980).

8. J. W. Mellor and R. Ahmed, eds., *Agricultural Price Policy for Developing Countries* (Baltimore: Johns Hopkins University Press, 1988).

9. G. J. Clark, "Economic Development: First Things First," in *Adjustment with Growth: A Search for an Equitable Solution* (Islamabad, Pakistan: North South Roundtable, 1984).

10. L. Chiarappa, "Reducing Crop Losses," in *Man, Food, and Nutrition,* ed. M. Recheigl, Jr. (Cleveland: CRC Press, 1973).

11. Council of Agriculture, *Post-Harvest Prevention of Paddy/Rice Loss* (Taipei: Council of Agriculture, 1986).

12. T. P. Ojha, "Improved Post-Harvest Technology to Maximize Yield and Minimize Quantitative and Qualitative Losses," in *Interfaces between Agriculture, Nutrition, and Food Sciences,* ed. K. T. Achaya (Tokyo: United Nations University, 1984), 120–33.

13. N. S. Scrimshaw, *Testimony before the National Bipartisan Commission on Central America* (Washington, D.C.: Superintendent of Documents, 1983).

14. "Urban Agriculture," *Food and Nutrition Bulletin* 9 (1987):2–41.

15. H. Alderman, M. G. Chaudry, and M. Garcia, *Household Food Security in Pakistan: The Ration Shop System,* Working Paper on Food Subsidies no. 4 (Washington, D.C.: International Food Policy Research Institute, 1988).

16. S. Reutlinger and M. Selowsky, *Malnutrition and Poverty, Magnitude and Policy Option,* World Bank Staff Occasional Papers no. 12 (Baltimore and London: Johns Hopkins University Press, 1976), 82.

17. FAO/WHO/UNU, *Energy and Protein Requirements,* World Health Organization Technical Report Series 724 (Geneva: WHO, 1984).

18. B. Torun, V. R. Young, and W. M. Rand, *Protein-energy Requirements of Developing Countries: Evaluation of New Data* (Tokyo: United Nations University, 1981), 268. W. M. Rand, R. Uauy, and N. S. Scrimshaw, *Protein-energy Requirements of Developing Countries: Results of International Research* (Tokyo: United Nations University, 1983), 369.

19. R. F. Chandler, *The Potential for Breeding Heat Tolerant Vegetables for the Tropics* (Taiwan: Asian Vegetable Research and Development Center, Tenth Anniversary Monograph Series, 1983).

20. N. S. Scrimshaw, C. E. Taylor, and J. E. Gordon, *Interactions of Nutrition and Infection,* WHO Monograph Series no. 57, 1968.

21. C. H. Shah, "The Demand for Higher-status Food and Nutrition in Rural India: The Experience of Matar Taluka. Basic Data and Interrelationship of Variables," *Food and Nutrition Bulletin* 8 (1986):4–23.

22. W. I. Torry, "Economic Development, Drought, and Famines: Some Limitations of Dependency Explanations," *GeoJournal* 12, no. 1 (1986):4–18.

23. D. Paarlberg, "United States Policy and Agriculture in Developing Countries," in *The Politics of Food: Producing and Distributing the World's Food Supply,* ed. D. J. Johnson (Chicago: Chicago Council on Foreign Relations, 1980), 16–35.

24. S. C. M. Scrimshaw and E. Hurtado, *Rapid Assessment Procedures for the Evaluation of Programmes of Nutrition and Primary Health Care: An Anthropological Approach to Programme Improvement* (Los Angeles: University of California Latin American Center Publications, 1987).

25. A. Sen, *Poverty and Famines: An Essay on Entitlement and Deprivation* (Oxford: Clarendon Press, 1981), 257.

26. N. S. Scrimshaw, "Testimony to the United States Senate on Bangladesh Refugees in India," in *World Hunger, Health, and Refugee Problems, Summary of Special Study Mission to Asia and the Middle East,* Committee on the Judiciary, United States Senate (Washington, D.C.: U.S. Government Printing Office, 1976), 118.

27. D. J. Johnson, "Increasing the Food Security of Low Income Countries," in *The Politics of Food: Producing and Distributing the World's Food Supply,* ed. D. G. Johnson (Chicago: Chicago Council on Foreign Relations, 1980), 183–206.

CHAPTER 2

Poverty, Hunger, and Food Security

Domestic Policies and Implications for External Assistance to South Asia

Uma Lele
Chief, Special Studies Division, Country Economics Department, The World Bank, Washington, D.C., United States

The largest concentration of poor and malnourished in the world is in South Asia—Bangladesh, India, Nepal, Pakistan, and Sri Lanka—where close to 300 million of the region's one billion people live below the poverty line. This fact is frequently forgotten in the international development community.

South Asia's population will rise to 1.5 billion by the year 2020 under the most optimistic assumptions; under more realistic assumptions, an increase to 1.8 billion is expected.[1] The response to the problem of growing population, malnutrition, and hunger will make a crucial difference to the quality and quantity of life on the subcontinent, as well as to world agricultural trade prospects. The complex interactions among education, employment, income, health, family planning, population growth, increases in food production, and food security need to be understood before their combined policy implications can be fully assessed.

Population, Education, and Infant Mortality

Population growth rates have dropped far more slowly in South Asia (Bangladesh, India, Nepal, Pakistan, and Sri Lanka) than in China, but more rapidly than in Africa. For the developing world as a whole, mortality rates have fallen faster than fertility rates. Reductions in fertility have been more rapid in areas where women's access to education and the access of the population at large to health and family planning have been greatest.

In South Asia, educational opportunity has expanded far more rapidly for women than for men, partly because it began from a very low base after independence. The religious and sociopolitical setting of a country has made a major difference in the extent of women's access to education. For instance, only 29 percent of eligible girls in Pakistan have access to primary education, even though the country has experienced the most impressive gross domestic product (GDP) growth rate in South Asia (see table 2–1). Sri Lanka's success in achieving universal primary education for girls is explained by its progressive social policies over several decades.[2] In India, which represents the middle ground, 75 percent of girls now have access to primary education, compared with 51 percent in Bangladesh and 47 percent in Nepal.

More generally, although South Asia's social conditions relative to income have improved substantially in recent decades, the progress has not been steady. Much of the decline in mortality rates, for example, can be explained by increased immunization for cholera, reduction in the incidence of malaria, and improvement in access to health services, rather than by major improvements in the nutritional status of populations—a factor that is determined by access to employment and food supplies.

Moreover, staggering differences exist both within South Asia and between the subcontinent and other regions. Infant mortality rates in Bangladesh, Nepal, and Pakistan are among the world's highest and are comparable to those in Africa, whereas Sri Lanka has a superior record (see table 2–1). Comparing South Asia with China highlights the former's relatively modest performance on this score: whereas China's infant mortality declined dramatically from 120 to 40 (per 1,000 births) between 1960 and 1980, South Asia's dropped to only 110 (albeit from a higher initial level of 155). Also, while less than 20 percent of children in China were reported underweight in 1986, the figure for South Asia was 70 percent.[3] Ideological differences between the South Asian countries and China may partly explain these disparities, yet Sri Lanka's example shows that it is possible to improve social conditions within a democratic and market-oriented framework.

Food Production, Employment, and Income

Unequivocal evidence now is available demonstrating the direct link between the decline in the proportion of the population living below the poverty line and the growth of food production and its effect on employment and incomes.[4] Since the mid-1960s, food production in South Asia

Table 2–1.

Social Indicators for South Asian and Six African Countries

Country / Year	Life Expectancy (years) Female	Male	Total	Infant Mortality (per 1,000)	Primary School Enrollment (%) Female	Male	Total
Asia							
Bangladesh							
1960	42.5	44.7	43.5	153	26	66	47
1970	44.1	45.6	44.9	na	35	72	54
1980	47.3	48.4	47.8	41	46	76	62
1985	51.2	49.9	50.6	123	51	73	60
% change	20%	12%	16%	−20%	96%	11%	28%
India							
1960	41.8	43.2	42.2	na	40	80	61
1970	46.8	48.1	47.3	na	56	90	73
1980	53.1	54.2	53.3	31	66	96	81
1985	55.6	56.5	56.0	89	73	105	90
% change	33%	31%	33%	na	83%	31%	48%
Nepal							
1960	38.0	39.0	38.4	na	1	19	10
1970	40.9	42.2	41.4	152	8	44	26
1980	44.3	45.8	44.9	147	48	115	83
1985	46.2	47.4	46.8	133	47	104	77
% change	22%	22%	22%	−13%	4600%	447%	670%
Pakistan							
1960	42.0	44.6	43.1	160	13	46	30
1970	45.0	47.2	46.0	142	22	57	40
1980	48.2	50.2	49.0	125	29	56	43
1985	50.2	51.8	50.9	115	29	54	42
% change	20%	16%	18%	−28%	123%	17%	40%
Sri Lanka							
1960	62.1	62.5	62.3	na	90	100	95
1970	64.7	62.3	63.5	na	94	104	99
1980	69.9	66.4	68.1	6	95	101	98
1985	71.9	67.7	69.8	36	101	105	103
% change	16%	8%	12%	na	12%	5%	8%
China							
1960	37.6	35.1	50.4	132	na	na	109
1970	60.8	57.6	na	69	na	na	89
1980	67.8	66.0	33.7	41	95	115	105
1985	70.0	67.8	68.9	35	107	129	118
% change	86%	93%	37%	−73%	na	na	8%

Country Year	Life Expectancy (years) Female	Male	Total	Infant Mortality (per 1,000)	Primary School Enrollment (%) Female	Male	Total
Africa							
Cameroon							
1960	44.7	42.1	43.4	161	43	87	65
1970	50.3	47.6	48.9	126	75	103	89
1980	54.8	51.3	53.0	106	95	114	104
1985	57.0	53.3	55.1	90	97	116	107
% change	28%	27%	27%	−44%	126%	33%	65%
Kenya							
1960	47.0	43.0	45.0	123	30	64	47
1970	52.0	48.0	50.0	102	48	67	58
1980	56.9	53.0	54.9	83	99	109	104
1985	59.0	55.3	57.1	82	91	97	94
% change	26%	29%	27%	−33%	203%	52%	100%
Malawi							
1960	38.5	37.4	37.9	206	na	na	na
1970	41.1	39.7	40.4	193	na	na	na
1980	44.9	42.6	43.7	169	49	74	61
1985	46.9	43.9	45.4	164	53	71	62
% change	22%	17%	20%	−21%	ERR	na	na
Nigeria							
1960	41.3	38.2	39.7	189	27	46	36
1970	45.3	42.1	43.7	158	27	47	37
1980	49.4	46.1	47.7	118	84	110	98
1985	51.8	48.4	50.1	107	81	103	92
% change	25%	27%	26%	−43%	200%	124%	156%
Senegal							
1960	40.4	38.8	39.6	179	17	36	27
1970	43.6	41.6	42.6	164	32	51	41
1980	46.3	44.1	45.2	147	36	55	46
1985	48.4	45.1	46.7	128	45	66	55
% change	20%	16%	18%	−28%	165%	83%	104%
Tanzania							
1960	42.3	39.1	40.6	146	18	33	25
1970	46.8	43.6	45.1	132	27	41	34
1980	51.4	48.0	49.7	119	86	100	93
1985	53.9	50.4	52.1	102	85	90	72
% change	27%	29%	28%	−30%	372%	173%	188%

na = not available.

% change calculation based on first and last available years.

School enrollment rates exceed 100% in some cases due to number of enrolled students exceeding population in primary school age. In some cases, Primary School Enrollment indicators are for other than given year; all are within two years.

Source: World Bank social indicators database.

has markedly increased as a result of the Green Revolution (generated by agricultural scientists such as Norman Borlaug, Robert F. Chandler, Jr., and M. S. Swaminathan, among others), increased investment in irrigation, and the positive agricultural policies governments have pursued. Despite abysmal poverty, the starvation due to drought and famine, formerly so widespread in the region, has been virtually eliminated, and chronic malnourishment has begun to decline. The estimated 40 percent of the population that lived below the poverty line in the 1960s has declined to 30 percent in the 1980s.

Massive poverty and hunger persist, however, and again regional differences are striking. For instance, India, Pakistan, and Sri Lanka have performed better than Bangladesh, Burma, and Nepal, although Bangladesh's performance has improved substantially in recent years. A study of agricultural growth rates in 282 of India's 360 districts in the 1970s revealed that only 48 districts had sustained growth in agricultural production of over 4.5 percent; nearly 50 percent had agricultural growth rates well below population growth rates.[5] Moreover, even where production has done well, the effects of new food grain technologies on employment and income have been weaker than expected in South Asia[6] and lower than in other regions, such as Southeast Asia.[7]

South Asia's performance lags for several reasons. First, the sheer incidence of landless people in many parts of the region, together with limited irrigation development, diminishes cropping intensity and retards crop yields. Second, governments have failed to invest adequately in rural infrastructure, communications, transport, and electrification—sectors that have been shown to directly increase employment as well as indirectly strengthen agricultural growth linkages. Third, improvement still can be made in providing small and marginal producers with access to services. Finally, more direct efforts to increase the food consumption of the poor are essential; providing employment for the landless is one way to increase their access to food.

Policies to Improve Food Access for the Poor

Government policies to improve the access of poor people to income and food have taken many forms. In Sri Lanka, consumer price subsidies have been the most important by far, first through rice rations and more recently through food stamps. Equitable food distribution has been pursued through "fair price" shops in India and Bangladesh, along with employment- and income-generating rural public works programs. School feeding programs in Tamil Nadu and Andhra Pradesh states in

India are examples of effective food access strategies. On the other hand, nutrition programs (including food fortification and nutrition education) deserve far more attention.

These programs, however, constitute an enormous burden on government budgets. In Sri Lanka, for example, food subsidies consumed 14 percent of annual government expenditures during the 1971–77 period; they dropped to 6 percent during the period of structural adjustment, 1978–85. Nevertheless, even in the latter period, Sri Lanka spent an annual average of nearly $7 per capita (or around $50 million) on food subsidies for the 50 percent of its population of 16 million that benefited from such programs.[8] The effect of subsidy reduction on the poor continues to be controversial, but World Bank economist Surjit Bhalla concludes that a more critical indicator, the real consumer price of rice—crucial in determining the incomes of the poor—was the same in the mid-1980s as it had been in the early 1970s, despite substantial growth in the demand for food. This outcome reflects government investment to increase productivity (including expansion of irrigation and input supply), which has greatly increased domestic rice production and made Sri Lanka self-sufficient in this area.

Sri Lanka's successful shift from providing symptomatic relief for hunger (through food subsidies) to removing its basic causes (through increased employment, income, and rice production) prompts an examination of the contribution that employment guarantee schemes (EGS) can make in this context. Unlike recurrent food subsidies, which can only improve human capital (and only as long as they last), EGSs that create productive physical assets hold the promise of generating additional income streams in the future.

An EGS in Maharashtra State in India, the largest such scheme in the world, provided employment to 1.6 million people in 1987–88 for 180 million person-days at a cost of only $1.1 per person-day, or a total cost of $205 million annually. It involved small-scale irrigation, road construction, reforestation, and soil conservation projects. About 60 percent of the $205 million took the form of direct wages to the poor, while the remaining 40 percent was spent on skilled labor, materials, land acquisition, maintenance, and planning and implementing the various schemes.

Using a conservative assumption for the income elasticity of demand (meaning percentage change in demand in relation to percentage change in income), poor households would spend an estimated $60 million, or 0.5 percent of the incremental wages from such schemes, to purchase nearly 300,000 additional tons of food grains. A conservative estimate of the cost of extending an EGS to reach one adult in each household of the 300 million poor in South Asia as a whole would run to $7 billion in annual wages at current wage rates; more liberal assumptions could increase this figure to $29 billion. (The average wage cost for

EGS workers was $0.6 per person-day, but it has increased to $1.2 per person-day since 1988–89 with the revision in wages of agricultural labor.)

Assuming an average household of five members, 60 million people would have to be employed. Their employment for 100 days at $1.2 per person-day would cost nearly $7 billion. Employing two adult members for 100 days—a more realistic assumption in the case of the poor, as most have no land to cultivate and need regular employment—could cost $28.8 billion annually.

If these investments were to yield a 10 percent annual rate of return, by no means an overoptimistic assumption in South Asia, the cost of EGSs would be recovered in ten years. Nearly $3.5 billion of the estimated $7 billion might be used for incremental food purchases involving additional food consumption of a minimum of 17.5 million tons. (Overall EGS costs and food consumption levels are highly sensitive to assumptions about wage rates and income elasticities of demand for food. The numbers used here should therefore be considered ballpark estimates and not firm figures.) Most of the food for this increased consumption would have to be imported, at least initially, increasing current world trade in cereals by about 8 percent and creating markets for the surpluses in Organization for Economic Cooperation and Development (OECD) countries.

The Role of External Assistance

Given their current GDP and revenue levels, South Asian governments cannot afford to make such large expenditures on their own, nor to import food on such a scale year after year. This is one reason for the lack of progress in expanding access to incomes, for the perplexing conjunction of problems of agricultural surplus disposal in the OECD countries, and for the declining levels of assistance to South Asia. Food aid to the region declined from 3.6 million tons in 1970–71 to 2.3 million tons in 1985–86. Transfers of official development assistance (ODA) with a grant element of 25 percent or greater per capita rose from $2.20 in 1973 to $4.47 in 1985; per capita assistance in 1983–85 was only 75 percent of its 1973–75 levels in real terms.

ODA has also become less evenly distributed in recent years. In India per capita ODA declined from a peak of $2.97 in 1976 to $1.96 in 1985, while in the rest of South Asia, it increased from $4.51 to $11.14. Overall, however, per capita ODA has risen much less in South Asia than in subsaharan Africa, where it grew from $6.50 in 1973 to $22.47 in 1985 (see figures 2–1 and 2–2).[9] Increasing per capita ODA in South Asia

Figure 2–1.

Total Food Aid for Subsaharan Africa and South Asia

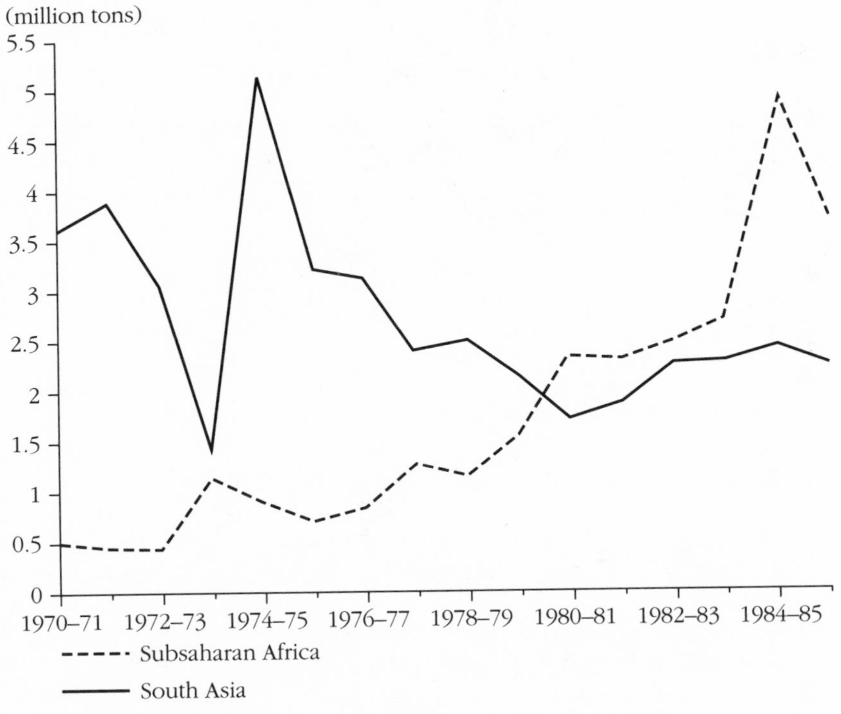

Source: compiled by author (see n.9).

to levels similar to those in Africa would imply additional donor commitments of $18 billion per year, which would roughly cover the region's need for a robust, productive rural employment generation scheme.

Analysis of aid effectiveness shows consistently high relative returns on aid to South Asia. This is partly due to the higher quality of donor assistance, in turn reflecting South Asia's good endowments of development planning and implementing capacity. Taken overall, South Asia's record demonstrates that countries with favorable conditions at independence can easily absorb very large quantities of aid.[10] The converse also holds, however, at the other end of the spectrum of initial endowments; thus, in a major study of the effectiveness of aid to African agriculture involving eight donors and six African governments, I have stressed that it is crucial to channel aid increases to Africa into building human and

Figure 2–2.

Official Development Aid Per Capita for Subsaharan Africa and South Asia

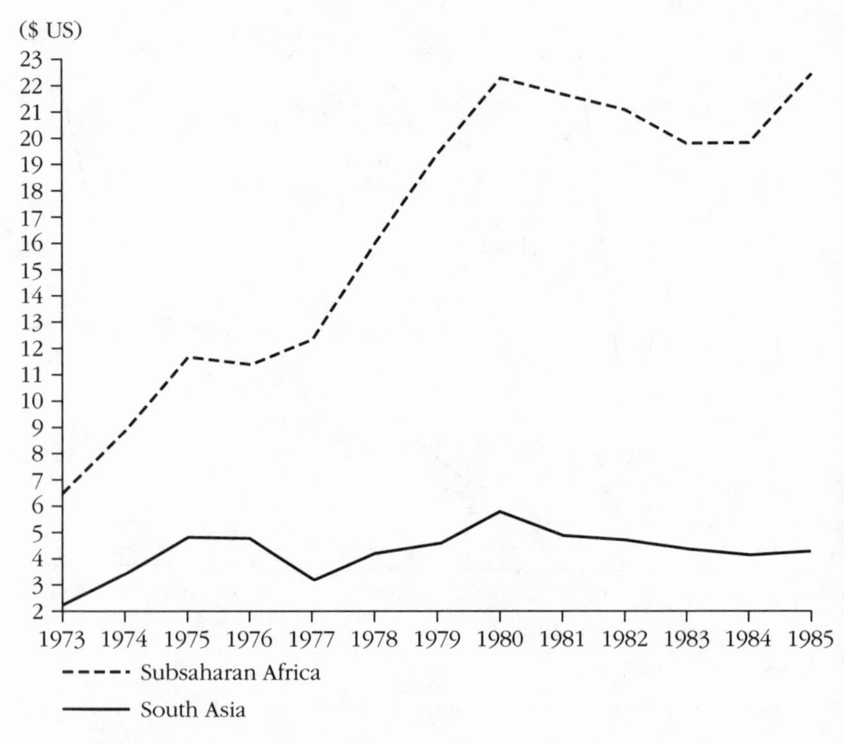

Source: compiled by author (see n.9).

institutional capital on a massive scale if they are to yield returns as high as those in Asia.[11]

Meanwhile, given the tremendous human and institutional capital in South Asia, the availability of additional ODA or food aid (or a combination thereof) on a reliable, consistent, and nonpartisan basis will expand markets, not only for cereals but also for other goods and services produced in OECD countries. More importantly, it will help to improve the quality of life for the growing segment of South Asia's population living in degradation and squalor, and it could solve the problems of hunger and unemployment by the beginning of the twenty-first century.

Notes

1. World Bank, *World Development Report, 1984* (New York: Oxford University Press, 1984).

2. Surjit S. Bhalla and Paul Glewwe, "Growth and Equity in Developing Countries: A Reinterpretation of the Sri Lankan Experience," *The World Bank Economic Review* 1 (September 1986):35–63.

3. United Nations, *First Report on the World Nutrition Situation,* November 1987.

4. John W. Mellor and Gunvant M. Desai, eds., *Agricultural Change and Rural Poverty: Variations on a Theme by Dharm Narain* (Washington, D.C.: International Food Policy Research Institute, 1985).

5. I. J. Singh, *Small Farmers and the Landless in South Asia* (Washington, D.C.: Development Research Department, World Bank, 1987).

6. John W. Mellor and Uma Lele, "Growth Linkages of the New Foodgrain Technologies," *Indian Journal of Agricultural Economics* 28 (1973):35–55.

7. Romeo M. Bautista, "Agricultural Growth and Food Imports in Developing Countries: A Reexamination" (Paper presented for the festschrift in honor of Professor Shinichi Ichimura, Kyoto University, June 1988).

8. Surjit Bhalla, "The Politics and Economics of Agricultural Price Policies in Sri Lanka" (Paper prepared for "A Comparative Study of the Political Economy of Agricultural Pricing Policies," September 1988).

9. Organization for Economic Cooperation and Development, *Geographical Distribution of Financial Flows,* issues from 1977 to 1986.

10. World Bank, *Tenth Annual Review of Project Performance Audit Reports* (Washington, D.C.: Office of Economic Development, World Bank, August 1984).

11. Uma Lele, "Agricultural Growth, Domestic Policies, the External Environment and Assistance to Africa: Lessons of a Quarter Century," in *Trade, Aid, and Policy Reform: Proceedings of the Eighth Agriculture Sector Symposium,* ed. Colleen Roberts (Washington, D.C.: World Bank, 1988), 119–98.

CHAPTER 3

Food Production and Nutrition in Southeast Asia

Aree Valyasevi
Resident Coordinator and Founding Director, United Nations University Institute of Nutrition, Mahidol University, and

Pattanee Winichagoon
Assistant Professor, Mahidol University, Bangkok, Thailand

The governments of Southeast Asia during the past few decades have embarked on aggressive efforts to alleviate malnutrition in their countries. In retrospect, however, most of these measures appear to have been only stopgap measures. They have consisted of short-term actions and interventions to deal with critical problems, but such efforts have not been sustainable without external assistance. The challenge for governments is to establish nutrition improvement strategies and programs that are self-sustaining and sustainable: programs carefully designed for and integrated in particular communities so that their operation and evaluation eventually become the responsibility of the communities themselves. In the latter case, external assistance, including technical know-how and training, is important at the beginning, but gradually more and more functions are taken over by local people.

This paper will describe the food and nutrition situation in Southeast Asia and focus on Thailand's food and nutrition program as an example of a promising strategy for sustaining nutritional well-being for people in developing nations. To understand the nature of sustainable nutrition programs, we will closely examine the entire range of the food chain, from production to consumption, and then pinpoint the problem areas that have to be solved.

Trends in Food Production

The production of major food crops—cereals, pulses, and roots and tubers—doubled in many countries of Southeast Asia between 1961 and

Table 3–1

Production and Average Annual Growth Rate of Crops in Southeast Asia (thousand tons)

Countries	Cereals 1961	Cereals 1981	Cereals Average Annual Growth	Pulses 1961	Pulses 1981	Pulses Average Annual Growth
Burma	6,940	15,812	3.3	222	671	3.1
Kampuchea	2,557	2,092	−0.8	193	37	−3.8
Indonesia	14,367	45,046	4.7	181	354	2.5
Laos	.557	1,527	4.1	10	26	3.5
Malaysia	1,097	1,885	2.2	—	—	—
Philippines	5,176	13,506	3.9	38	42	1.3
Thailand	10,748	23,703	3.2	49	414	6.7
Vietnam	9,290	16,850	2.4	73	158	2.8

Countries	Roots & Tubers 1961	Roots & Tubers 1981	Roots & Tubers Average Annual Growth
Burma	79	262	14.5
Kampuchea	79	139	1.7
Indonesia	15,592	17,200	0.6
Laos	42	169	12.5
Malaysia	495	505	−0.4
Philippines	1,828	3,374	4.8
Thailand	7,485	20,411	9.2
Vietnam	2,311	5,335	4.8

Source: FAO, Regional Office for Asia and the Pacific, Bangkok.

1981 (see table 3–1).[1] Indonesia had the largest increase in cereal production, followed by the Philippines; Thailand, the largest increase in pulses; and Burma, in roots and tubers. Only in Kampuchea did the production of cereals and pulses decline.

The region actually produced a surplus of cereals over the twenty-year period (see table 3–2).[2] Indonesia and the Philippines decreased their dependency on food aid, especially on the U.S. Food for Peace (P.L. 480) Program. Nevertheless, these countries still import various other food commodities from each other as well as from developed countries.[3] In addition, the need for external food aid in Kampuchea and Vietnam is expected to continue for some time.

Table 3–2.

Production, Consumption, and Net Importation of Cereals in Southeast Asia (million metric tons)

Year	Production	Consumption	Net Exports
1984/85	40	33	7
1985/86	41	33	8
1986/87*	39	33	6
1987/88*	40	34	6

*Projection
Source: USDA, *World Food Needs and Availabilities, 1987/88* (1987).

Substantial Increases in Dietary Energy

During the early 1960s, Malaysia was the only country in the region with adequate available dietary energy. The other countries had an average daily deficit of 200 to 300 calories per person (see table 3–3).[4]

In the late 1970s, however, the food situation substantially improved throughout the region, and today the dietary energy available for consumption exceeds the required national average in most countries. Even Laos and Kampuchea, which had large deficits during the Vietnam War, came close to meeting national average requirements in the early 1980s.

Caloric availability from rice consumption markedly increased in Burma and Indonesia in the 1982–84 triennium over 1961–63.[5] In Burma caloric intake from pulses and beans increased threefold, while in Indonesia intake from nuts and oils jumped 1.6 times. Caloric intake from animal products increased strikingly in Laos (79 percent) and Malaysia (84 percent), and, to a lesser extent, in the Philippines (24 percent). However, animal foods intake decreased in Kampuchea and Indonesia.

Rice is still the major source of calories throughout the region, supplying from 60 to 79 percent of total available energy in all countries except Malaysia and the Philippines (see table 3–4).[6] Animal products and pulses and beans, however, contributed less than 13 percent, indicating that the quantity of protein in the Southeast Asian diet may be inadequate. Fats and oils, including nuts and oil seeds—typically a small proportion of the Asian diet—comprised only 12 percent of the total.

Table 3–3.

Daily Per Capita Availability of Dietary Energy in Southeast Asia (Kcal)

Countries	National Average	1961–63	1964–66	1969–71	1974–76	1979–81	1982–84
Burma	2,160	1,913	1,980	2,185	2,217	2,420	2,502
Kampuchea	2,220	2,189	2,110	2,187	1,841	—	2,064
Indonesia	2,160	1,944	1,874	1,976	2,113	2,372	2,433
Laos	2,220	1,835	2,001	2,098	1,989	—	2,089
Malaysia	2,230	2,438	2,458	2,508	2,565	2,518	2,549
Philippines	2,260	1,872	1,928	1,982	2,101	2,405	2,399
Thailand	2,220	2,095	2,187	2,285	2,269	2,330	2,322
Vietnam*	2,160	2,100*	2,102*	2,178	2,096	—	2,184

*North Vietnam.
Source: FAO, Regional Office for Asia and the Pacific, Bangkok.

Sugar and honey comprised a large share of dietary energy in Malaysia, the Philippines, and Thailand.

Thus, although the macrolevel data indicate that Southeast Asia is doing all right in food production, there are certainly problems needing attention in various links along the food chain.

Constraints on Food Supplies: Issues Affecting the Food Chain in Three Nations

This section focuses on Indonesia, the Philippines, and Thailand as regional examples, since data are more readily available from these countries. Moreover, four-fifths of the population of these countries live in rural areas, reflecting the distribution in the region as a whole.

Land and labor are the basic resources in Southeast Asian agriculture. Thailand has far more land under cultivation than Indonesia and the Philippines. In Indonesia and the Philippines, on the other hand, the cropped land (i.e., land that is planted) expanded at a much faster rate than cultivated areas (i.e., land prepared for cultivation, but not yet planted). This suggests a decline in the land available for agricultural

Table 3–4.

Percentage of Daily Per Capita Caloric Availability by Food Group and Country in Southeast Asia (1982–84)

	Burma	**Kampuchea**	**Indonesia**	**Laos**
Rice	73.3	78.8	60.6	72.3
Other cereals	3.8	5.5	9.6	2.9
Roots & tubers	0.5	2.1	7.5	3.6
Pulses & beans	4.1	1.7	0.7	2.3
Animal products	4.1	3.5	2.3	9.6
Nuts & oil seeds	2.4	1.0	6.8	0.7
Fats & oils	6.3	1.2	4.9	2.5
Fruits & vegetables	2.9	3.0	1.9	2.8
Sugar & honey	2.1	2.7	5.9	0.8
Alcoholic beverages	0.04	1.2	0.04	1.7
Others	0.3	0.3	0.1	0.6

	Malaysia	**Philippines**	**Thailand**	**Vietnam**
Rice	39.4	39.0	59.9	70.2
Other cereals	11.8	20.6	1.2	3.8
Roots & tubers	2.7	6.0	2.7	8.1
Pulses & beans	1.2	0.2	0.7	0.9
Animal products	12.0	9.4	5.8	6.5
Nuts & oil seeds	1.8	0.8	4.2	1.1
Fats & oils	14.2	4.3	2.5	2.2
Fruits & vegetables	3.5	7.6	6.6	4.2
Sugar & honey	12.5	10.0	14.5	2.4
Alcoholic beverages	0.4	1.4	1.2	0.3
Others	0.8	0.2	0.5	0.2

Source: Modified from FAO, Regional Office for Asia and the Pacific, Bangkok.

production. In addition, the proportion of the labor force engaged in agriculture has declined in all three countries. This trend may be attributable to price instability, limited agricultural land, and a growing number of jobs outside of agriculture. Since most agricultural production in this region is labor intensive, productivity must be increased through other means such as improved agricultural technology to compensate for the decreases in land and labor.

Problems in the struggle to increase agricultural yields have per-

Figure 3–1.

Production Trends in Major Agricultural Commodities in Selected Southeast Asian Countries

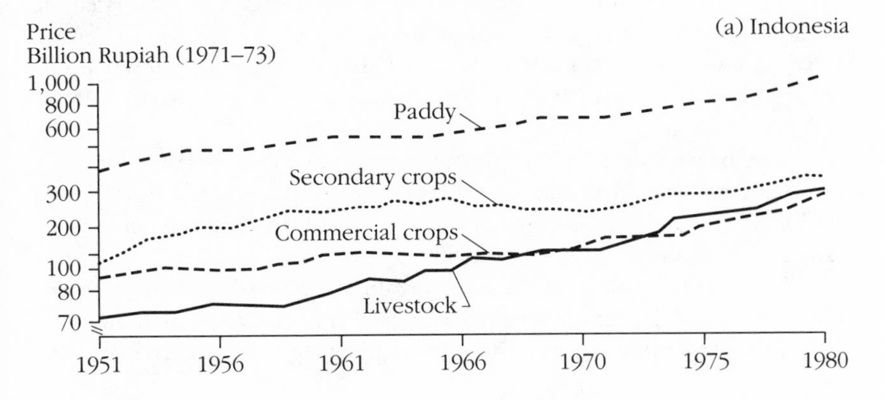

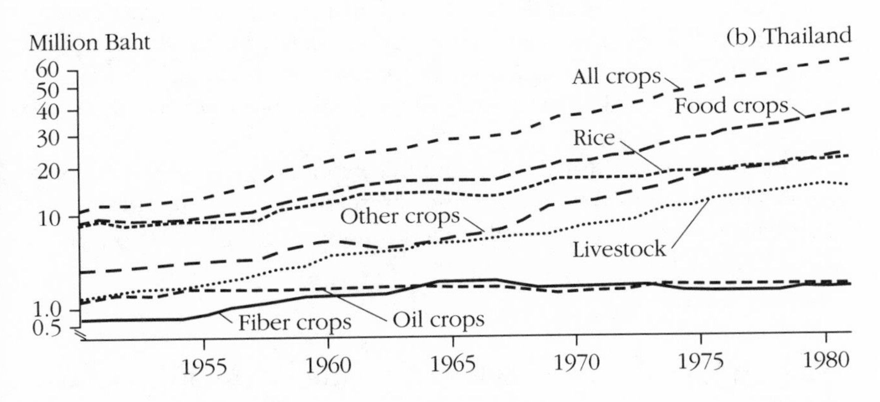

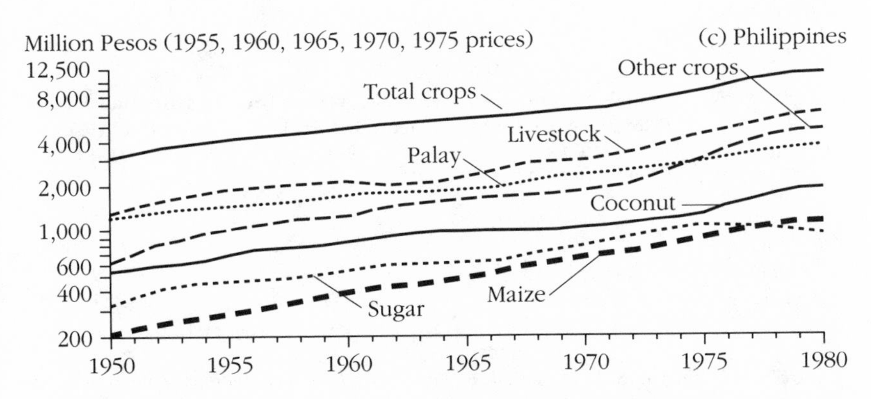

Source: Asian Productivity Organization, *Productivity Measurement and Analysis: Asian Agriculture* (1987), 230, 414, 417.

sisted for years. Rice has been the major crop in the region, although there is an accelerating trend toward more commercial crops (i.e., food crops other than rice as well as nonedible cash crops) particularly evident in the Philippines (see figure 3–1).[7]

The introduction of high-yield varieties substantially boosted rice yields in Indonesia and the Philippines (see table 3–5).[8] However, the new varieties were not accepted in Thailand, since the local varieties there are better in quality and more popular in the world market, despite their low yields.

Fertilizers and irrigation are also important factors contributing to increased productivity, but their use in the region has been limited so far. In Thailand, for example, farmers cannot afford the cost of fertilizer, so it is used far less than recommended.

Furthermore, the majority of farming is rainfed. Where irrigation has been available, the yields have increased substantially (see table 3–6),[9] on both the alluvial soil of the central plain and the sandy soil of the northeast.[10]

Postharvest losses in the traditional agriculture system are another common problem. Losses occur at various steps in the handling and storage of rice, for example (see table 3–7),[11] due to rodents, insects, and storage conditions. The magnitude of the losses, however, is difficult to determine.

In addition, the distribution and marketing systems as well as pricing policies at both the national and international levels constrain food availability in this region, as elsewhere.

Table 3–5.

Rice Paddy Yields in Selected Southeast Asian Countries (kg/ha)

Country	Annual Average for Triennium Ending 1971	Annual Average for Triennium Ending 1981	Compound Growth Rate (%) 1971–81
Indonesia	2,346	3,317	3.5
Malaysia	2,396	2,833	1.7
Philippines	1,655	2,196	2.9
Thailand	1,947	1,933	−0.1

Source: FAO cited in S. S. Puri, *Role of Agriculture, Food, and Nutrition Policies in Solving Nutrition Problems in Asia* (1983).

Table 3–6.

Irrigated Versus Rainfed Rice Yields in Thailand (kg/rai*)

Region	Irrigated	Rainfed	Regional Average
North	545	349	369
Northeast	390	140	244
Central	442	230	314
South	340	253	271

*Unit of land area (2.5 rais = 1 acre)

Source: Agriculture Development Council, *Food Policy Analysis in Thailand* (1985)

Table 3–7.

Reported Rice Losses in the Postharvest System

Country	Where Losses Occurred (% Loss)	Total % Weight Loss
Indonesia	Drying 2 Storage 2–5	6–17
Philippines*	a. Drying 1–5 Unspecified Store 2–6 Threshing 2–6	9–34
	b. Handling	3–10
Thailand*	a. On Farm Store 1.5–3.5 Central Store 1.5–3.5	8–14
	b. On Farm Store 2–15 Handling 10	12–25
Malaysia	Central Store 6 Threshing 5–13 Drying 2, on Farm Store 5 Handling 6	17–25

*More than one study reported

Source: E. R. Pariser, "Post Harvest Food Losses in Developing Countries" (1982).

As previously indicated, Southeast Asian countries seldom experience shortages in food production. Nonetheless, to ensure long-term food adequacy in the region, attention must be focused on making agricultural production more efficient, diminishing postharvest losses, improving distribution and marketing mechanisms, and updating pricing and agricultural policies.

As depicted in figure 3–2, good health and nutrition depend on the interaction of production, distribution, and consumption. At the individual level, food access and food choices determine the quantity and quality of the food consumed. While socioeconomic status affects an individual's purchasing power, culture and tradition are important factors in eating preferences and habits. In reality, all of these factors are

Figure 3–2.

Interaction among Determinants of Nutritional Status

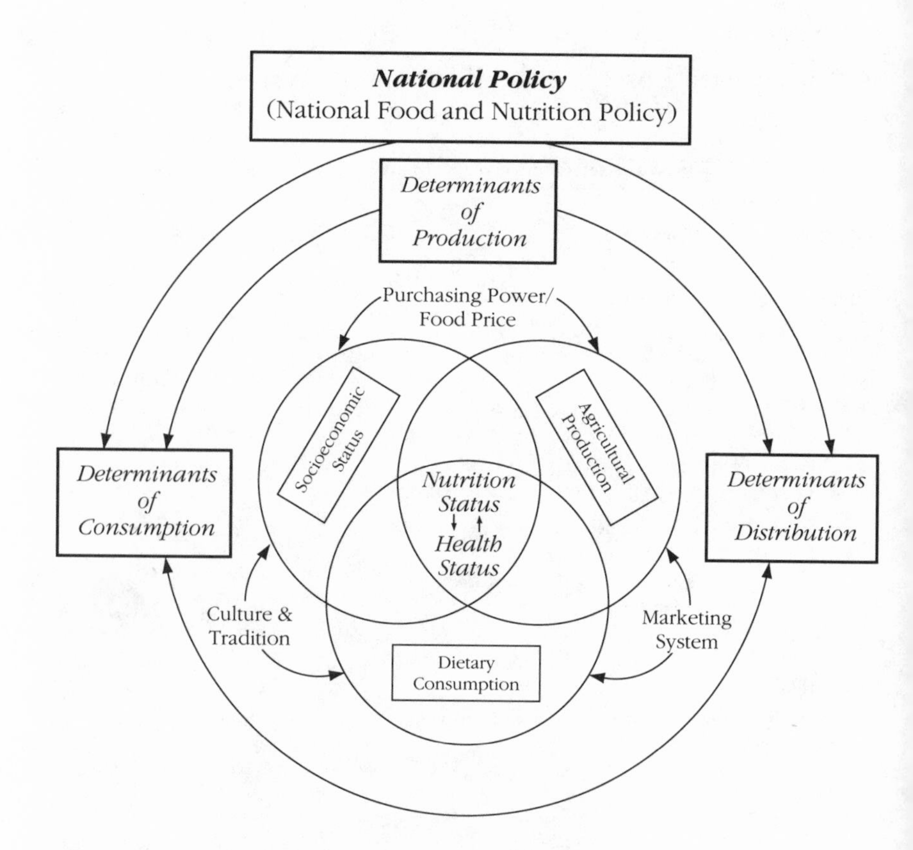

Table 3–8.

Percentage of Malnutrition among Children under Five in Selected Southeast Asian Countries

	Indonesia[1]		**Thailand**[2]		**Philippines**[3]	
Degree	**1980**	**1986**	**1982**	**1986**	**1982**	**1984**
Mild	na	40	36	22	na	na
Moderate	30	10	13	2.7	15.6	15.9
Severe	3	1.3	2	0.07	1.6	2.2

na = not available

Notes

1. Harvard standard, modified Gomez's criteria, MOH.
2. Thai standard, MOPH.
3. Philippines standard, PNP, Philippines.

Source: K. Tontisirin, "The Nutrition Situation and Nutrition Action Program in Four ASEAN Countries" (1985), and personal communication.

interwoven; therefore, the weight or effect of each one may not be readily quantifiable. Nevertheless, the interaction of these several factors has resulted in malnutrition in many developing nations, including the nations of Southeast Asia. The reader is alerted to the distinctions drawn between three forms of malnutrition—mild, moderate, and severe. *Mild malnutrition* refers to deficits in both protein and energy intake (PEM) and signifies a middle stage between normal and abnormal nutritional status. For example, in the average Thai diet, which is based on rice, deficits in available energy were found to be more serious than deficits in protein intake. Overall, the protein composition of the Thai diet is generally adequate; even among rural low-income households the importance of protein intake for child growth is widely recognized. However, further effort is needed to increase the energy density of the diets of children (see table 3–8).[12]

Thailand's Attack on Malnutrition

Thailand is known internationally as a major rice exporter with a 15 to 22 percent share of the world market.[13] Yet prior to the mid-1970s, more than 60 percent of Thai children under five years of age were found to be malnourished.[14] As a result of stepped-up research and advances in understanding the mechanisms for reducing malnutrition, the Government of Thailand, beginning in 1977, determined that nutrition education and improvement should become a leading component of social policy. Sound nutrition became recognized as a building block of public health and human resource development; conversely, malnutrition became identified as a leading public health problem. The first National Food and Nutrition Plan (NFNP) was incorporated into the nation's development planning, setting a precedent in which nutrition improvement became a responsibility of the government, specifically of its Ministry of Public Health.[15]

The NFNP was based on the premise that malnutrition is a consequence of disruption at different points in the food chain, and, therefore, a multisectorial approach was called for. Because resources were limited, the most vulnerable groups in the Thai population were targeted by the plan. Greatest emphasis was given to the needs of children five years of age or under; other target groups included school-age children and pregnant and lactating women. Rural, low-income areas, particularly in the northeast, became the focus of the earliest efforts. The strategy was directed at first eradicating malnutrition in the most severe stages of its development. The health care infrastructure was identified as the most appropriate channel for implementing nutrition activities.

To support the national plan, the Institute of Nutrition, Mahidol University, was established to carry out research and training for implementation of nutrition programs. A national food and nutrition committee was appointed to coordinate food and nutrition activities of various ministries and universities (see figure 3–3). Similar committees were set up at the provincial and district levels to coordinate and implement community programs. The relevant ministries and universities are jointly responsible for monitoring, evaluating, and conducting operational research.

The Institute of Nutrition emphasized four major components as critical in the effort to translate nutrition policy into action:[16] health care, food supply and availability, effective nutrition education, and income generation (see figure 3–4). Furthermore, community participation, leadership, and self-reliance were deemed essential for the success of the programs.

Curative health care was found to be an effective entry point for introducing nutrition into the community, since it serves the immediate needs of people. Further action programs, including primary health care, then can be introduced. It must be recognized that nutrition by itself is a rather abstract notion in villagers' minds, and therefore it should be tied

Figure 3–3.

Organization of Thailand's National Food and Nutrition Committee

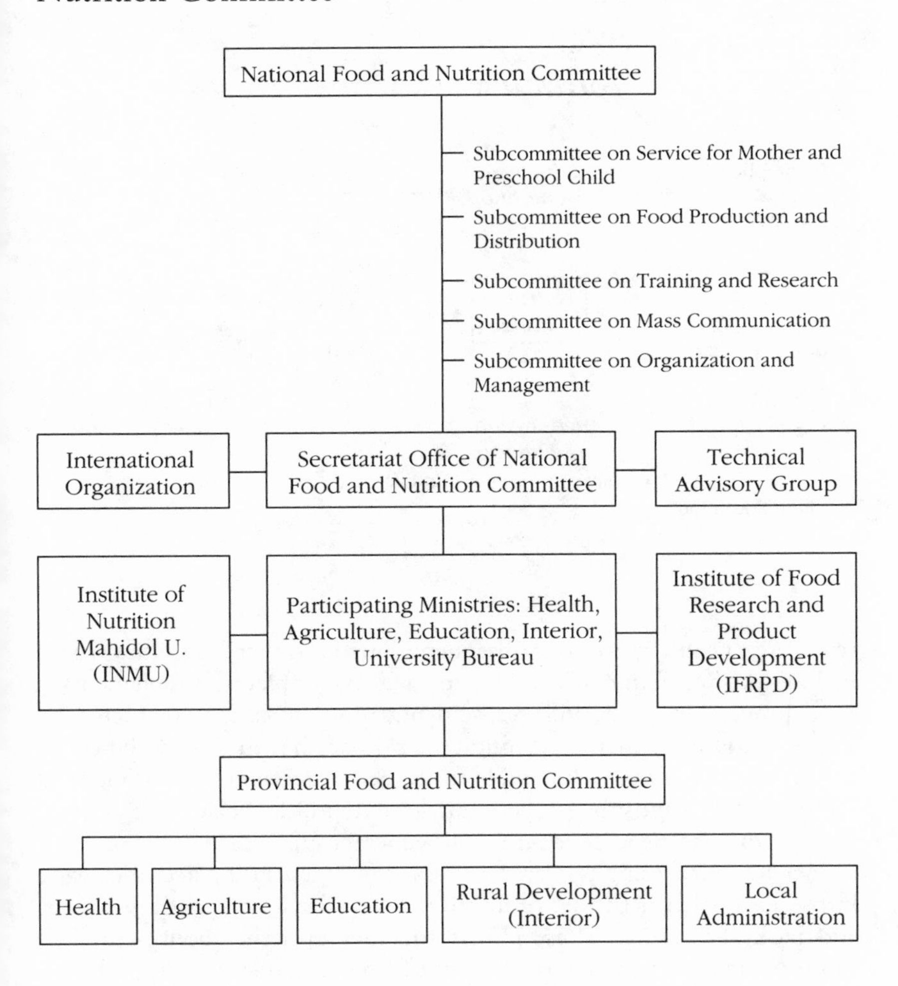

Figure 3–4.

Four Integrated Components for Improving Nutritional Status in Thailand

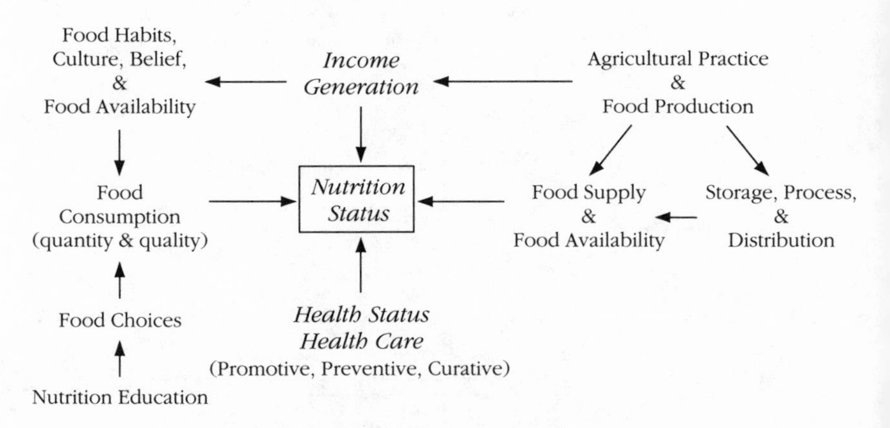

to broader health concerns. Subsequent nutrition-related activities would include the weighing of children to identify problems, supplementary food processing in the villages, and nutrition education conducted by villagers and implemented through the primary health care system. Nutrition education can help people make better decisions regarding food selection, but it must be properly integrated into the health care system. In addition, means were identified to generate supplemental income and to increase purchasing power. Several income-generating activities were introduced, such as the use of improved weaving looms, batik painting, and basket weaving. These efforts together brought about a marked improvement in the nutritional status of children under five (see table 3–9).[17]

In most Asian countries, rice is readily available, particularly in rural areas, but there are shortages of other nutritious foods, especially those essential for the normal growth of young children. For example, the poor commonly lack sufficient protein foods, as stated previously. Thus, supplementary food processing was introduced at the village level, using a locally available and affordable rice-legume combination—a nutritious alternative for young children in rural areas.[18]

Table 3–9.

Percentage of Protein-Energy Malnutrition in Thai Children under Five

Degree of PEM	1982	1984	1986	1987
Mild (1°)	35.7	25.0	21.7	21.0
Moderate (2°)	13.0	4.3	2.7	2.4
Severe (3°)	2.1	0.3	0.07	0.06

Source: Department of Health, Thailand Ministry of Public Health

National Implementation of the Model

When these concepts were first adopted as part of the fourth national development plan (1977–81), the multisectorial approach was not used effectively. In the fifth development plan (1982–86), however, the government adopted a rural development policy for the reallocation and management of resources. The efforts of all the appropriate ministries were focused on rural poverty areas, which are mainly in the northeast region. Primary attention was given to strengthening the village committees so they could make decisions as well as monitor the community programs.

Thailand's experience with nutrition education indicates that gaps along the food chain must be carefully identified and remedied if malnutrition is to be eradicated. This requires, in addition, the strong commitment of the top levels of government. Through its ministries and agencies, the Government of Thailand was intensively involved in implementing the national food and nutrition plan, and the experience showed that a holistic approach was critical in improving nutrition. At later stages, leaders in the nutrition program recognized that community initiative and participation were vital to making nutrition improvement a self-sustaining part of life. Efforts were made to strengthen the ability of communities to develop effective nutrition information and education programs, and to adopt new technologies for alleviating malnutrition. These programs succeeded in several rural communities, in which villagers participated in planning, monitoring, and evaluating the nutrition programs in their communities.

Today, nutrition forms an integral part of the basic minimum needs policy that the Thai government is implementing through the sixth national development plan (1987–91) (see figure 3–5). Initially, this program was conceived of as a set of short-term, stopgap measures to respond to the high incidence of moderate and severe malnutrition found in the population, particularly among children of five years of age or less. This vulnerable group has shown considerable improvement in their nutritional status, yet the problem of mild malnutrition, as well as low birthweight, still persists and requires further action. Research is being carried out to develop a long-term, sustainable strategy for coping with remaining food and nutrition deficits in children, as well as adults.

Closing the gaps in the food chain is centrally important to the struggle against hunger and malnutrition. Although Southeast Asia continues to have a food surplus, attention needs to be directed to the problems relating to food distribution, marketing, and postharvest storage. Thailand's experience has shown that efforts to reduce malnutrition must be undertaken in the context of total development. In most countries, however, attempts to improve nutrition have consisted of short-term measures to cope with immediate problems. More comprehensive alternatives need to be investigated and implemented in the struggle to find a permanent means of eradicating hunger and malnutrition in Southeast Asia.

Figure 3–5.

Basic Needs for Decent Quality of Life in Thailand

Notes

1. Food and Agriculture Organization (FAO), "Food Production for Nutritional Adequacy in Asia-Pacific Region" (Paper presented at Nineteenth FAO Regional Conference for Asia and the Pacific, Bangkok, July 1988).

2. United States Department of Agriculture, *World Food Needs and Availabilities, 1987/88* (Washington, D.C.: USDA, August 1987).

3. A. Booth et al., *Food Trade and Food Security in ASEAN and Australia*, ASEAN-Australia Joint Research Project (Kuala Lumpur and Canberra: Australian National University, 1986).

4. FAO, "Food Production."

5. Ibid.

6. FAO, *Availability of Dietary Calories* (Bangkok: Regional Office for Asia and the Pacific, 1988).

7. Asian Productivity Organization, *Productivity Measurement and Analysis: Asian Agriculture* (Hong Kong: APO, 1987), 230, 414, 447.

8. S. S. Puri, *Role of Agriculture, Food, and Nutrition Policies in Solving Nutrition Problems in Asia: Proceedings of the Fourth Asian Congress of Nutrition* (Bangkok, 1983), 30–35.

9. Agricultural Development Council, *Food Policy Analysis in Thailand*, ed. T. Panayotou (Bangkok: Allied Printers, 1985).

10. Ibid.

11. E. R. Pariser, "Post Harvest Food Losses in Developing Countries: A Survey," in *Nutrition Policy Implementation Issues and Experiences*, ed. N. S. Scrimshaw and M. B. Wallenstein (New York and London: Plenum Press, 1982).

12. K. Tontisirin, "The Nutrition Situation and Nutrition Action Programs in Four ASEAN Countries," *ASEAN Food Journal* 1, no. 4 (1985):162–68.

13. Booth, *Food Trade and Food Security*.

14. *National Nutrition Policy in the Fourth National Economic and Social Development Plan* (Bangkok, 1977).

15. Ibid.

16. A. Valyasevi, "Public Health Program to Promote Nutrition in Rural Areas—Thailand Experience," in *Nutrition and Food Science, Vol. 1*, ed. W. Santos et al. (New York and London: Plenum Publishing Corp., 1980), 527–45. S. Dhanamitta, S. Virojsailee, and A. Valyasevi, "Implementation of a Conceptual Scheme for Improving the Nutritional Status of the Rural Poor in Thailand," *Food Nutrition Bulletin* 3, no. 3 (1981):11–15.

17. Division of Nutrition, Thailand Ministry of Public Health, *Nutrition Surveillance Report*, various years.

18. K. Tontsirin, B. Moaleekoonpairoj, and A. Valyasevi, "Formulation of Supplementary Infant Foods at the Home and Village Level in Thailand," *Food Nutrition Bulletin* 3, no. 3 (1981):37–40.

CHAPTER 4

Food Security and Nutrition in the Arab World

Mohamed A. Nour
Assistant Administrator, United Nations Development Programme, New York, United States

The Arab world faces many constraints in its struggle to achieve food security and provide all of its people with access to sufficient food for an active, healthy life. Some of these are beyond human control, although their impact could be minimized if warning signs were heeded. Others, such as war and mismanagement, are self-inflicted. The net result, however, is that governments fail in their efforts to alleviate the suffering of the poor, the deprived, and the hungry.

This paper covers twenty-two Arab nations spread over a variety of geographic and climatic zones. In population size, they range from less than half a million to more than 50 million. The population growth rates are among the highest in the world, an average of 3 percent annually, compared with 1.7 percent worldwide and 0.6 percent in the developed countries. The total population of these nations was 192 million in 1985—some 70 percent in Africa and 30 percent in West Asia—and is expected to reach 290 million by the year 2000.

The gross national product (GNP) per capita ranges from $290 in Somalia to $23,770 in Libya, Kuwait, Saudi Arabia, and the United Arab Emirates. Despite the relative affluence of the region, the rapid population growth threatens to outstrip any advances in food production. For this reason, family planning is a high priority in development strategies. Arab countries also vary in the extent to which their populations are urbanized, from less than 40 percent in Mauritania, Somalia, Sudan, and Yemen, to more than 75 percent in Djibouti, the Gulf States, and Lebanon. The average of 45–50 percent is higher than the world average of 41 percent and the developing countries' average of 31 percent. At the present high rate of rural-to-urban migration, urbanization will reach 60–70 percent by the year 2000, exerting even greater pressure on the food supply.

Food Resources and Food Imports

Food security is nonexistent for a third of the population in the developing world (excluding the People's Republic of China), and half of those people are acutely undernourished. Not surprisingly, food policy is a central issue in many Arab countries. Unfortunately, their strategies to achieve food security are often neither cost-effective nor successful in reaching the target populations.

The outlook for food self-sufficiency in the Arab world is not bright. Most countries are experiencing difficulty in expanding food production. With a deteriorating global economic environment, commodity prices have fallen and debt problems have risen. Sluggish economic growth in the industrial countries has negatively affected the developing world. The slowdown in worldwide economic growth has intensified the estimated 2 or 3 percent decline in the national income of developing countries, which, in turn, is likely to lead to a 10–15 percent drop in the incomes of the poorest people.

Some Arab countries depend on imports to supply half or more of their grain for domestic consumption; and three-quarters of all imported grain is wheat. Cereal grains supply most calories and protein in the Arab world. In fact, poor people obtain 60 percent or more of their food energy and protein from bread, which justifies fortification of bread with nutrients like iron, vitamins, and certain amino acids that may be missing from their diets.

The Mashreq and Maghreb countries of the Near East and North Africa are deficient in cereal feed, food grains, and livestock products (meat and milk), a deficit that is expected to continue to grow. Syria's production of cereal grains fell short of consumption by 1.4 million tons between 1984 and 1986, a gap that will double by the year 2000.

Escalating expenditures on food imports devour a large portion of national incomes, raising the pressure on balances of payment and constraining development in other sectors. Food imports will cost the Arab states $200 billion by the year 2000, compared with $30 billion in 1984, according to a recent study by the Chambers of Commerce Union of the Gulf Cooperation Council. For this reason Arab countries are pursuing policies to achieve greater self-sufficiency in food production. However, only the oil-exporting countries with low agricultural potential can afford to provide and maintain adequate food supplies at relatively low prices, while improving distribution systems.

Some observers argue that many Arab countries should not even bother to feed themselves, since their resources could be used more effectively in other areas of development. But this presupposes the continuing availability of worldwide food surpluses on the international market and subsidized production among the countries that export food.

Land Use and National Food Policies

The trends cited above can be reversed only by undertaking new food production policies. Recent studies by the International Centre for Agricultural Research in the Dry Areas and by Syrian scientists reveal that a 50–70 percent increase in barley yields is possible if farmers were simply to adopt existing technologies. Livestock production, mainly involving sheep, could be doubled by better management of natural pastures, which in Syria constitute 73 percent of the total land area.

Land is inadequately used and often misused in the Arab world. Only 40 million of an estimated 198 million hectares are under cultivation, mainly in rainfed agriculture. In Algeria, the 260,000 hectares that are cultivated constitute only 4 percent of the potentially cultivatable land—the lowest ratio in the Arab world. Planners aim to expand the cultivated area of Algeria to 720,000 hectares by the year 2000. In Egypt, on the other hand, only 6 percent of the land is arable, and nearly all of it is under cultivation.

Desertification has damaged up to 80 percent of rangelands and rainfed croplands and 30 percent of irrigated land in some of these countries. The Sahara desert is spreading southward at the rate of 2–5 kilometers per year. From the air, Al Fasher, for example, a town in western Sudan formerly surrounded by farmland, looks like a city besieged by sand. Human beings play a large role in the desertification process and the exhausting of the land. Since 1950, livestock herds have doubled in the Sudano-Sahelian countries, leading to extensive overgrazing. In Somalia, where 90 percent of exports are derived from livestock, the rangeland is deteriorating from overuse. The rangelands of Jordan, Oman, Saudi Arabia, and Syria, among the driest areas in the world, are continuously grazed by domestic livestock. The conversion of rangelands to dryland farming has aggravated an already difficult situation in Iraq and Syria. Excessive woodcutting has contributed to the loss of topsoil in Oman, Syria, and the Yemen Arab Republic.

Fish Production

As the arable land shortage hinders agricultural productivity in Arab countries, the seas could present an important alternative food source. Fish and fish products provide a large share of the diets in developing countries. In Asia alone, an estimated one billion people rely on fish as their primary source of protein. The countries of Western and Eastern Europe, North America, and Japan harvested the bulk of the world's fish in the 1950s and 1960s. This situation has changed dramatically during the 1970s and 1980s. Developing nations now account for 47 percent of the world catch, although these resources are underutilized in many countries.

Recent surveys have shown that Arab fisheries account for approximately 8.7 million tons of fish stock. The Atlantic fisheries of Mauritania and Morocco are the most productive with more than 50 percent of the total stock; the Gulf and Arabian Sea fisheries have 23 percent, followed by the Mediterranean and Red Sea fisheries with 14 and 3 percent respectively. Egypt was the leading fish producer in 1983, with catches totaling 140,000 tons, and the Egyptian government has embarked on a variety of schemes to increase the annual catch. The other Arab countries, with the exception of the United Arab Emirates, have not fully exploited their potential in fisheries. However, production could meet or exceed consumption with the introduction of efficient fish farming technologies and fishery operations.

Fish and marine life in these regions tend to form a single biological mass. Therefore, the fisheries of neighboring countries are interdependent and based on the same ecological and biological conditions. It is important that these countries coordinate research in order to conserve stocks and increase fish production.

Nutritional Considerations

Young children are the group most vulnerable to malnutrition because of their extra nutritional requirements. In Arab countries, 40 percent of the population is under sixteen years of age; another 20 percent is between fifteen and twenty-four years old. Anthropometric measurements of children indicate a high incidence of malnutrition. For instance, a 1979 national nutritional survey in the Yemen Arab Republic indicated that the average rural child reached only 65 percent of the expected height for age, and 66 percent of rural children were below 80 percent of expected weight. In Syria, a 1979 survey showed that 20 percent of rural children were malnourished. A survey in Sudan's southern region in 1979–80 showed that as many as 39 percent of children up to the age of four suffered from protein and caloric malnutrition.

The studies of children and special nutritional surveys demonstrate that malnutrition and undernourishment are prevalent in the Arab world, worse in rural areas than in urban areas. Poverty looms large as a cause of malnourishment. Available data for seven countries in the region (Egypt, Democratic Yemen, Jordan, Morocco, Somalia, Sudan, and Tunisia) indicate that nearly 40 million rural people live in poverty—mainly the landless, wage laborers, nomads, small farmers, the unemployed, and the disabled. Yet poverty is not the only reason for malnourishment. Libya has malnutrition despite the fact that families are economically well off and foods are readily available. Lack of education and information about nutrition and health also are significant factors. Studies have shown that nutritional status can be improved when economic advances are accompanied by progress in education and health care. Food security, of course, can be achieved through measures that promote economic growth. Yet this is a long-evolving process in which the purchasing power of the poor is increased only slowly or hardly at all. Education and training must accompany economic development strategies.

Training, Employment, and Human Resources

Arab countries as a whole lack sufficient numbers of trained people, a prerequisite for the economic growth needed to stabilize food supplies. Many Arab countries employ foreigners in jobs ranging from laborer to scientist and engineer. To reduce this dependency on overseas workers and to promote industrialization, Arab governments should assign a higher priority to the training of scientists and researchers, especially in fields like biotechnology and electronics. The Arab world must be ready to capitalize on scientific advances in genetic engineering and biotechnology in general.

A few Arab countries, notably Egypt, train many scientists and other university graduates, but they have a high unemployment rate. Nearly 400,000 new graduates of Egyptian middle and vocational schools and universities seek employment each year, and, currently, an estimated 2 million graduates are unemployed. Many Egyptian scientists seek work abroad, especially in the Gulf States, Iraq, and Jordan. Unemployment among university graduates also is emerging in Sudan and Syria. Policies to advance industrialization have to be implemented to utilize these graduates; moreover, their training has to be better targeted to existing development needs and programs.

Women in Economic Development

According to a United Nations Development Programme (UNDP) study, women comprise about one-third of the labor force worldwide, yet they perform two-thirds of all the work, as measured in work hours. Overall, women receive only 10 percent of the world's income and own less than 1 percent of the property. International Labor Organization figures for 1950–75 and projections for 1975–2000 classify 35 percent of women as "economically active." This is deceptive, however, because the figures omit arduous and time-consuming domestic tasks that are particularly prevalent in developing nations, such as gathering, producing, and processing food for the family, caring for children, and fetching fuel and water. Women's participation in the work force in Arab nations is very low, according to official estimates, averaging only 8 percent. It is lowest in the Gulf States, Mauritania, and Saudi Arabia, higher in Lebanon, Morocco, Sudan, Syria, and the two Yemens, and highest in Algeria and Somalia (30 and 35 percent, respectively).

Some observers argue against raising Arab women's participation in the work force, because of prevailing high unemployment. This should not deter policymakers, however, from promoting female employment. Increased numbers of women in the work force would produce several socioeconomic benefits, including a drop in the population growth rate, a decline in female dependency, and advances in the education and training of women.

Price and Trade Policies

Farmers often fail to adopt new production practices because of misguided price policies. For example, Jordan in 1988 imported a large supply of meat just as local sheep owners were preparing to slaughter their lambs. As a result, the price of lamb dropped in the local market, leading sheep owners to use forage resources to maintain their animals. Eventually, they were forced to sell at lower prices. The experience has discouraged them from expanding their herds.

Jordan has implemented a pricing policy that encourages farmers to grow wheat in areas where barley yields are consistently higher than wheat yields (wheat yields are as much as 30 percent lower than barley yields). Wheat prices in Jordan are usually 60 percent higher than barley prices and, in the world market, roughly 30 percent higher. This policy encourages farmers to grow wheat in areas better suited to barley. The result is that Jordan, which imports both wheat and barley, is using more foreign exchange for cereal imports than is necessary, because price policies do not reflect the comparative advantages of growing specific crops.

Environmental Resources

From the standpoint of agriculture, the Arab countries represent a variety of environments, ranging from irrigated fields to deserts. Each environment could be better utilized by optimizing the cropping systems. High-intensity agricultural and livestock systems could be employed in areas with good water resources. The dry areas and even the Badia (i.e., rangeland in Syria, Jordan, and Iraq) have tremendous potential for increased forage production for sheep and other livestock. Convincing evidence from Iraq, Jordan, and Syria indicates that the control of grazing in the Badia can increase the animal-carrying capacity of the rangelands by up to 300 percent. The availability of livestock products can be increased by improving rangeland management.

Practices such as cultivating marginal lands around the desert for grain crops that provide low yields (and in some seasons no yields) merely accelerate desertification. Instead, shrub planting (already practiced in Iraq, Jordan, and Syria) should be increased. Jordan's efforts to grow grazing barley in areas with an average annual rainfall of 200 millimeters should be expanded with the aim of producing self-regenerating pasture barley that requires no cultivation. This can be done by using the available germplasm in the region (e.g., wild barley or its crosses with cultivated barley). In addition, solar energy resources could be better exploited, especially in agricultural areas where incomes are low, to expand the availability of hot water in both cities and remote villages.

Increasing Food Availability in Arab Countries

Because agroclimatic conditions, per capita GNP, and other economic factors vary among Arab countries, policies to promote food security in the Arab world cannot be uniform. Two classes of countries have to be considered: those with oil revenues but limited agricultural resources and those with few financial resources but high agricultural potential.

Countries with high oil revenues and low agricultural potential, including the Gulf States and Saudi Arabia, should avoid using their enormous oil revenues to produce crops like wheat that are readily available in international markets. This is uneconomical in the long run, especially if oil revenues diminish. On the other hand, fresh vegetables and milk, which involve high transportation costs, can be produced locally. The limited grazing lands must be fully exploited. These countries instead should use their oil revenues and low-cost energy to manufacture goods for local consumption and export. Well-planned and

-managed industries would increase job opportunities for skilled labor and university graduates, paving the way for the introduction of high technology in the Arab world.

The poorer countries with low oil revenues and high agricultural potential should concentrate their human and financial resources on agriculture. This can be done by growing crops that have a comparative advantage in each region, improving management of the environment, promoting trade and distribution of products within countries and among Arab nations, and establishing price policies that ensure high, stable incomes for farmers. Oil-rich countries could increase their assistance to agriculture-rich countries in return for crop and livestock products that their own countries do not produce.

Agricultural Research

Research is an essential first step to increasing crop yields and agricultural production. Despite the remarkable research progress in some Arab countries in the 1970s, there is still a great need to strengthen research institutions and build and retain the pool of scientists and other trained professionals.

Numerous constraints retard the progress of agricultural research in Arab countries and developing countries in general. For example, few Arab countries can afford to allocate the target 0.5 percent of the agricultural domestic product to agricultural research, as suggested at the 1974 World Food Conference. The information gap between research centers and the end users of research—the farmers—is a major constraint. In this connection, the transfer of research results and improved technologies to the farmers is essential. Two-way communication and feedback between them requires strong agricultural extension services. The most serious constraint on research is the continuous changes in government policies on and commitments to agricultural research. The resulting uncertainty and instability depress morale among research staff and precipitate the flight of specialists to other countries. Shifting policies also thwart efforts to link together the research enterprise with national priorities, the planners with the policymakers.

Cooperative Ventures

Sa'ad Al Din Ibrahim, a prominent Jordanian economic development expert, has advised Arab states to establish regional unions similar to the

Gulf Cooperation Council. This council started as a defense pact but successfully developed into a broader economic union of the Gulf States and Saudi Arabia that cooperates in various economic and social efforts.

Algeria, Libya, Mauritania, Morocco, and Tunisia in 1988 have seriously studied the potential for a Maghreb union and established committees to work out the details. A similar regional cooperative council could be set up for the countries of the Fertile Crescent: Iraq, Jordan, Syria, Palestine, and Lebanon. Jordan and Iraq cooperated closely in the Iraq-Iran war. Jordan and Syria have recently improved their relationship, and Syria and Iraq may be ready to settle their ideological differences. Another regional organization can be developed from the traditional cooperation between Egypt and Sudan in the Nile Valley and expanded to include Djibouti and Somalia.

The UNDP Regional Bureau for the Arab States fostered a strategy for subregional cooperation at an intergovernmental meeting held in Casablanca in March 1988. However, past experience indicates that intercountry cooperation may at times produce delays or even negative effects, and these have to be examined. Nevertheless, UNDP favors adoption of a subregional strategy for the Arab states along geoecological zones: the Gulf States, the Fertile Crescent, the Horn of Africa, the Maghreb, and the Nile Valley. UNDP also is promoting closer cooperation between Arab countries and Euro-Mediterranean countries through joint development programs.

In conclusion, agriculture and food security in Arab nations will continue to deteriorate unless corrective policies are developed and adopted in a timely manner. There is tremendous potential to increase food availability and security through proper use of agriculture, human resources, oil revenues, and, above all, by means of stronger cooperation among Arab countries.

Readings

Calal, O. 1987. "Qualitative Approaches for Security in the Moslem World."Paper presented at a seminar on Food Security in the Moslem World, Amman, Jordan.

Cornia, Giovanni Andrea, Richard Jolly, and Frances Stewart, eds. 1987. *Adjustment with a Human Face.* United Nations International Children's Emergency Fund (UNICEF).

Dinham, Barbara, and Colin Hines. 1983. *Agribusiness in Africa.* Trenton: Earth Resource Publications.

The Economic Arab Report. 1986. Kuwait: The Arab Fund.

Kandyoti, Denise. 1985. *Women in Rural Production Systems.* United Nations Education, Science, and Cultural Organization (UNESCO).

Khaldi, N. 1984. *Evolving Food Gaps in the Middle East/North Africa.* Washington, D.C.: International Food Policy Research Institute (IFPRI).

Lappe, F. M., and J. Collins. 1980. *Food First.* New York: Abacus.

Omran, A. R. 1988. *Population of the Arab World, Past and Present.* United Nations Fund for Population Activities.

CHAPTER 5

Perspectives on African Agriculture and Food Policy

Thomas R. Odhiambo
Director, The International Centre of Insect Physiology and Ecology, Nairobi, Kenya

Africa cannot feed itself. This was the unfortunate conclusion reached by the African heads of state at their economic summit in October 1985—a sequel to the devastating African famine of 1983–85—as they prepared for an emergency effort to mobilize the continent's political will and the world's opinion and resources in the task of restoring agriculture to its prime role in Africa's economic development. Their forthright conclusion was presented to the Special Session of the United Nations General Assembly in June 1986 in a document entitled, "Africa's Priority Programme for Economic Recovery, 1986–1990 [APPER]," as follows:

> Agriculture, which is the dominant sector in our economies, has rapidly deteriorated in recent years. The already declining trend in the production and productivity of the sector, which was noticeable since the beginning of the 1970s, has been dramatically aggravated by drought and natural calamities compounded by the problem of refugees and displaced persons, thus making almost half of the Member States of our organization dependent on food aid.[1]

APPER appealed to the world community for a net financial inflow of $286 billion over the 1986–90 period as a financial base for initiating the economic recovery program. The program called for the African nations themselves to rapidly increase expenditure on agriculture from the then prevailing 5 to 15 percent share in national budgets to at least 25 percent by 1989.

The financial aid that was promised has not materialized, however. Annual grain imports have reached 8 million metric tons. Only a few countries in Africa are self-sufficient in food, and none can produce enough wheat and rice—the grains that are rapidly becoming convenient staples in the rapidly urbanizing continent.

Providing a bleak counterpoint to the pervasive food insecurity is the growing poverty of the continent, which is worsening despite the deep structural adjustment programs that have been installed in country after country by the International Monetary Fund, the World Bank, and, lately, the African Development Bank.

Africa's debt burden has become almost intolerable. The total external debt had reached $218 billion by the beginning of 1988, equivalent to approximately 44 percent of the gross domestic product (GDP). Annual debt service obligations now cost between 100 and 300 percent of export revenues. Debt service obligations may well reach $45 billion a year by 1995, a burden that would certainly halt any economic growth, particularly since net financial flow into Africa falls far short of outgoings (i.e., outflow). In 1987, the estimated net inflow amounted to $20.5 billion, while the debt service obligation totaled $29 billion, making Africa, in effect, an exporter of financial resources, mostly to the industrial North. Africa's accelerating poverty cannot, therefore, be considered separate from its increasing food insecurity.

Most of the agricultural commodities, including food commodities, are exported by Africa as raw materials, without value added through processing and packaging. Thus, agricultural production is considered in isolation from agroindustrial production and processing. The interaction between agriculture and industry in Africa needs to be examined carefully, as it has proved to be a potent factor in economic development in other world regions. Africa has met a major roadblock in this area: Nontariff barriers against exports from African countries to Western Europe and North America (the continent's major trading partners) substantially increased between 1981 and 1986; they were particularly severe on processed commodities of cocoa, coffee, cotton, fruits, sisal, sugar, tobacco, and vegetables. Consequently, the export of raw materials has been encouraged over domestic processing. Even so, the prospects for coffee, cocoa, and other commodities on which Africa relies to create export-led economic growth are not encouraging. The average price index for these commodities was lower in 1987 than in any year since 1975, and the medium-term trends point to a continuing decline. These trade and external economic factors compound the problem and forestall any simple solutions.

At the same time, domestic policies relating to agriculture have fueled food insecurity in most African countries. African governments have neglected to cultivate domestic sources of agricultural innovation (through scientific research and technological development) or to develop a domestic infrastructure for agricultural production and marketing (by providing the resource-poor farmers with agricultural advice, credit, inputs, and markets).

Meanwhile, the North has clung to its own domestic food self-sufficiency and high-profile protection of its agricultural production despite their comparatively high cost. Farm subsidies to maintain low domestic prices and export subsidies to artificially lower the international prices of agricultural commodities (and thereby enable the main agricultural producers of the North to compete successfully for stagnant world markets) have distorted the world food commodity trade over the last two decades.

The consequences of these developments are that food imports have become comparatively cheap for Africa; food aid has become a profitable convenience for both parties; and Africa has thus lost the incentive to strive for food security. If the main international food producers within the Organization for Economic Cooperation and Development were to terminate farm subsidies (about $229 billion a year), the developing world as a whole would gain an estimated $26 billion a year.[2]

Yet agriculture will continue to be the dominant economic sector in most of Africa for at least the near future. Except for a few countries (Algeria, Djibouti, Gabon, Libya, Réunion, Seychelles, Zambia, and Zimbabwe) where the contribution of agriculture to GDP is relatively small (from 3 to 15 percent), a substantive 40 to 60 percent of Africa's GDP arises from agriculture.[3]

Some 71 percent of Africa's labor force work in agriculture; 77 percent of the population live in rural areas; and the health, nutrition, and income of the majority, who are overwhelmingly resource-poor farmers, are inseparably linked to the performance of agriculture.[4] It is estimated that the number of Africans in absolute poverty rose from 205 million in 1974 to 258 million in 1982 in a total population which has now reached 537 million.[5] Meanwhile, the number of malnourished has climbed from 81 million during the 1969–71 period to 99 million in the 1979–81 period.[6] Thus, Africa's inadequate food production and food entitlement are linked to its singular resource base and the interaction between its particular environment and human activities.

Africa's Fragile Resource Base

Africa's environment has never been an easy one for agriculture, except for the highland regions of East and Central Africa. For instance, the continent's soil resources are poor. Outside the fertile highlands, most of the soil, derived from ancient, weathered rocks, is low in nutrients and lower in clay content than that of most other tropical regions. As a consequence, its fertility and water-holding capacity are both lower: 55 percent of African soil shows severe or very severe infertility, while only 19 percent has no inherent fertility limitations.[7]

The low clay content and level of organic matter make much African soil highly susceptible to crusting or erosion once its vegetative cover is removed. Deforestation and overgrazing have resulted in widespread soil erosion throughout the continent. In Ethiopia, for instance, topsoil losses up to 296 metric tons per hectare have been reported on 16° slopes, and in West Africa up to 30–55 metric tons per hectare on 1–2° slopes.[8]

In addition, wind erosion and the resulting sand dune encroachment threaten many areas of irrigated cropland. In the Sudan, about 60 percent of the best irrigated agricultural land has been smothered by wind-blown sand; 40 percent of the inhabitants have left the affected area, mainly for the Gulf States.[9]

The climate prevailing in most of Africa is problematic. Outside the humid zones, rainfall is unpredictable, fluctuating by 20 to 40 percent up or down the annual mean. The risk of prolonged drought is high. In two-thirds of the land area, two or more successive dry years are likely to occur more than four times in a fifty-year period.[10] Botswana in southern Africa has just passed through five consecutive years (1982–87) without any rain. The Sahel faces unusually wet or dry periods persisting for one or two decades. Even during years of "normal" rainfall, the rains are spotty and sporadic.

It is possible that groundwater could prove to be a major resource for irrigating arable lands. For instance, only 30 percent of the available groundwater is being used in the Sudan, though preliminary studies indicate that it seems to cover the entire Nubian sandstone basin, half of which is located in the Sudan and the remainder in Egypt, Libya, and Chad. It is estimated that the level of this groundwater varies from near the surface to 100 meters below ground level, thus sustaining the supply to the artesian wells common in the area. A rational method of using this resource would be to acquire baseline information to determine the potential for exploiting it.

The harsh conditions stemming from the fragile soil and the problematic climate have perennially challenged African farmers to develop methods that would balance their economic livelihood with protection of the natural resource base. The traditional crop-growing methodology, commonly known as shifting cultivation, provided a thoroughly tested, ecologically appropriate response to this challenge. It specifically provided a period of recovery when the land was left to lie fallow for a number of seasons. In the process, the nitrogen level was enhanced, and organic matter from the decomposing vegetation was recycled into the soil; trees and shrubs leached nutrients from the lower soil and deposited them on the surface through the process of leaf fall; and the vegetative cover protected the topsoil against rain and wind erosion. The fallow areas provided grazing lands, fuelwood, and medicinal and other forest products. The farm implements used under shifting cultivation were simple and gentle in their impact on crop husbandry: Roots were left largely intact, and the cultivated soil was not deeply disturbed, thus reducing the potential for erosion.

Intercropping (the growing of more than one crop species at the same time on the same land) was almost universally adopted in shifting cultivation as well as in kitchen gardening. It preserved plant diversity, helped to exploit soil nutrients, and provided an environment significantly inimical to insect pests and plant diseases, while protecting the cultivated land against moisture stress and soil erosion.[11]

In precolonial times, the success of African traditional agriculture was largely dependent on shifting cultivation and its attendant intercropping and agroforestry. These methods led to the successful domestication of many important crops (coffee, cowpeas, and teff, for example), the conservation and husbandry of a large range of leafy vegetables that are a mainstay of the rural community, and ecologically sustainable agriculture.

The crucial failure of twentieth-century African household farming results from the agricultural scientist's contemptuous dismissal of shifting cultivation and intercropping and failure to understand their underlying cultural and ecological circumstances. The agricultural scientist lost a historical opportunity to scientifically rationalize these processes and to reassure the African farming households that the agricultural scientist is indeed a partner in their agricultural endeavor.

Shifting cultivation depended on abundant land for the stability and sustainability of production. As Africa's population and needs have grown, fallow periods have gradually been shortened to the point at which restoration of soil fertility and the provision of seasonal grazing grounds have virtually ceased, except in the large, humid lowlands of Central Africa. It has become necessary to intensify agricultural production on more or less the same land. Yet the appropriate technology to sustain productivity on fragile African soils has yet to be developed and tested.

One should observe that the African age-old tradition of communal land ownership may have contributed, at least partly, to soil conservation in the past, through a communal responsibility to use the land well for the present and future generations; however, farming households no longer have any long-term interest in this practice. Since political independence, there has been a progressive shift toward individual land ownership.

Equally significant has been the tendency of most African governments to invest little in agriculture. Government-supported parastatal agencies responsible for marketing agricultural produce have generally paid low prices for crops in order to provide the growing urban population with cheap food. Furthermore, high levies and taxes on farm produce have siphoned off a significant percentage of cash receipts from rural farmers, which has decreased the value of cash crops (tea, coffee, cocoa, cotton, oil palm, etc.) while making food imports artificially cheap and easily available. As a result, the shift to wheat and rice has accelerated, particularly in West Africa—even though these food crops are usually difficult to grow in most African countries because of their ecological requirements—while the depressed markets for the traditional staples (bananas, maize, millet, sorghum, tubers and roots) have discouraged entrepreneurial farming, other than for family subsistence. As a consequence, African farmers—except in a few countries such as Cameroon, Côte d'Ivoire, Kenya, Malawi, and Zimbabwe—have had no incentive to increase their agricultural production and to maintain the productive resources of their farmlands.

Africa thus finds itself in a dilemma. The need to find a long-lasting solution is urgent. The continent must increase its food production (the aggregate total of production), which has recently become uncoupled from its traditional knowledge base; but it must also enhance its capacity to rapidly increase its food productivity (the optimal yield per unit area) in the face of a Green Revolution technology that is rapidly becoming obsolete even in those countries that have so successfully practiced a high-input industrial agriculture. The recent drought in the American Midwest and the weakening natural resource base of the developed countries have sharply put into relief the lack of on-the-shelf technology to bring about a second Green Revolution in industrial agriculture. Lester Brown puts it in dramatic terms:

> Unfortunately, there are no identifiable technologies waiting in the wings that will lead to quantum jumps in world food output such as [are] associated with the spread of hybrid corn, the ninefold increase in fertilizer use between 1950 and 1984, the near tripling of irrigated area during the same period, or the relatively recent rapid spread of the high-yielding wheats and rices in developing countries. These technologies are playing out in some situations with no major new technologies emerging to take their place.[12]

Africa must employ novel technologies to improve the incomes of the rural majority, thus enhancing access to food and services in an international environment that has severely circumscribed its trade options. It must do this within a framework that conserves the agricultural resource base and halts and then reverses the environmental degradation that has become so pervasive in the continent.

The Beginnings of a Solution

Five key practices of African agriculture today seem to be unsustainable:

First, it is unsustainable to continue to employ technologies appropriate for other regions of the world in Africa, with its fragile soils, uncertain rainfall, and slender farming resources.

Second, it is unsustainable to rely on expatriate agricultural scientists, planners, and policymakers to develop farming strategies in an environment alien to them, as if the technologies were neutral with regard to their locale.

Third, it is unsustainable for African countries to ignore their traditional food profiles in developing food policy strategies. Central Africa, for instance, depends on bananas and root crops as staples. There is a vast domestic market, hardly recorded formally by economists, in bananas, sweet potato, and cassava. Yet there is hardly any research and development investment in bananas; and roots and tubers only recently began to command some resources.

Fourth, it is unsustainable to set food crops into competition with cash crops, since rural households can obtain access to food and social services only if they have the economic means to purchase them.

Fifth and finally, rural health in the African tropics is an overarching concern. Because acute problems of rural health were disposed of in the waning years of the nineteenth century in the industrialized North, they have attracted low priority when considering rural farming strategies in Africa. The reality is that infectious diseases—malaria (which comprises 60 percent of clinical cases diagnosed in rural health centers in Africa), river blindness, sleeping sickness, leishmaniasis, and childhood diarrheal and respiratory diseases—are a major constraint in rural productivity.

For this reason, the recent establishment of the Independent International Commission on Health Research for Development, based at Harvard, is a breath of fresh air. The commission comprises an impressive array of world health research and management experts from the developing regions as well as the industrial world, with the purpose of putting together a long-term program for capacity building of research and development in the health field in the tropical developing countries themselves (as reported in the British medical journal, *The Lancet*, of November 7, 1987). The highest priority should be given to building research capacity in the developing countries so that they can deal with these problems themselves. Leaders must be trained, and research and development institutions must be established and sustained. Often, rural health research and development programs are the first to be cut when there are budget restrictions; yet many rural development projects (e.g., irrigation projects, new agricultural production projects, and rural industrial projects) have been abandoned because of a failure to recognize the critical importance of tropical diseases in rural Africa.

Africa desperately needs to develop an array of agricultural technologies in order to address the singular tropical farming problems it is encountering under changing circumstances that require the intensification of cropping, while the productivity of the natural resource base is maintained. The essence of practices like intercropping, agroforestry, and minimum tillage, which made traditional African agriculture successful and sustainable in centuries past, must be revived and incorporated into innovative technologies yet to be developed, within a fragile environment and in circumstances that cannot be reproduced again easily: abundant land, a vigorous domestic market, and a traditional food preference profile.

What are the chances of bringing about this second farming epoch in Africa? Some observers think it cannot be accomplished within the next generation. One such knowledgeable writer, Carl Eicher of Michigan State University, states:

> After a third of a century of independence, there is a growing awareness in many circles that Africa may be generations, and perhaps centuries, behind Asia and Latin America in terms of its stage of scientific and human development and political and institutional maturity. . . . The level of development of the continent's nation-states was still roughly equivalent to that of Europe or China in the fourteenth and fifteenth centuries—and certainly no later than the seventeenth century.[13]

This is too pessimistic a view based on an argument that is too scanty to warrant close analysis. But it does focus on the crucial need to develop African institutions, including those dedicated to knowledge services. As the Brundtland Report, entitled *Our Common Future,* so cogently puts it, expanding knowledge increases the productivity of resources.[14]

African governments must create an environment in which creativity is rewarded and innovation is directed toward the major problems that constrain national development. The population debate in Africa ought not to focus solely on numbers. Poverty and resource degradation can exist in thinly populated areas, such as drylands and humid tropical forests. Surely, people (and especially the young) are the ultimate resource. Improvements in education, health, and nutrition allow them to better harness their skills and resources and stimulate and encourage them to experiment and raise their ingenuity above the mundane level of striving to survive. Similarly, the sustainable use of resources is as threatened by inequalities in access to resources and ways in which they are used as by the sheer number of people.[15] Thus, concern over the rate of African population growth must be accompanied by concern for human progress and equity. Governments should work on several fronts: to manage population growth; to provide people with forms of social security other than a large number of children; and to realize human potential so that people can better husband and use natural resources.

There is no doubt that Africa cannot simply transfer the know-how from other climates and cultures to its own environment, particularly in areas such as tropical agriculture and food technology, which are colored by the nature of the specific ecosystem and related culture. The creation of a critical human mass of excellence for scientific research and technology development in African agriculture is now the most urgent task facing Africa today. As I stated earlier this year:

> Technical assistance by itself has failed, over the last quarter century, to create this necessary condition for sustainable agriculture in Africa. Time and again, the history of science-oriented transformation of societies has shown that the development of indigenous human capital dedicated to the long-term tasks of national development goals and motivated by incentives to reach the highest levels of excellence and relevance, has proved a pivotal factor in sustaining such transformation.[16]

Notes

1. Organization of African Unity, *Africa's Priority Programme for Economic Recovery, 1986–1990* (Rome: Food and Agriculture Organization of the United Nations, 1985).

2. Centre for International Economics, *Macroeconomic Consequences of Farm Support Policies* (Canberra: CIE, 1988).

3. E. P. Pallangyo and L. A. Odero-Ogwel, "The Persistence of the Food and Agriculture Crisis in Africa," in *Economic Crisis in Africa: African Perspectives on Development—Problems and Potentials,* ed. A. Adedeji and T. M. Shaw (Boulder, Colo.: Lynne Rienner Publishers, Inc., 1987), 169–86.

4. *Financing Adjustment with Growth in Sub-Saharan Africa, 1986–1990* (Washington, D.C.: World Bank, 1986), 96.

5. M. Hopkins, "Employment Trends in Developing Countries, 1960–80 and Beyond," *International Labour Review* 122, no. 4:474.

6. Food and Agriculture Organization of the United Nations, *Fifth World Food Survey* (Rome: FAO, 1985), 26.

7. United Nations Environment Programme, *Map of Desertification Hazards* (Nairobi: UNEP, 1978).

8. C. Reij and S. Turner, *Soil and Water Conservation in Sub-Saharan Africa* (Rome: International Fund for Agricultural Development, 1985).

9. African Academy of Sciences, *Report on Long-Term Project on Drought, Desertification, and Food Deficit (DDFD) in Africa* (Nairobi: African Academy of Sciences, 1988).

10. Food and Agriculture Organization of the United Nations, *Crisis of Sustainability, Africa's Land Resources Base* (AGD/801/1) (Rome: FAO, 1985), 13.

11. L. Fussell and P. Serafini, "Crop Association in the Semi-Arid Tropics of West Africa" (Niamey, Niger: International Crops Research Institute for the Semi-Arid Tropics, Sahelian Centre, 1985, Unpublished Draft).

12. L. R. Brown, "World Food Supplies Tightening," *World Watch* (September–October 1988):10–18.

13. C. K. Eicher, "Food Security Battles in Sub-Saharan Africa" (Address to the Seventh World Congress for Rural Sociology, Bologna, Italy, June 26—July 2, 1988), 42.

14. World Commission on Environment and Development, *Our Common Future* (Oxford: Oxford University Press, 1987).

15. Ibid.

16. T. R. Odhiambo, "Transformation of an Idea into an Advanced Institute for Development-Oriented Research" (Address presented at Symposium on African S&T Institution-Building and the Role of International Cooperation, Bellagio, Italy, 1988).

CHAPTER 6

The Ecology of Food and Nutrition in Latin America

J. E. Dutra de Oliveira
Professor of Clinical Nutrition, Medical School of Ribeirão Preto, University of São Paulo, Ribeirão Preto, Brazil

The Latin American ecology of food and nutrition is certainly similar to that of the other less developed regions of the world. Hunger and chronic malnutrition are prevalent among the great majority of the people. Many countries of the region are not even dealing with a complete food chain but only with unconnected links; their people struggle to feed themselves without the benefit of a coordinated national plan. International and national action must be undertaken immediately to improve the food and nutrition situation in these nations.

However, a few Latin American countries have managed to break the pattern and make impressive progress toward closing gaps in the food chain, even under adverse economic conditions. There seems to be no particular political environment or form of government that typifies the countries that have successfully upgraded the nutritional status of their populations. Thus, it appears that improvements in the food chain are feasible within a variety of political and economic settings.

A Regional Overview

Bolivia and Haiti are among the Latin American countries that rank with the worst in the world in terms of general health and nutrition. For example, infant mortality in Bolivia was around 170 (per 1,000 infants) in 1960; it declined during the next decade and a half but only to about 113 by 1986. The population of the country increased from 5.8 million to

6.5 million, while the per capita GNP decreased from $600 to $470 between 1981 and 1986.

Other Latin American countries that are slightly better off than Bolivia and Haiti nonetheless rank very low in the food and nutrition status of their populations. Infant mortality in Peru, for instance, was around 90 in 1986, similar to the rate in 1981. In Honduras, it was 71 in 1986, a little lower than in 1981, and in Guatemala, it decreased from 71 to 61 in the 1981–86 period.

Average life expectancy was around sixty years in the three countries in 1986, an increase of only one or two years over the last five years. The literacy rate of the Peruvian population was relatively good at 91 and 78 percent for men and women respectively, a real improvement when compared to the 1970 rate. In Honduras and Guatemala, however, the literacy rate was only 61 and 58 percent and 63 and 47 percent, respectively. In these countries, first-degree malnutrition (i.e., 10–25 percent weight deficit according to the Gomez classification) is still common among children under five, and the rate of calories available daily per capita is very low.

Over the last five years, the rate of population growth decreased to 2.3 percent in Peru but increased to 2.9 percent in Guatemala and 3.5 percent in Honduras. In these countries, the use of contraception is much lower than in the developed, or industrialized, countries; the practice of breastfeeding, however, is much higher.

In 1985 the per capita GNP was a little over $1,000 in Peru, $720 in Honduras, and $250 in Guatemala. Women's life expectancy in these countries was a little higher than men's and their literacy level lower compared to men's.

In most Latin American countries (Argentina, Brazil, Colombia, El Salvador, Ecuador, Guyana, Mexico, Panama, Paraguay, Venezuela, and Uruguay), infant mortality ranged from 61 to 23 in 1986, a decrease from the 109–138 range in 1960. Life expectancy ranged from sixty-five years in Colombia, Ecuador, and Mexico, to seventy-two years in Panama.

Brazil, with the largest land area in Latin America (larger than the United States without Alaska), belongs in the above group of nations (in the middle range of social conditions) but has extreme variations geographically. Southern Brazil is well developed, with an advanced industrial center located in the state of São Paulo. Indirect nutritional indicators for the region have improved; infant mortality, for example, dropped from 116 in 1960 to 65 in 1986.

The northeastern part of the country, on the other hand, ranks with the least developed nations in socioeconomic indicators. The 36.5 infant mortality rate in 1984–85 in the city of São Paulo contrasts sharply with that in northeastern Brazil, where infant mortality frequently exceeds 150.

A significant report on improving health conditions has emerged from a community with a population of 11,000 Brazilians of low socioeconomic level in which the Medical School of Ribeirão Preto has been working for at least ten years in a primary health care program. The infant mortality rate has been reduced to below 16, showing the marked difference that attention to health needs can make, even in a community in which poverty is widespread.

An especially heartening situation exists in five countries (having very diverse political systems), the health and nutrition indices of which rank among the best in the world: Costa Rica, Chile, Cuba, Jamaica, and Trinidad-Tobago. The first three had infant mortality rates in 1986 of 20, 18, and 15 respectively, a significant decrease from the 114, 84, and 62 of 1960. Low birthweight is not a significant problem in these countries, and all three have a good per capita supply of food calories. The population growth rate is higher in Costa Rica (2.7 percent) than in Chile (1.7 percent) and Cuba (0.8 percent), according to 1986 data. In 1985 the per capita GNP was $1,430 in Chile, $1,300 in Costa Rica, and presumably around the same level in Cuba, although the actual figure is unavailable. It is noteworthy that the United States and Canada with per capita GNP of U.S. $16,690 and U.S. $13,680 respectively, or ten times higher than the countries referred to above, have rather similar profiles of health and nutrition indicators, or levels.

The favorable indicators in food and nutrition are far better than one would expect in countries with relatively low per capita incomes, underscoring the fact that government decisions to assign a high priority to health and nutrition can produce impressive results, regardless of the governments' political and economic structures.

No Single Cause

The Latin American food and nutrition situation is linked to a range of factors, including the size of the country, population, the economic situation, and food production. The available data show that widespread malnutrition is usually accompanied by a high mortality rate (among infants, children under five, and mothers), low per capita GNP, short life expectancy, and poor school attendance, mainly among girls. Moreover, these countries have lower rates of expenditure on health and education, faster population growth, less use of contraceptives, low status of women, and generally poor economic conditions.

This recurring pattern demonstrates that the problem of hunger and malnutrition has complex and multiple causes. Certainly, the solution cannot be found solely in health, agriculture, economics, or any other single sector.

Practical short-term action is urgently needed. Regional and local factors have to be analyzed, and the most appropriate multisectorial solutions have to be applied to each country. We cannot wait for the poor to become rich or for income to be distributed more equitably. We must stop merely talking about hunger and instead take action based on the premise that adequate nourishment is a basic human right. It is intolerable that thousands of children starve to death or eat barely enough to survive each day and that this is no longer news in the world. Unless we begin very soon, we will fail to bring about any substantial abatement in the worldwide incidence of hunger and malnutrition in our lifetime.

A Plan of Action

In devising a plan of action, one of the most important tasks is to develop local expertise, especially professionals who can recognize the multisectorial aspects of food and nutrition problems. Nations must not only train experts in food and nutrition but take measures to prevent the brain drain of specialists to other places. The nutritional status of the population will never improve if the country lacks sufficient numbers of well-trained local personnel. The public and private sectors should support local universities and research institutes in training professionals. Local and international organizations must promote the interaction of specialists within less developed countries instead of permitting them to emigrate to the industrialized countries.

In Brazil, a one-year, postgraduate interprofessional and multidisciplinary teaching program in nutrition is offered at the University of São Paulo in Ribeirão Preto. The program trains physicians, economists, sociologists, nurses, nutritionists, and other professionals. From its beginning in 1968, its main objective has been to demonstrate that food and nutrition are multisectorial concerns.

Despite this effort and the existence of a few comparable programs, multidisciplinary expertise in food and nutrition education and training is very limited in Latin America. In the past ten to fifteen years, a reasonable number of individuals have undergone training in nutrition, but only a few are still working in this field.

Specialists should not be trained exclusively in the developed countries, as is the present practice; rather, their experience should be diversified through a network of countries, particularly in the less developed ones. Professionals should learn about food problems in their own countries, close to the problems, and apply locally appropriate solutions.

A good starting point for this effort is to redirect and strengthen the work of international organizations. The number of groups that are working worldwide to combat hunger and malnutrition is considerable.

Anyone in the field can easily name at least ten to fifteen of them. Their headquarters are generally located in the industrialized countries. Their search for indigenous experts often results in a brain drain of the few specialists available in the lesser developed countries. These organizations send "advisers"—who are itinerant experts—to consult with host-country people and organizations (though they are not always appropriate and effective advisers). Their efforts have failed to reverse the world food crisis. Most of these organizations claim they have insufficient staff and funding to deal with so immense a problem worldwide. Some of them made progress in the past, as in the fight against goiter, but times have changed. The centralized nature of these organizations, with their top-heavy headquarters staff, has rendered them less productive, and alternative strategies must be developed.

There is a need for these international organizations, governmental or not, to pool their data, expertise, and funds, and to work more directly with local country institutions in the developing countries. Collaboration and coordination need to be strengthened with the goal of assisting these countries to develop national leaders and national solutions in food policy and nutrition. Implementation of policies within the developing nations has to be emphasized. An important task of international organizations should be to alert the world to the urgent problems of hunger and malnutrition that threaten the majority of the human race and to encourage all governments to assign to this problem the highest priority—the same priority that current campaigns to eradicate smallpox or AIDS enjoy. The advantage of this approach is that it could be carried out with available data and relatively small staffs.

With the impetus provided by indigenous expertise and the collaboration of international organizations, each country could improve the nutritional situation through the following additional steps:

1. It has to be accepted as a principle that every individual has the right to a well-balanced daily diet.

2. Government and public officials must become well informed about the precarious food and nutrition situation of the population.

3. The people should understand that the right amount and type of food have to be produced and consumed daily to prevent disease and promote health.

4. Developing country governments that favor cash crop exports must understand that reducing the amount of land devoted to food crops contributes to the spread of hunger and malnutrition. They must ensure local food crop production with prices comparable to those of cash crops and a good system for distributing food to the consumer.

It bears repeating that countries or regions with quite adverse economic conditions and very different kinds of political structures have managed to improve the health and nutritional status of their populations. Therefore, it is impossible to reach a solution by classifying hunger and malnutrition as an exclusively political or economic issue or by concluding that the only solution is a change of government.

The precarious food and nutrition situation in Latin America can be improved through a coordinated and concentrated effort of the international organizations working alongside the governments in the region. Trained specialists working in their own countries, with the assistance of international experts, is the long-range goal. However, each country should assume the responsibility for producing and distributing the food needed for its own population.

In conclusion, I want to summarize my point of view in two ways:

1. The most effective strategy to resolve food and nutrition deficiencies and problems in developing countries is to train and support indigenous specialists and professionals, who work with the problems at hand and who derive appropriate local and national solutions.

2. Ample food supply and healthy diets can be achieved in countries with very different political and economic structures, as long as their leadership has made a commitment to assign a high priority to food sufficiency and good nutrition. Even nations with relatively low per capita income still can improve the food and nutrition situation if a national commitment exists.

And last but not least, I want to say that human beings and the political systems they have built are responsible for having created the world food crisis; only they can develop the necessary solutions, and they must do so.

Readings

Dutra de Oliveira, J. E. 1988. *Food and Nutrition Policies in Brazil.* Ribeirão Preto, Brazil: Manuscript Nutrition Library, Faculty of Medicine, Ribeirão Preto.

First Report on the World Nutrition Situation. 1987. Rome: ACC/SCN.

Infant Situation in the World 1988. 1988. Translated and reported by the UNICEF Office, Brasilia.

Monteiro, C. A. 1988. *Children's Health and Nutrition in the City of São Paulo.* São Paulo, Brazil: HUCITEC-EDUSP.

Pan American Health Organization (PAHO)/World Health Organization (WHO) Consultation Group Report on the Regional Network of Food and Nutrition Institutions. 1984. Washington, D.C.: PAHO/WHO.

PAHO/WHO Program Policies Report in Food and Nutrition. 1988. Washington, D.C.: PAHO/WHO.

Santoro, J. R. In press. *Infant and Pre-School Mortality in a Small Town in the State of São Paulo.* Ribeirão Preto, Brazil: Faculty of Medicine, Ribeirão Preto.

CHAPTER 7

Overcoming Food and Economic Dependency in the West African Sahel

Anne de Lattre
Special Advisor, Club du Sahel Secretariat, Organisation for Economic Cooperation and Development, Paris, France

Food production and consumption trends in the West African Sahel have been disappointing since these countries achieved independence almost thirty years ago. A few facts based on foreign trade statistics, which are more reliable than national food production data, illustrate the magnitude of their food production and consumption problems.

Drought, Food Aid, and Economic Stagnation

In the early 1960s, the commercial and food aid imports of the West African Sahel countries averaged only 200,000 tons annually. In the acute drought years of 1974, 1981, and 1984, they varied between one million and 1.7 million tons. During the 1970–86 period, however, they averaged approximately 750,000 tons annually, even in the years of good rainfall.

Rice and wheat account for the bulk of imports. Urban consumers are constantly demanding more of these cereals. Yet local farmers continue to grow traditional crops of millet and sorghum; they have failed to produce much rice and cannot grow wheat because of climatic conditions.

The figures that have been quoted demonstrate two principal trends. First, the region is vulnerable to climatic variations. Pronounced drought leads to soaring cereal imports. Imports fail to prevent shortages, malnutrition, and even famine in some areas and among vulnerable population groups. Second, the Sahel's dependence on outside food aid is rising, irrespective of drought-related factors. Imports have risen by an estimated 8 percent per year over the last twenty-five years. Food aid accounts for a growing percentage of food imports. Unknown before 1970, food aid deliveries amounted to 100,000 tons in 1970 and 750,000 tons on average each year after the severe drought of 1973.

What conclusions can be drawn from this record? In the West African Sahel, food production is not keeping pace with population growth, which is estimated to be approximately 3 percent per year—among the highest in the world. Nor is local food production meeting the preferences of urban dwellers, who demand increasing volumes of rice and wheat. Furthermore, Sahelian governments no longer have the foreign exchange to pay for the imports to meet these needs. The principal cash crops of the Sahel—groundnuts and cotton—have fared poorly on world markets. Industries capable of producing and exporting manufactured goods have not been created. The demand for Sahelian minerals (copper, iron, phosphates, and uranium) has declined, as have their prices.

Cattle raising, another resource of Sahelian countries, has also performed poorly. Traditional herding methods still are prevalent but have reached their limits in a degraded environment. New techniques that would enable herders to meet the needs of the growing population are yet to be introduced. Meat consumption is falling in the Sahel from an estimated 18 kilograms per head per year in the 1960s to around 13 kilograms today.

Sahelian food production, on the whole, has remained traditional, inefficient, and vulnerable to drought. It has adapted in neither quantity nor quality to the needs of a population that has doubled in size since independence. It has adjusted still less to the needs of an urban population whose numbers have multiplied five-fold since independence. The Sahel region is increasingly dependent on external resources, particularly food aid. The recent return of favorable climatic conditions has not reduced this dependency.

Understanding Sahelian Food Dependency

The causes of Sahelian food dependency are multifaceted and deep-rooted. Scholars have probed the reasons for the poor performance of these states. Many of them have made valuable contributions. Their observations can be summarized in a nutshell: Sahelian societies are in a state of crisis, which has intensified over time. Historical, political, social, economic, technological, environmental, and other factors have combined to prevent these states from making the transition from traditional to modern societies. The economic development policies adopted since independence reflect this crisis.

The precolonial and colonial heritages are a component of the present crisis. At independence, Sahelian societies were still largely rural and traditional. Colonization brought the seeds of change to these relatively stable societies: sharp population growth, urbanization, and new values. These changes destabilized the historical social pattern. New classes arose, including a new political class strongly influenced by Western schooling and culture. Disruption of the fragile ecological balance began, although the signs of environmental degradation went unnoticed at the time.

The transition from the colonial era to independence was peaceful. The power base was formed from the political class that had emerged under colonial rule. The policies of the new leaders mirrored a Western-style development model—either liberal or socialist according to the country. Foreign aid encouraged the chosen model, emphasizing the priorities of industrial development; infrastructure to export cash crops, minerals, and industrial goods; expansion of social services; and imports of Western-style consumer goods. Food production was not considered a development priority. The state was expected to be the prime mover and the population was to follow its leadership. In the 1960s, these policies led to development and increasing prosperity.

Early in the 1970s, the oil shock, declining markets for groundnuts, and consecutive droughts revealed the weaknesses and contradictions of the development system. State-managed economic plans resulted in high taxation on farmers' incomes. Overtaxed farmers tended to withdraw from the official market into an underground economy. Agricultural and food production stagnated. Industry stagnated or shrank because national markets were small and fragmented, production costs high, and consumer purchasing power declining. The burden of expanding public sectors and social services became unbearable—far out of proportion to the limited growth of the productive sector. Pressure on incomes derived from productive activities mounted, demand for foreign aid increased, and rising external indebtedness became a temporary solution to financial stress. Development along Western lines failed to involve the populations, which became dispirited and fragmented. Policies had heavily favored the political class, its clientele, and a privileged urban minority. No organized power emerged to scrutinize and criticize the development policies that governments had chosen to implement.

New external shocks in the 1980s—the rising value of the dollar, rising interest rates, and two consecutive years of acute drought—exacerbated the situation. Conditions have improved since 1985, but previous trends have not been reversed. For the most part, the economies of the Sahel are disjointed and fragmented along urban and rural lines.

Conditions favorable for increasing food production do not yet exist despite the structural adjustment programs imposed on Sahelian governments by outside funding sources. The gap is widening between economic realities and the aspirations of a population attracted by the Western consumption model.

Yet, despite a disturbing picture, there are some positive developments in Sahelian countries that may augur well in coming years. In rural areas, traditional cropping patterns are being modified to incorporate new food and vegetable crops. Efforts are underway to fight soil erosion and deforestation. Improvements in and new combinations of food crops and cash crops are bringing results. In Mauritania private investors are successfully growing rice, millet, and vegetables on irrigated perimeters.

In cities, jobs are being created for new urban-dwellers, and goods and services at prices adapted to the low consumer purchasing power are emerging—a result of enterprise outside of government control. Productivity remains low, yet Sahelians are demonstrating that despite government policies, they are open to change and innovation.

The Role of Foreign Assistance

Official development assistance to the West African countries of the Sahel has been generous in the past fifteen years. It rose from $750 million in 1974 to about $2 billion in 1980 and stabilized around that figure between 1981 and 1986. Expressed in constant prices, aid commitments rose by an average of 3 percent a year between 1975 and 1980 and by an average of 7 percent between 1980 and 1985. Aid disbursements have more or less followed the same pattern. In addition to external development assistance, private sector flows, which are significant but hard to quantify, are augmented by a growing number of nongovernmental organizations involved in a wide gamut of projects.

The Sahel ranks among the biggest recipients of foreign aid in Africa: approximately $60 per capita compared with $30 in Egypt and $19 in subsaharan Africa, excluding the West African Sahel. However, an increasing number of donors are questioning the volume of aid given to the West African Sahel and the accomplishments of that aid. A growing number of observers regard Sahelian food production and consumption trends as highly discouraging, suspecting that the countries of the region are doomed to become perpetual basket cases ever in need of food aid. Battles are lost, however, when everyone accepts dependency as an inescapable destiny.

The time has come to develop convincing arguments to counter this conventional wisdom. The West African Sahel is in a position to increase local food production and productivity as well as food security. While it is clear that countries can only save themselves through their own efforts, overseas donors should engage in hard thinking about their aid policies and practices. These policies and practices have inhibited sound development more often than they have promoted it.

Donors should draw the attention of the Sahel to the impossibility of emulating the Western development model, which they so unwisely encouraged after independence. Considerable efforts must be directed to the bulk of the population, to the small farmers, to locale-specific food research, and to rainfed agriculture; so far, this has not been done. Food aid requests must be scrutinized and evaluated. Donors have over-responded to food requests because of the abundance of subsidized food in Western countries. There is an acute need for food aid discipline that would draw the line between increasing dependency and providing food security.

The results of development projects in all sectors have never been adequately evaluated to draw useful lessons of success, failure, and sustainability over the long term. Research needs to be undertaken without delay to improve understanding of the political, social, and economic realities in the Sahel and its capacity to adjust to change.

Despite the appeals for caution, economy, and wise management made by the International Monetary Fund over the years, the state apparatus has been supported, financed, and expanded. The adjustment process will be painful and difficult. Nevertheless, financial adjustment must be pursued whatever the risks because there is no alternative. The risks are high, yet financial adjustment must be turned into structural adjustment over a period of ten to fifteen years.

Few hard questions or interesting insights are being raised about the place of the West African Sahel in the world economy. Can market forces enable the Sahel to reduce its food dependency? Should not donors support the reversal of consumption patterns so heavily weighted in favor of imported rice and wheat? Should not the objective of sustainability become the principal force behind aid programs? Should not donors encourage private agriculture, private industry, private trade—all the forms of private initiative that have been so successful in their own countries and that have led, over time, to democratic government?

Readings

Giri, Jacques. 1983. *L'Afrique en Panne: Vingt Cinq Ans de Développement.* Paris: Karthala.

______. 1983. *Le Sahel Demain: Catastrophe ou Renaissance?* Paris: Karthala.

Huddleston, B. 1984. *Closing the Cereals Gap with Trade and Food Aid.* Washington, D.C.: International Food Policy Research Institute (IFPRI).

Organization for Economic Cooperation and Development. 1988. *The Sahel Facing the Future: Increasing Dependence or Structural Transformation.* Paris: OECD.

Timberlake, Lloyd. 1985. *Africa in Crisis: The Causes and the Cures of Environmental Bankruptcy.* London: International Institute for Environment and Development.

U.S. Department of Agriculture. 1985. *Sub-Saharan Africa: Outlook and Situation Report.* Washington, D.C.: USDA.

CHAPTER 8

The Energy Gap as a Factor in Nutrition and Food Policy

John C. Waterlow
Professor Emeritus of Human Nutrition, London School of Hygiene and Tropical Medicine, University of London, London, Great Britain

The concept of this colloquium on completing the food chain is to combine the knowledge and insights of several disciplines that are concerned with different links in the chain. In my experience nothing is more difficult to do properly, and seldom is it really successful unless specialists from different backgrounds are actually working together on a practical project for a reasonable length of time.

I am sorry to begin on what may seem a negative note, but I find it so hard to master all that is relevant in my own field, which I would call nutritional physiology, that I am left with no time or energy for incursion into other fields. Even if one makes the attempt, as I sometimes have, the knowledge gained is often superficial, and this may be more dangerous than useful. I propose here, therefore, to stick to my own discipline but to focus on some themes that are of obvious relevance for those concerned with the other links in the food chain.

How Much Food Does Man Require?

"How much food does man require?" was the title of a letter that some friends and I addressed to *Nature* fifteen years ago.[1] Some progress has been made toward an answer, largely through the belated intervention of modern technology, but much remains to be done. The question about humans' need for food, which basically means the need for energy, is clearly a physiological question. Some people believe that the figures obtained in response to this question have no real relevance or real use. Be that as it may, many agencies, such as the United Nations Food and Agriculture Organization (FAO), the UN World Food Programme (WFP), and the World Bank, seek after these figures or believe that they need them, and it is our job, as nutritionists, to respond.

The basic questions are: how many undernourished people are there in the world or any particular part of it, and what is the size of their energy gap or deficit? FAO has made a valiant attempt to answer these questions in its Fifth World Food Survey.[2] Although I differ with the findings in some respects, nevertheless it is an important and forward-looking document. The FAO approach involves three steps. The first is to estimate from surveys the distribution of food intake—or some proxy for food intake such as income—between different households in a given population. This task is difficult and complicated. The second step is to determine the distribution between households of energy requirements. The third step is to match the two distributions in order to estimate the number of households, and hence of people, whose intake is likely to fall below their requirements. This statistical exercise results not in an absolute number, but in a statement of probability.

My concern here is with the second step as it relates to adults. Since 1985, when an expert consultation convened by FAO, WHO, and the United Nations University produced a lengthy report on the subject,[3] the method used has been to estimate the basal metabolic rate (BMR) from body weight, age, and sex. This can be done from relationships established on the basis of the world literature.[4] It is then proposed that the *minimum* energy requirement should be taken as 1.4 times the BMR, which also is referred to as the *maintenance requirement*. This is a level of energy intake that will cover the needs of people who are minimally active, and it has a coefficient of variation of about 10 percent. Of course, people's needs will be greater if the nature of their lives requires them to be more active. Nevertheless, it is quite logical for FAO to take this level of 1.4 BMR as a cutoff point. If the intake does not provide such a level of energy, it can reasonably be called inadequate except for very sedentary people, who would then be classified as energy deficient or "undernourished."

There are three difficulties in this approach. First, the expected BMR is based on body weight, but many of us weigh more than we ought to, or at least more than we need to. FAO would calculate my requirement not on my actual weight, but on the lower limit of what has been called the "acceptable" weight for a person of my height. Unfortunately, as we shall see, we do not really know what this lower limit should be.

The second difficulty is that the relationships between BMR and weight have been established largely by measurements of people in well-to-do countries. There is a good deal of evidence, especially from India, that in Third World countries the BMR for a given body weight may be some 10 percent lower than for individuals in Europe or the United States.[5] This may seem a small amount, but 10 percent of world food supplies is a great deal.

Possibilities for Adaptation to Low-Energy Intakes

I mentioned above that some measurements in the Third World indicate that BMRs, which form the major part of total energy expenditure, may be significantly lower than those of people in industrialized countries. This finding raises what is now one of the key questions in nutritional physiology: to what extent can people adapt their energy expenditure in the face of a restricted intake? I am not here talking about an acute restriction, as in the case of the volunteers studied by Keys and co-workers[6] in the last war, or in obese people on lower energy diets; rather, I am talking about people who all their lives have been exposed to marginally low intakes.

The third difficulty, then, is that 1.4 × BMR is too low for people who are more than minimally active physically. Such people probably still constitute a majority of the world's population, though perhaps not for much longer. It is obvious that if a person's actual daily expenditure is 2 × BMR, 1.4 × BMR will not be adequate. There is evidence that adults can tolerate an imbalance such as this over short periods, as in a hungry season, but then, when the harvest comes in, they will make up for it.[7] Measurements at a single point in time may be quite unrepresentative.

Until quite recently, the only way of measuring a person's actual energy expenditure, including physical activity, over a twenty-four-hour period was by an extremely tedious timed-activity procedure, in which the energy cost of each activity is measured and its duration recorded for every minute throughout the day. It is only recently that a new method based on isotopically labeled water has been introduced, by which it is possible to integrate total energy expenditure over ten to fourteen days.[8] This method can easily be applied in the field, provided that the technology is available for the isotope measurements. Unless some unforeseen difficulties arise, it probably represents the most important breakthrough in nutrition since the last war.

Adaptive Processes for Economizing Energy

A true adaptation would be represented by an increase in efficiency, that is, the same output at less energy cost. Of course, one could reduce one's physical activity—what is known as *behavioral adaptation*—but this would hardly be a satisfactory method for those, like farmers in the Third World, whose livelihood depends on physical work. There may, however, be ways of carrying out the same task more economically. For example, to carry a load a given distance it is more economical to do the job slowly rather than fast. Thus there is a choice: to save energy or to save time? To operate slowly would be a successful adaptation to a shortage of energy intake, but the trade-off or cost is less time for other kinds of productive activity. Other factors that could be important for economizing the costs of movement are stride-length and gait. There is need for a much wider application of the science of ergonomics in the Third World.

There may also be biochemical and metabolic mechanisms for economizing energy, but we know very little about whether they actually occur. The possibilities have been discussed by this author.[9] In any event, it will take a long time for research on adaptive mechanisms to bear fruit.

Enumeration of the Undernourished

Without waiting for further research, there is a simpler approach to FAO's problem of estimating the number of malnourished—so simple that it seems absurd. Why should we not apply to adults the classical approach that has been used for children and take the body weight as an indicator of nutritional status? Weight can be normalized for height by the body mass index or BMI (Wt/ht^2). In Great Britain the average BMI of healthy and fit adults, soldiers of both sexes, for example, is 22–24 kg/m^2, according to age. In many Third World countries the average BMI is about 20, and in some it is as low as 18. A BMI of 16 is about the lowest that has been observed in people leading an apparently normal life; a figure of 14 is characteristic of anorexia nervosa; at 12 one is on the verge of death.

Observations of this kind, crude though they are, give us a kind of scale: below 16, frank undernutrition; 16–18, zone of increased risk; 18–20, possibly mild undernutrition; 20–25, no problem; above 25, excess.[10] Of course, different cutoff points could be chosen. The simplicity of this approach is that it is concerned only with the end result, the actual nutritional state, and not with the way by which that state was reached, whether through inadequate food intake or failure to adapt. Those are second-line questions, to be tackled when the undernourished have been identified.

Stunting of Growth in Children

In children the situation is complicated by the fact that they grow in height as well as in weight. A low weight in relation to height (i.e., wasting) can be used as a measure of current undernutrition. But what are we to say about the child who is simply small in size, with a normal weight for height (i.e., stunted)? This is an important question for planners, because in Third World countries 30–60 percent of preschool children may fall into this category. When I say "small," one may well ask, by what standard? Is it an appropriate standard? There is now wide agreement that the potential for linear growth in young children is very much the same in different ethnic groups and that genetic differences, which certainly do exist, are nevertheless small compared to those imposed by the environment. The obvious ethnic differences that are seen in adult stature are, I suggest, programmed at puberty.

If we accept that many young children are not fulfilling their growth potential, does it matter? D. Seckler, an economist, regards it as an adaptation that enables children to survive under scarcity conditions, because, being small, they need less food.[11] Small people also need less clothing and less space. One could argue that the secular increase in height in many countries represents a drain on natural resources almost as serious as the growth of population. The only *direct* disadvantage of being small that has been demonstrated without doubt is a reduced absolute capacity for physical work.[12] One report from India revealed that youngsters who were short in height had greater difficulty in getting employment as farm laborers.[13] This sequence of events would lead to a vicious circle: no work, no money, children (when they come) underfed and stunted, no work when they grow up.

The retardation in mental development that frequently accompanies stunting can hardly be a direct consequence of it; both kinds of retardation, physical and mental, result from impoverishment and deprivation—of food, of sanitation, of adequate psychological and social stimulation. Stunting is an index of poverty, but this does not get us very far. Everyone knows that there are countless people who live in a state of deprivation. The question that I ask the planners is this: would it help to know in more detail what kind of deprivation leads to stunting? There must be some defect at the nutritional or metabolic level that leads to impairment of the normal biological process of growth. I myself believe, perhaps unorthodoxly, that impairment results from a deficiency of good-quality protein, or of substances associated with protein in foods, such as calcium or zinc. Would it be of practical use, as opposed to academic interest, to try to establish this hypothesis? If so, there is a clear indication for further research.

I have dwelt on this subject because it affects so many children, and because it presents us with value judgments that are exceedingly difficult. One might take the line that, according to the UN Declaration of Human Rights, every child should have the right to full development of his or her genetic potential for both physical and intellectual growth. The latter we all accept: every child has a right to education. But what about the former? In my view, stunting may have to be accepted in the short term as a survival mechanism. The biological point of view has been well put in a recent review from which I quote: "Taking a more evolutionary viewpoint, we may ask ourselves if this condition of 'nutrition at risk' is not the living condition for which nature has prepared the human race: setting a high genetic potential, knowing by experience that the environment may thwart some of this potential."[14] However, is it too idealistic to assert that in the long term this dominance of the environment is not acceptable? Put in another way, the question for the planners is: are you planning for survival or planning for improvement?

Conclusion

In this contribution to the multidisciplinary debate, I have made no attempt to cover the whole field of nutrition, which would be impossible. I have tried to do two things. The first is to draw the attention of scientists and scholars further up the food chain to the basic biological problems, the solution of which seems to me important for rational planning.

I mentioned earlier that progress has sometimes been held up by the absence of adequate techniques. The doubly labeled water method for measuring total energy expenditure is a good example. The principle of this method was published more than forty years ago, but it has only recently been applied to humans. The reason for the delay was that the cost of making measurements in humans was prohibitively high, until the development of more sensitive mass spectrometers that made analyses possible with much smaller quantities of isotopes. This is a purely technical problem, one that I believe could have been solved much earlier if there had been an impetus to solve it. I believe further that the impetus was lacking because of the tendency of international funding agencies to emphasize support of applied research on Third World problems that has immediate short-term payoffs, and to regard basic or strategic research as academic and inappropriate. We may yet pay dearly for this.

My second objective is to ask the planners how they see these problems—as priorities or as peripheral? If we could come up with answers to biological questions, such as the capacity for adaptation, or the nutritional cause of stunting, would these answers be of any relevance to them, and if not, why not? The answers are very important to us nutritionists, because it is the planners who hold the purse-strings.

Notes

1. J. V. G. A. Durnin, O. G. Edholm, D. S. Miller, and J. C. Waterlow, "How Much Food Does Man Require?" *Nature* (London) 242 (1973):218.

2. *The Fifth World Food Survey* (Rome: FAO, 1985).

3. *Energy and Protein Requirements.* Report of a Joint FAO/WHO/UNU Consultation. Technical Report Series 724 (Geneva: World Health Organization, 1985).

4. W. N. Schofield, C. Schofield, and W. P. T. James, "Basal Metabolic Rate—Review and Prediction, Together with an Annotated Bibliography of Source Material," *Human Nutrition: Clinical Nutrition* 39C, suppl. 1 (1985):5-41.

5. C. J. K. Henry, "A Preliminary Analysis of Basal Metabolic Rate and Race," in *Comparative Nutrition*, ed. K. L. Baxter and I. A. Macdonald (in press).

6. A. Keys, J. Brozek, A. Henschel, O. Mickelson, and H. L. Taylor, *The Biology of Human Starvation* (Minneapolis: University of Minnesota Press, 1950).

7. A. Ferro-Luzzi, G. Pastore, and S. Sette, "Seasonality in Energy Metabolism" (Paper presented at the meeting of the International Dietary Energy Comparative Group [SCN/UNU], Guatemala, 1987).

8. D. A. Schoeller, E. van Santen, D. W. Peterson, W. Dietz, J. Jaspan, and P. D. Klein, "Total Body Water Measurements in Humans with ^{18}O and ^{2}H Labelled Water," *American Journal of Clinical Nutrition* 33 (1980):2686–93. W. A. Coward and A. M. Prentice, "Isotope Method for the Measurement of Carbon Dioxide Production in Man," *American Journal of Clinical Nutrition* 43 (1985):659–61.

9. J. C. Waterlow, "Mechanisms of Adaptation to Low Energy Intakes" (Paper presented at a symposium of the Society for the Study of Human Biology, Oxford, July 1988).

10. W. P. T. James, A. Ferro-Luzzi, and J. C. Waterlow, "The Definition of Chronic Energy Deficiency," *European Journal of Clinical Nutrition* 42 (1988):969–82.

11. D. Seckler, "Small but Healthy: A Base Hypothesis in the Theory, Measurement, and Policy of Malnutrition," in *New Concepts in Nutrition and Their Implications for Policy,* ed. P. V. Sukhatme (Pune: Maharashtra Association for the Cultivation of Science, 1982), 127–37.

12. G. B. Spurr, J. C. Reina, H. W. Dahners, and M. Barac-Nieto, "Marginal Malnutrition in School-Aged Colombian Boys: Functional Consequences in Maximum Exercise," *American Journal of Clinical Nutrition* 37 (1983):834–37.

13. K. Satyanarayana, A. Nadamuni Naidu, and B. S. Narasinga Rao, "Agricultural Employment, Wage Earnings, and Nutritional Status of Teenage Rural Hyderabad Boys," *Indian Journal of Nutrition and Dietetics* 17 (1983):281–85.

14. J. Ghesquiere and C. D'Huist, "Growth, Stature, and Fitness of Children in Tropical Areas," in *Capacity for Work in the Tropics,* ed. K. J. Collins and D. F. Roberts (Cambridge: Cambridge University Press, 1988), 165–80.

CHAPTER 9

Molecular Biology and Agriculture

The Need for Global Strategies

Pablo A. Scolnik

Research Supervisor, Plant Science Section, E. I. du Pont de Nemours & Co., Wilmington, Delaware, United States

The second half of the twentieth century is witnessing a revolution in the life sciences that will substantially alter our societies. Originating with the discovery of the structure of deoxyribonucleic acid (DNA), the molecule that contains genetic information, this revolution entered the field of applied technology when in vitro manipulations of DNA, generally known as recombinant DNA (rDNA), became possible. Biotechnology—the set of techniques involving the manipulation of live organisms for commercial purposes—includes but is not limited to rDNA. Agricultural biotechnology can be classified according to whether the techniques involve the use of rDNA. This article discusses my views on the impact of biotechnology on agriculture, particularly in the context of global strategies for agricultural research and development.

Biotechnology and Agriculture

The main characteristic of biotechnology is its integrative nature—its role as a clearinghouse for technologies developed in many different areas of the life sciences. It is therefore difficult to forecast the overall impact of biotechnology on food production in general and agriculture in particular. However, certain ideas are already entering the product development stage and can be used as the starting point for this analysis.

Several products that are currently being tested are based on genetic engineering, which consists of introducing rDNA into genomes to generate transgenic organisms. This technique can enhance the ability of crop plants to resist herbicides, environmental stress, and bacterial, fungal, insect, and viral attack. Obviously, the success of genetic engineering programs depends on our ability to obtain transgenic plants.

Transformation and regeneration of plants was first accomplished with model systems of little or no commercial importance. However, progress on the transformation of crop species has been rapid: success has already been reported with rice, soybeans, and tomatoes, and progress is now being made with maize. It is realistic to expect that transgenic plants of most major crops will be available by the early 1990s.

Biotechnology can also be used to design sensitive diagnostic tools. It is possible, for instance, to detect the presence of a plant pathogen by searching for its specific DNA sequences. The sensitivity of these assays allows for detection of the pathogen at the onset of infection, and protective measures can be taken before extensive damage occurs. In addition to the detection of plant pathogens, DNA molecular probes can be used in plant breeding. A technique known as restriction fragment length polymorphism (RFLP) can be used to correlate the presence of a certain DNA sequence with desirable quantitative and qualitative traits. Using RFLPs, the breeder can screen the progeny of a genetic cross without having to wait for the phenotype (i.e., the visible properties of an organism) to be expressed.

Plant tissue culture and micropropagation are the two most important techniques that do not require rDNA. Plant tissue culture is essential for generating transgenic plants. Also, mutations arise in the course of regenerating plants from tissue culture. This process, generally termed *somoclonal variation,* can provide new and useful traits to be incorporated into breeding programs. Micropropagation is a branch of plant tissue culture that can provide a large number of disease-free, genetically identical plants. Although at the present time micropropagation is used primarily as a research tool or a means of propagating expensive ornamentals, automating the process could lower production costs to the point of making the use of seeds unnecessary.[1] Tissue culture can also be used to preserve germplasm that is difficult to maintain in the form of seeds.

The information generated by biotechnologists has to be transferred to the plant breeders, who are ultimately responsible for introducing useful traits into the appropriate germplasm. Systematic preservation of germplasm, using tissue culture if necessary, preserves genetic diversity, and it is, therefore, essential for the future of agricultural biotechnology.

Both transgenic plants and the systematic use of RFLPs in breeding should bring significant increases in both the quantity and quality of food crops and increases in agricultural productivity. However, these approaches have limitations. The number of genes that can be beneficial to plants and that have been cloned or replicated is relatively small, and progress in increasing that number is rather slow. RFLP technology is limited to mutations that have already occurred in nature. In the long run, transgenic plants will provide the major breakthrough in the agricultural uses of biotechnology, but we must first clone and learn to manipulate more genes for agriculturally important traits.

When we examine the strategies for genetically engineering plants with traits as complex as improved quality of oils and proteins or enhanced yields, we realize that the major stumbling block is our general paucity of knowledge in plant biology. It is interesting to note that although basic observations in biology, such as the laws of heredity and the existence of transposable elements (i.e., pieces of DNA that can "jump" around the genome), were made with plants, our society still undervalues plant science in favor of animal and human research. However, the industrialized nations will have to realize that, sooner or later, the technological challenges posed by the need to feed an exploding global population can be met only by mounting a massive and comprehensive effort to explain the major biosynthetic and regulatory processes of plants at the molecular level.

Evolution of Agricultural Biotechnology in the United States

The biotechnology industry has become a reality in less than a decade—since the first research papers on recombinant DNA were published. The speed with which this process has taken place exemplifies the dynamism of scientific research in industrialized societies.

An analysis of the primary forces behind agricultural biotechnology in the United States can provide additional insights for implementing international programs in this area. The basic principles on which biotechnology is based had already been identified, and a sense of excitement about the economic possibilities of these techniques pervaded the scientific community. However, the know-how in biotechnology resided primarily in non-land-grant (or private) universities (NLGUs), while land-grant universities (LGUs), which had been established for the study of agriculture, were largely unable to respond rapidly to the changes taking place in biology.

Successful application of biotechnology to agricultural problems depends ultimately on the plant breeds that should be the final focus of the collaborative efforts of molecular biologists, biochemists, and plant physiologists. This process of interdisciplinary integration is difficult but essential for the future of agricultural biotechnology.

At the same time that NLGU researchers were starting to focus on problems of plant molecular biology, the private sector moved feverishly into biotechnology. As usual, the investment was primarily in biomedical technology, but several companies focused on biotechnology, which, even by conservative estimates, should eventually account for a $100 billion-plus market. Multinational corporations started such programs, which, in some cases, are complemented by active efforts in basic research. These corporations regard biotechnology as a natural extension of their agrichemical divisions.

The birth of the scientist-entrepreneur was also a phenomenon of the early 1980s. Excitement over the economic promises of recombinant DNA drove many university professors to the emergent field of industrial biotechnology. Companies financed by venture capital were created at such a pace that keeping track of their acronyms was almost impossible. The expertise was provided by university professors, who dedicated part or all of their time to these ventures. The classical distinction between "pure" and "applied" research became very blurred, and industry and academia began to form close ties.

Federal research funding for plant sciences constitutes only a small fraction of the amount required to cover the technological needs of the next decade. The private sector continues to carry out much of the development in biotechnology, and the pressure to utilize limited resources efficiently favors interactions between industry and academic laboratories. These interactions take the form of scientific-industrial parks and joint programs financed at least partially by federal grants.

Academic biologists, in other words, were the main driving force behind the development of agricultural biotechnology in the United States; they gave birth to plant molecular biology as a discipline and in a number of cases pioneered commercial applications. Another important element in this development, which is unlikely to become profitable in the immediate future, is the support of venture capital. Contract work with larger corporations also plays a role. Thus, basic research and product development are following a parallel and very interactive path.

Most fears expressed early in the process have not materialized. Universities have not been depleted of molecular biologists. Multinationals have not swallowed the small biotechnology companies, which, with some ups and downs, have managed to survive and in some cases to prosper. Regulatory and environmental concerns have focused more on genetically engineered microbes and ethical aspects of human and animal genetics than on transgenic plant development.

Barriers to Biotechnology in Developing Countries

A consensus of opinion is emerging around the major political and economic trends for the balance of the twentieth century that favors attention to the needs of the developing countries. First, the economic importance of national boundaries appears to be declining rapidly, and both marketing and manufacturing are becoming increasingly global in scale. Second, the main sources of political conflict appear to be shifting from East-West to North-South; the superpowers' conflict is likely to be overshadowed by the urgent issues of underdevelopment, of which food production is the most pressing. To ensure long-term peace and stability, we must develop strategies to integrate developing countries into the global economy. From the point of view of biotechnology, international research and development can spearhead a wider economic integration in the future.

However, several obstacles have to be dealt with before biotechnology can advance in the developing world. Common to all nations is the fact that the plant breeder is the ultimate recipient of new knowledge. Molecular biology research is not widespread in the developing world, and most technology will probably have to be imported from abroad. Nor is the lack of significant efforts in molecular biology research limited to developing countries facing economic crises. Newly industrialized countries of Asia also have neglected this area of technology.

The education of young scientists from developing countries is, of course, a prerequisite for future development. Training opportunities exist in both American and European laboratories, generally in the form of graduate or postgraduate studies. Already, American universities train students from virtually every nation in the world. However, many brilliant scientists do not return to their native countries or, if they do return, do not find the support needed to compete at the international level. Appropriate funding of individual laboratories does not seem to change this situation. Bureaucratic barriers in developing countries, as well as problems of isolation from the world's scientific community, also conspire against scientific production in developing countries.

Venture capital, which played an important role in the development of American biotechnology, is difficult to obtain in the developing world. This problem is complicated by the fact that many multinational corporations exclude developing countries from their international biotechnology programs, and, thus, interactions that could occur between local companies and the multinationals do not.

The exclusion of developing countries from international marketing strategies deserves further analysis. Current market analyses are based on the purchasing power of people in different countries. It is perceived that agricultural biotechnology will increase the quality of agricultural products for both developing and developed nations but that the return on investments will come mostly from industrialized nations. Although this corresponds to obvious economic realities, it would be naive to overlook the precarious social and political conditions in developing countries that threaten to disrupt economic transactions with industrialized nations. To adapt to new global realities, development agents will have to be trained to consider not only economic but also political and social factors in their planning.

It is important to note that markets that today seem unattractive because of the time scale and the net value of returns can become important in the future. Also, as manufacturing and processing become global, numerous countries can play roles in global production. For example, germplasm available in one country can play a major role in generating new product lines that can be successfully marketed worldwide.

To summarize, biotechnological progress in developing countries faces several problems. First, the lack of capital and the limited markets undermine efforts to attract researchers to join the enterprise. Second, molecular biology research costs considerably more than any other area of biological research. The generally weak economic situation of developing nations thwarts the emergence of such research programs. Third, even when individual laboratories are properly financed, restrictions on imported equipment, travel, and transfer of knowledge, as well as political conflict and other factors conspire against the establishment of successful programs.

A possible solution is for both academic and private laboratories in the United States, Europe, and Japan to actively collaborate on research with the best scientists in developing countries. For these collaborations to be effective, researchers from developing nations must be allowed to communicate freely with their counterparts in the industrialized world, to exchange visits to complete work initiated abroad, and to participate in scientific meetings and training courses.

As a scientist involved in basic research in plant biology, I am convinced that molecular biology will be the driving force behind the next Green Revolution. However, the effort must be interdisciplinary, and researchers of diverse backgrounds, particularly breeders, must be brought together under the general umbrella of biotechnology.

The funding dedicated to basic research in plant biology is presently well below the minimum required to ensure significant increases in food production by the end of this century. The presence of agricultural surpluses in the United States has been used as an argument against increasing funding for agricultural research. However, as demonstrated by the 1988 drought in the U.S. Midwest, the surplus safety blanket is illusory. Crash programs, implemented after a crisis has already developed, do not work very well in biology or biotechnology. What is needed is creative, stable, long-term support.

Any significant initiative in agricultural biotechnology must include the developing world. Harmonious worldwide economic and political growth depends on policies that stimulate technological progress in the developing countries. Since agricultural problems are global in nature, this solution demands global cooperation. It is time to realize that feeding the world will not be easy in the twenty-first century. As scientists, we can accept the challenge if we receive appropriate support for our work.

Notes

1. R. L. M. Pierik, *In Vitro Culture of Higher Plants* (Dordrecht, Netherlands: Martinus Nijhoff Publishers, 1987), 229–30.

Readings

National Research Council. 1987. *Agricultural Biotechnology: Strategies for National Competitiveness.* Washington, D.C.: National Academy Press.

———. 1984. *Genetic Engineering of Plants: Agricultural Research Opportunities and Policy Concerns.* Washington, D.C.: National Academy Press.

CHAPTER 10

Food Science, Technology, and Agroindustry

Ricardo Bressani
Research Coordinator in Food Science and Agriculture, Instituto de Nutrición de Centro América y Panama, Guatemala City, Guatemala

Science and technology have contributed significantly to improving food systems. This paper discusses the potential of food science and technology in two specific areas: the development of standards to measure food crop quality and the use of agroindustries to improve the food system.

To be successful, both tasks require the active participation and exchange of ideas and experiences of professionals from a number of disciplines. In addition, both tasks require active participation by consumer groups, who must decide what improvements they would like and how they can help achieve them. In addition, market forces must be carefully considered throughout the process. In fact, balancing market and consumer concerns is the most difficult problem facing a developing country in its efforts to improve food systems.

The Food Chain

At the most basic level, achieving food and nutrition security means increasing food production. A more complex explanation takes into consideration a number of components, including the food chain.[1] The interrelationships of various disciplines and their activities and outputs are shown in figure 10–1. The environment's capacity to produce is linked with the environment of the consumer population, which should be able to utilize the outputs of the entire system.[2]

Figure 10–1.

The Food Chain: A Multidisciplinary System to Deliver Food and Nutrition to Consumers

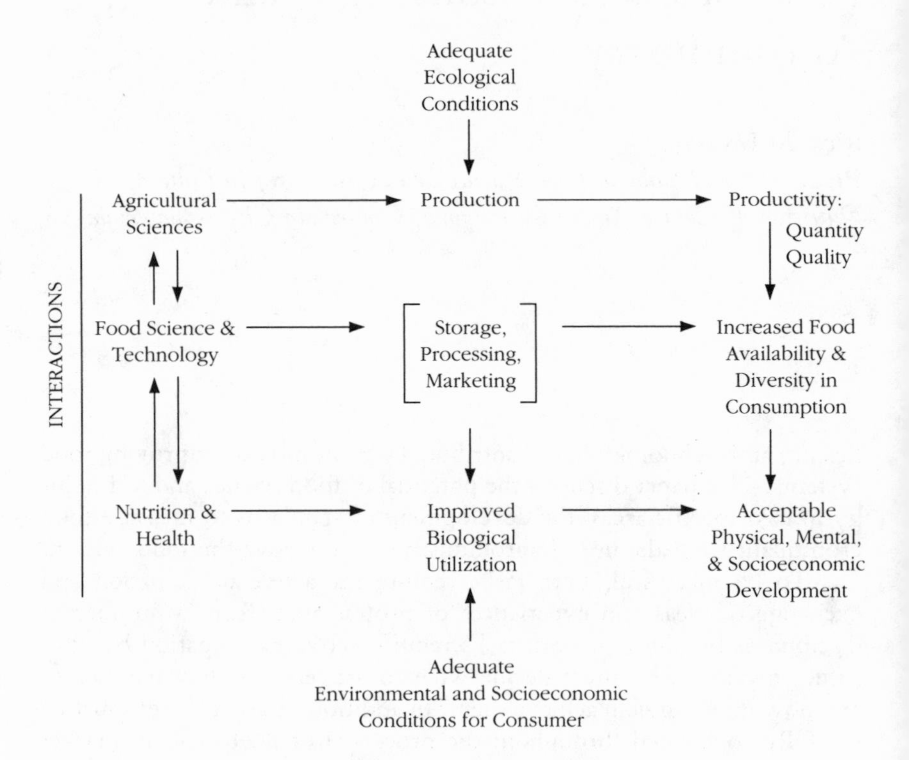

Food Crop Quality Objectives

Until very recently, the main objective of agricultural scientists was to increase productivity, or production per unit of land, by applying scientific and technological research findings. Although no one can deny the significance of this objective, these efforts failed to take into consideration the needs of the target population, such as decent conditions for production, food acceptability, and nutritive value.[3] These are the elements that determine food crop quality. Food science and technology can contribute significantly to food quality by identifying, defining, and developing methods to evaluate food storage, processing, acceptability, and bioutilization.

Grain quality characteristics for common beans, for example, are shown at different points on the food chain in figure 10–2.[4] At the production stage, farmers expect high and stable yields, which are obtained through proper breeding and disease-resistance measures and acceptable cultivation practices. At harvest time, farmers want pods of uniform size and color that reach physiological maturity at the same time, and grain that separates easily from the pod. At the storage stage, farmers want insect-resistant beans that retain their color and that develop slowly to the hard-to-cook condition—namely, qualities that the consumer finds acceptable.

The user, whether a housewife or a food industry, wants to process a bean with a thin seed coat, stable color, rapid hydration, short cooking time, and a thick-cooking liquor. Processing should be effective enough to eliminate antinutritional factors without affecting the bioavailability of other nutrients. The bean nutrients, particularly protein, should also be highly available and effectively supplement other staple foods.

The task is to identify and define these attributes and to develop appropriate methodology for selecting and evaluating their presence in

Figure 10–2.

Grain Quality Attributes for Common Beans

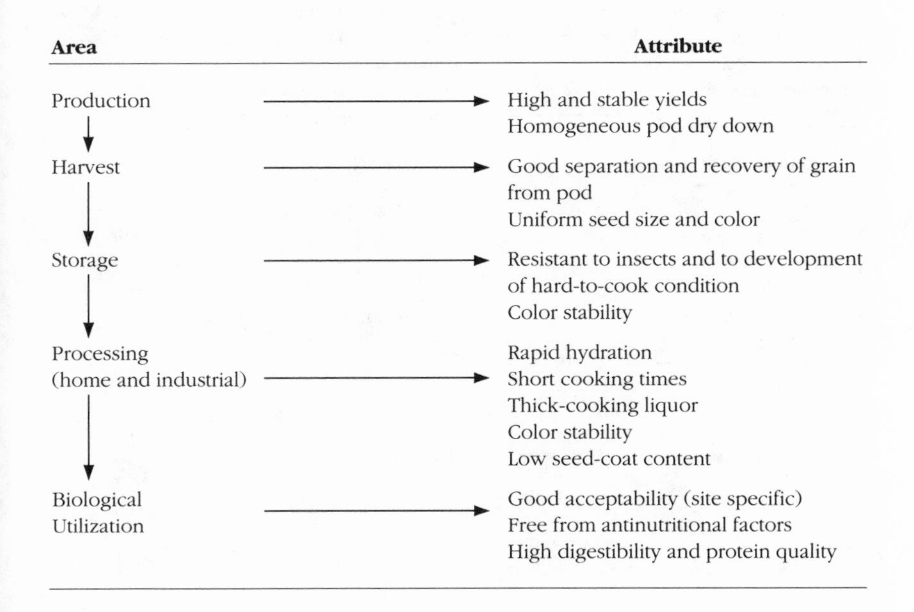

Figure 10–3.

Chemical Compounds and the Food Chain

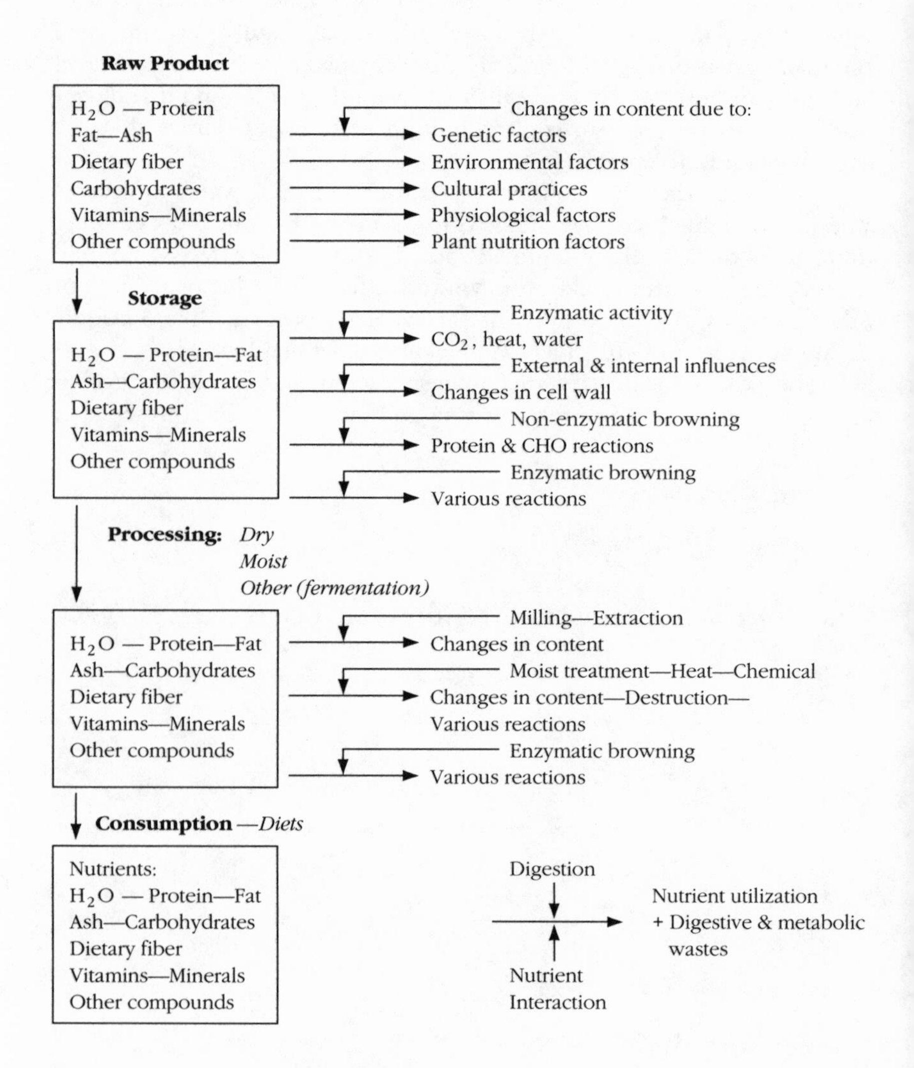

the grains. This requires a multidisciplinary approach involving agricultural scientists, food scientists and technologists, and nutritionists.

This approach is so vital to achieving high quality in food grains that it is necessary to expand on it, even though it may seem obvious.[5] Figure 10–3 shows the different steps in the food chain and lists the major chemical compounds present in food. These compounds are responsible for the characteristics shown in figure 10–2. The compounds are affected by many factors, such as genetic makeup, environmental conditions, cultivation practices, and disease and nutrition of the plant or animal. The seed is biologically active during storage, which influences the stability and content of the chemical compounds. External factors also influence the biological activity of the grain, but those changes may be subtle and difficult to evaluate. The same chemical compounds are susceptible to change during processing, but these changes can be controlled. Finally, the chemical compounds become nutrients when the individual consumes the food.

Utilization of the nutrients in the food depends on both the individual effects of external factors particular to each link of the food chain and on the interaction of the nutrients in the foods making up the diet. The chemical compounds offer the means to evaluate and quantify grain quality factors.

Thus, to attain high-quality food crops, the concerted effort of many disciplines is required. The food scientist develops the methodology to evaluate the crops, although the ultimate evaluation comes in the marketplace.

Food Science, Technology, and the Role of Agroindustry

Another important role of food science and technology is to improve food systems in the areas of production, marketing, and bioutilization. These include increased opportunities for crop utilization as food; increased efficiency in weak links of the food system, such as better storage to retain grain integrity and to reduce food losses; processing of feed and nonfood products for other production-processing systems; and the incorporation of food processing at home or in industry for better use of food crops and/or preservation for future consumption.

Agroindustries are often mistakenly perceived as processing units, rather than as important components in a food system. However, when they are integrated into food systems, they can complement both production and marketing activities. Conceived in such a way, agroindustries not only contribute to economic development, but also help solve the population's nutritional problems.[6]

Agroindustry's role is also commonly misconstrued as limited to processing and converting crops to food products for human consumption. Too little attention is directed to processing activities designed to utilize residues and by-products in nonfood products, thus enhancing the value of the entire system.

Agroindustries can significantly improve the food system in a number of ways. Figure 10–4 shows areas in the food chain where agroindustries could be involved.[7] They may, for example, be useful in selecting and storing seed for improved production or improved marketing schemes.

Common agroindustry practices are to market select agricultural products in different sizes, shapes, and colors; to charge more for a product when it is fresh; and to label processed products as second or third class. The development of storage facilities so the product can be marketed off season is another approach. Processing can serve to reduce losses at times of high production. It is also important to remember that the processed foods should be included in the diet of the rural population as well as marketed elsewhere.

The market and agroindustry considerations are fundamental to food system improvement. Both can play an important role in promoting the quality and quantity of agricultural production based on market demands. Breeders, agronomists, food technologists, and food scientists, as well as marketing specialists, can work together with organized production and processing groups (cooperatives, for example).

It is common for fruits, vegetables, and other perishable crops to be transported to market by truck. The produce is piled relatively high and the weight of the products, the bouncing of the truck, and the exposure to sun and rain cause much damage. Thus, important improvements could be made in packaging for transport.

It is also common to see immature maize piled in the market to be consumed as ear corn. Farmers can easily obtain three to four times more for corn sold in this manner than for corn sold dried or mature. The losses are very high due to the lack of cool storage or any storage facilities at all. Processing of this immature corn would be a profitable activity, particularly if the green plants left in the field were used to feed animals and the fresh green husks and ears entered other production systems.

Studies should be conducted on how the local people use particular crops. For example, sorghum is considered a second-class grain, but many products are made from its flour or grain in the regions that produce it. A popular example is popped sorghum grain. (Popped corn using imported grain also has become a popular snack food.)

Agroindustries that process agricultural residues can significantly

Figure 10–4.

Agroindustries in the Food Chain

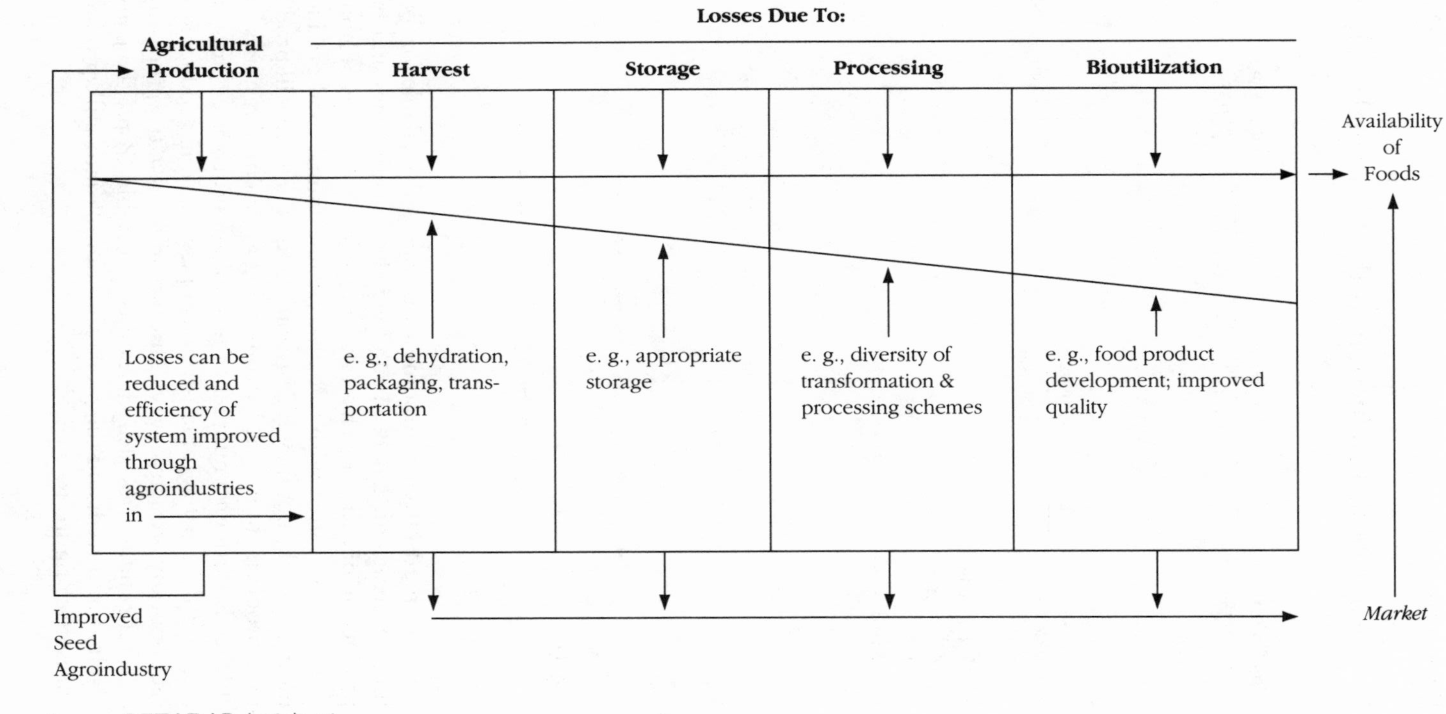

Source: RETADAR (1985): 16.

Figure 10–5.

Increasing Milk Production in the Guatemala Highlands

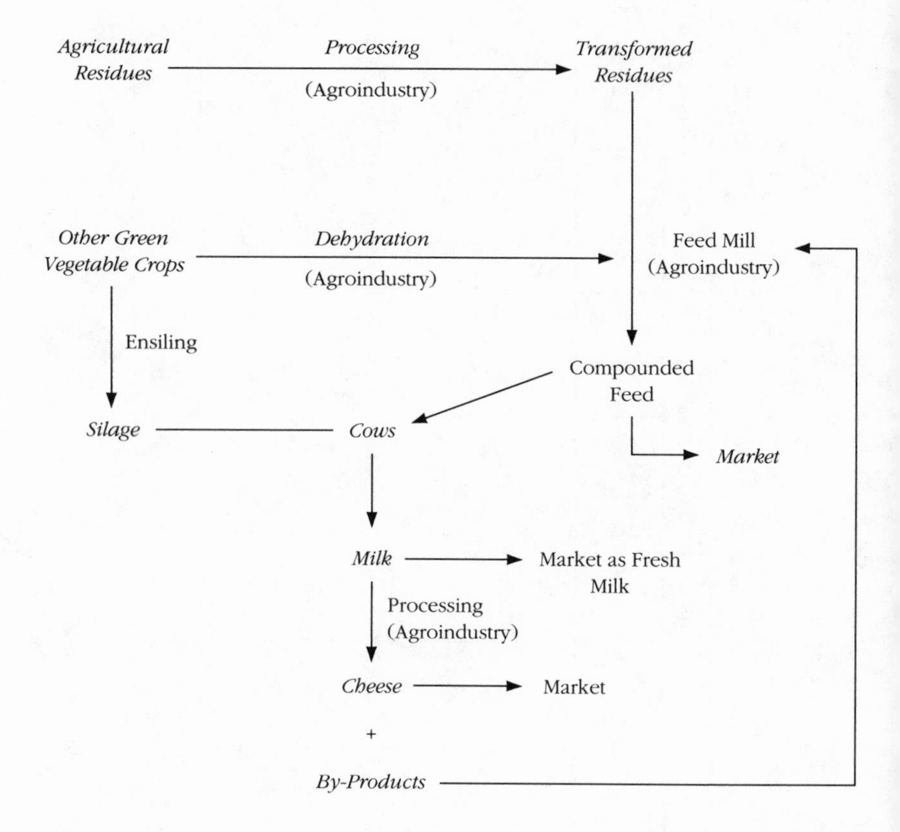

improve food systems. In some areas, the land available for food crops is limited because it has been subdivided so many times and because the production of cash crops has taken precedence. Owners of land dedicated to food crops often wish to have available animal food products such as meat and milk, but they lack grazing land. They can still produce animal food products, however, by converting agricultural residues into acceptable feeds through a number of technologies such as ensiling. For example, four different agroindustries can play a role in producing milk in an economically attractive way. This would involve the processing of agricultural residues; the dehydration of vegetable crops; the conversion of residues into feed; and the processing of milk into milk products such as cheese (see figure 10–5).

Food and nutrition programs can be undertaken in different regions of a country by using the specific crops of a region to prepare flours with a high energy and protein content. These can be made more acceptable in quality through the joint efforts of producers, processors, and consumers by producing better quality raw materials, using adequate processing, and selecting for food characteristics that combine consumer preference and nutrient value.

Although the above examples apply to rural populations, urban groups involved in food processing and distribution can also benefit from food system improvements. A recent study on food vending in Guatemala City cited many appealing processed foods. The quality of these foods can be upgraded by improvements in the raw materials, processing techniques, packaging, and by distribution to a wider market.

Agroindustry has tremendous potential to improve food and nutrition through advances in food systems. It is important, however, to develop a methodology to select the more successful techniques and to collaborate with various disciplines in the effort to improve the well-being of malnourished people in developing countries.

Market Development

There is no doubt that agroindustrial development is an important activity that is very often ignored in food system development. The fact that most of the world's successful agricultural economies also happen to be industrialized is not purely accidental. Expanding the technological capacity of farmers is vitally important to agricultural production, and diversification of production appears to strengthen technological capacity. It is important to remember, however, that agroindustrial development tends to be a long-term process, one that yields results only after years of careful planning.

An important step to accelerate agroindustrial development is identifying and developing markets, as well as increasing the purchasing power of the consumer. Important market considerations include the advantages of an assured market, such as school feeding programs, and export demands where high quality is a fundamental factor. The product, whatever it is, must have a clear identity derived from the need that it fulfills in the marketplace.

Agroindustries must then be created and developed on the basis of need. One obvious need is to strengthen national economies through agroindustries that increase exports or decrease imports. There is also a need to ensure the availability of seasonal foods (such as fruits), to reduce harvest losses, or to use products such as fresh foods that do not meet all quality standards. A further need is to develop products to be used in specific food and nutrition programs, such as highly nutritional foods for infants, preschool children, and pregnant and lactating mothers. Government-sponsored school feeding programs may market such foods.

Also important is the conversion of agricultural residues for use in other food production systems. For rural societies that depend on farming for their livelihood, this type of agroindustry is essential. Agroindustries should be able to produce and make available intermediary products, or food product ingredients such as human-grade cottonseed flour. Ingredients can be produced to enhance color, flavor, and texture; to fill gaps in the food chain; to preserve the environment; and to produce useful products. Agroindustries should preserve and improve native technologies, particularly for products that are popular in the local diet.

A final and important point is the need to analyze the reasons for the low incidence or complete absence of agroindustries in developing countries. Understanding this phenomenon should facilitate the development of food and feed agroindustries. One possibility is that at one time foods were readily available in these countries most of the year, thereby making unnecessary the processing of foods by agroindustries. Additional possible explanations include the lack of household equipment for food storage and processing, the absence of consumer markets as a result of poverty and diminished purchasing power, and, in addition, insufficient supplies of food beyond that used on a daily subsistence basis.

Integrating Production and Consumption Systems with Food Processing

Food science and technology can play a key role in improving nutrition by linking food production, food processing, and food consumption.[8] The food production system of farmers with small or medium capacity to invest has the objective of maximizing land use by growing a variety of compatible crops and ensuring food security and income. Production will vary, depending upon the particular food crops, or combination of crops and livestock production. The underlying goal of food consumption systems, of course, should be improved nutrition—not only by maximizing nutrient bioutilization, but also by educating the consumer about nutrient deficiencies in foods and how to correct them by consuming other foods.

In the example given in figure 10–6, protein quality responses to a number of common maize-bean mixes are shown. Two combinations of maize and beans representing the present intake (D) and the optimum

Figure 10–6.

Nutritional Improvement of the Maize-Bean Consumption System

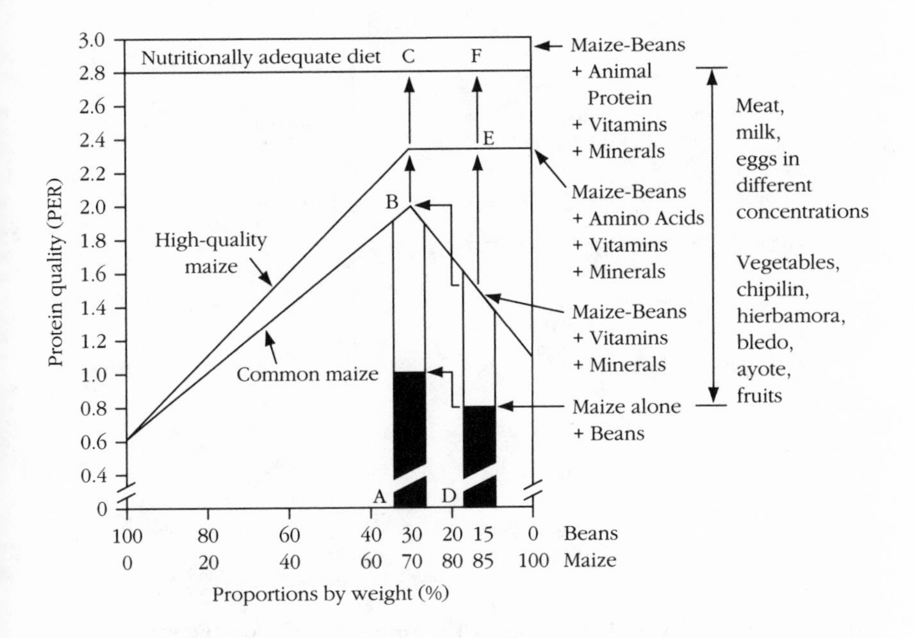

intake (A) have been supplemented with different foods shown at the far right of the figure. These provide the nutrients that would improve the quality of the basic maize-bean mixture. Changing the ratio of maize and bean intake from D to A and adding food sources of vitamins and minerals, such as green vegetables, increases the quality to point B. Point E can be reached by replacing common maize with high-quality protein maize,[9] while points C and F can be reached by consuming small amounts of animal food. Achieving better nutrition and food consumption through the production of animal products as components of farm systems has proved to be technically and economically feasible, at least under experimental conditions.[10]

Agricultural production and food consumption can be further improved by the use of a variety of food processing techniques. An example is shown in figure 10–7. Nutritional studies have shown that a food high in protein and relatively high in fat is obtained when maize and soybeans are mixed in a seven-to-three weight ratio through industrial processing. However, the same food can be obtained through proper training within

Figure 10–7.

A Food Processing System Based on Maize and Soybeans

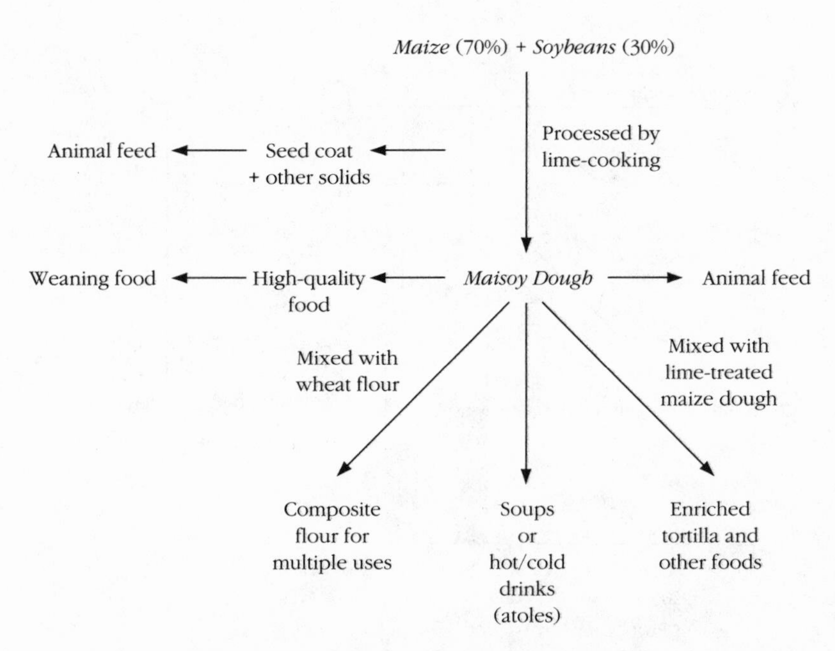

the household, provided soybeans become available and people learn to process them. For example, lime cooking, one of several technologies tested, can be applied to the raw grains and results in a dough with multiple applications ranging from foods used for weaning infants to animal feeds. It can also be mixed with wheat flour, maize, and other grains to produce foods such as cookies, soft-dough breads, and tortillas, which will introduce variety in the meal and improve nutrition.[11]

Furthermore, maize and beans and other crops grown on small areas of land can be used to produce animal feed products. The theoretical example in table 10–1 demonstrates that with integrated approaches, it is possible to achieve diets that respect dietary habits, offer a variety of foods, and provide good nutrition.[12] The crops used in this example are grown on many small farms; if environmental conditions do not permit their production, alternatives can be found. Such systems have not been tested in an integrated form, although it would be worth the effort to test them in practical situations. Education must also be carried out along with agricultural activity and processing. Finally, an economic evaluation of these systems presents opportunities for multidisciplinary solutions to the problems of food deficits and nutritional deficiencies.

Table 10–1.

The Integration of Food Production and Consumption to Provide Highly Nutritious Diets

	Foods (grams/person/day)					
Food Consumption	**Maize**	**Beans**	**Plantain**	**Soybean**	**Meat**	**Protein-Rich Vegetables**
Maize-beans	59.5	19.5	—	10.5	—	—
Maize-soybean (gruel)[2]	35.0	—	—	15.0	—	—
Beans-plantain	—	20.0	80.0	—	—	—
Maize-soybean (tortilla)	85.0	—	—	15.0	—	—
Meat-maize-beans[1]	72.0	8.0	—	—	20.0	—
Vegetable-maize-beans[1]	85.5	9.5	—	—	—	5.0
Total/person/day	422[2]	57	80	55	20	5
Total/family/year (kg)	411	55	78	54	20	5
Hectares of land	0.34	0.11	—	0.03	14 p	—

Protein content total: 81g; 12.7%

Utilizable protein content (%): 65g; 10.2% (80% BV)

Calorie content total: 2292 cals;[3] cals/100g: 360

Digestible calories content: 2177 cals; cals/100g: 342 (95% utiliz.)

Relationship protein calories/total calories: 12[4]

Notes

1. Can be rice-beans.
2. Average 18 tortillas/day (adult).
3. The calories increased with the consumption of other foods not considered within the food consumption systems, such as sugar, fat, vegetables, and fruits.
4. Reduced to 9 when caloric content increased.

Notes

1. R. Bressani, "La Seguridad Alimentaria en el Desarrollo de los Países de Centro América y El Caribe, Consideraciones sobre Valor Nutritivo y Uso de Recursos Fitogenéticos" (Paper presented at PCCMCA XXXIII Reunión, Guatemala, March 30–April 3, 1987).

2. R. Bressani, "La Filosofía de la Cadena Agroindustrial y Alimentaria" (Paper presented at II Congreso Panamericano de Ingeniería Agronómica y de Alimentos, UPADI-86, Guatemala, August 25–27, 1986).

3. Ibid; R. Bressani, "Una Vista Integral del Problema Agroindustrial Alimentario Latinoamericano, Algunas Consideraciones sobre el Desarrollo Agroindustrial Latinoamericano" (Paper presented at seminar "Desarrollo Agroindustrial Rural en América Latina," RETADAR, San José, Costa Rica, April 15–20, 1985).

4. R. Bressani, "Overview on Bean Quality" (Paper presented at First International Workshop on Nutrition and Acceptability Parameters of Common Bean, CIAT, Cali, Colombia, October 1988).

5. Ibid.

6. R. Bressani, "Una Vista Integral." R. Bressani, "Situación Actual y Problemas de Fomento Agroindustrial en Guatemala" (Paper presented at seminar "Sobre Análisis y Estrategias para el Desarrollo de la Agroindustria en Guatemala," Guatemala, June 1988).

7. R. Bressani, "Una Vista Integral."

8. R. Bressani, "Situación Actual." R. Bressani, "Sistemas de Producción, Alimentación, y Nutrición" (Paper presented at seminar "Taller Regional sobre Elaboración de Hojas de Balance de Alimentos," CADESCA, Guatemala, July 27–31, 1987).

9. National Research Council, *Quality Protein Maize* (Washington, D.C.: National Academy Press, 1988).

10. R. Bressani, E. Ibáñez, and J. M. González, "Small-Scale Integrated Agricultural Production," *Family Farm, Food, and Nutrition Bulletin* 8 (1986):30–36.

11. R. Bressani, "Sistemas de Producción." Bressani, Ibáñez, and González, "Small-Scale Integrated Agricultural Production." N. H. Khan and R. Bressani, "Preparation and Nutritional Quality of High Protein Food Extracts from Immature Corn, Whole Soybeans, and Dry Whole Milk," *Plant Food for Human Nutrition* 37 (1987):141–49.

12. R. Bressani, "Situación Actual."

CHAPTER 11

Broadening the Food Development Agenda

Richard R. Harwood

Regional Director, Asia, Winrock International Institute for Agricultural Development, Morrilton, Arkansas, United States

This colloquium is a vivid reminder that countless millions of human beings in the world are hungry and malnourished. Hunger and malnourishment are affected principally by the quantity and quality of available food at the global, national, and regional levels and by family income and access to food. We struggle to find the ways in which agriculture can respond. Should agriculturists focus solely on food production? It seems evident that production alone cannot feed hungry people. As we commit resources to agricultural development, the concern for the sustainability of agricultural advances further complicates the challenge.

Sustainable agriculture can be defined as an agriculture that evolves toward greater human usefulness, greater efficiency in the use of resources, and a balance with the environment that is favorable to both humans and most other species. The social and political aspects in particular make such an agriculture very nation-specific and location-specific within nations. National agendas for agricultural development continue to evolve in ways that more accurately reflect the full range of national needs. Those agendas have five elements in common:

1. To increase the utility of agriculture, for which production and employment are the dominant features. Provision of a diversity of wholesome foods at reasonable prices is another major objective.

2. To increase agricultural productivity, for which efficiency of resource use is critical.

3. To maintain a favorable environment, with water quality ranking high on the list of environmental goals.

4. To assure the capacity of agriculture to evolve indefinitely, with maintenance of soil quality and genetic potential the dominant concerns.

5. To develop a geographical distribution and scale of agriculture, along with its associated industries, consistent with the achievement of the first four objectives.

These five broad categories cover a wide range of specific items with the agendas of industrialized countries tending to be more specific in the first four. No country is really doing a good job of rationalizing geographical distribution and scale of agriculture.

Universal Guidelines

Several common development themes are emerging from national agendas:

1. Food production must continue to increase over the next several decades to meet the demand of rapidly expanding populations.

2. Given the rapid population growth in developing countries, total agricultural employment as well as individual incomes derived from agriculture must expand greatly if rural people are to have the means to obtain adequate food and nutrition.

3. Efficiency in the use of capital, land, and production inputs must increase substantially.

4. Nutrient flow loops of agricultural systems must be progressively closed. For instance, the cycling of plant nutrients from crop residue to the soil and then on to a subsequent crop must be increased in efficiency with a reduction in losses due to erosion or to a downward movement into groundwater.

5. Production systems must be structured to involve as little use of pesticides as possible; pest management must be "internal" to the production system. This can be achieved through genetic resistance in the crop, by means of certain culture controls, or by altering the pest-predator balance. Once a balance is achieved with these methods, no further inputs are needed.

6. Areas rich in soil and water resources will continue to produce much of the needed food, yet increasing numbers of people depend on agricultural systems in low-resource areas, the development of which is a high priority.[1]

No country demonstrates these needs more than India, where agricultural production has increased at a compound rate of 2.5 percent per annum over the last three decades. Food grain production increased from 50.8 million tons in 1950–51 to 144.1 million tons in 1986–87, with a peak of 152.4 million tons in 1983–84. Population almost doubled, growing from 361 million in 1951 to 685 million in 1981, with the result that agricultural growth per capita is lower.[2]

India's population is expected to reach one billion shortly after the turn of the century. Well over half of those people will reside in rural areas, depending on agriculture for their livelihood and their nutrition. "Agricultural development in India," a 1988 Indian Council of Agricultural Research report concludes, "will be critical to various other sectors of activity including generation of employment and alleviation of poverty in the rural sector. The cost of creating jobs in industry is infinitely higher than producing jobs in agriculture. Lack of dynamic agriculture will lead to rural violence."[3]

National development agendas are increasingly specific and demanding, and certain problems can be dealt with at the national and international levels by means of carefully directed research and resource allocation. However, other issues are local in nature and require very specific analysis and targeted action. The Green Revolution technologies were highly successful in advancing production in high-resource environments. It remains to be seen whether technologies generated at the national and international levels can meet the needs for employment production and environmental protection in low-resource areas.

The Need for an Integrative Approach

We must adapt agricultural science and research in order to bridge the gap between national agendas and technology selection at the field level. New technologies not only must be integrated at the local level but also must fit the broader national mandate. Existing analytical tools are crude and seldom used in technology selection and assessment.

The farming systems approach is the most commonly used to test and apply technologies to on-farm environments.[4] In the most advanced form of this approach, the farmer is a full partner in research planning, technology evaluation, and application and change. Because of limited resources, research usually focuses on technology testing and adaptation within the context of the whole operating system of a farm. This assumes the setting is a true reflection of the social and biological interactions of the farm.[5] Farming systems research and extension have been highly effective in bringing the farmer into the planning, technology, testing, and extension process.

Nevertheless, the farming systems approach so far has fallen short in analyzing the relationship between national development agendas and farm-level activities. For instance, labor requirements of new technologies, as applied to crop patterns or crop-livestock systems, are nearly always carefully assessed in on-farm research. Yet labor is regarded as any other cash input to be added to production cost. A "net return," the amount remaining after total production cost is subtracted from the selling price, is then calculated as profit to a farm enterprise. Labor use or "employment" is considered, along with other cash inputs, as an external cost to be minimized in the interest of profit. Family labor is treated as if it were just another "input" procured from outside the farm; it is not differentiated from hired labor. It is assumed that reduction in the cost of family labor is the same as reduction in the cost of other cash inputs when, in fact, the opportunity cost of family labor is often extremely low—particularly in low-resource areas. In other words, there may be few if any employment opportunities off the farm. Therefore, on-farm family employment should be considered as a benefit rather than a cost in such farming systems. Seldom is "return to labor" listed as a separate factor, and almost never is the employment effect of a new technology assessed, even at the farm level.

If employment and family income are critical to food consumption and family nutrition in rural areas, and if agriculture is to be responsible for absorbing at least part of the growing rural work force, why are these employment and income criteria not incorporated more systematically into the farming systems agenda? Perhaps it is because national agendas are not designed adequately to relate to the work of development workers at subnational levels and in specialized fields.

As an agronomist concerned primarily with farm-level production, I see little evidence yet of a real commitment to increasing farm employment on the part of international development agencies and scientists. Perhaps as a result of Western labor-saving notions, labor is regarded as just another input cost to be reduced to a minimum. We have yet to learn that labor efficiency (and return to labor) as well as total farm employment may be more important factors than total production.

The Challenge of Agroecology

Agroecology is emerging as an area of scientific research and development applying the principles of ecology to the study of agricultural systems at the field level. A recent World Resources Institute report sums up the purposes of agroecology:

> All that ecologists study—the distribution, abundance, and interactions of organisms in space and time; the interrelationships between organisms and the physical environment; and the flows of energy and materials through ecosystems—bears on our understanding of agroecosystems as

whole systems and on the development of new technologies to support a sustainable agriculture.[6]

The analytical tools of agroecology are best suited to investigating areas of strongest interaction (i.e., the field level) but can be adapted to relationships at higher as well as lower levels.[7] Agroecological research is well suited to analysis of relationships between economic and sociopolitical factors at the national and international levels and the biological-social-physical interactions of the farm and field. It is highly conducive to systems integration at any level, although it works best at the farm level, measuring interactions within the farm and flows between the farm and its environment. Unfortunately, we have yet to create an effective process in most countries, including the United States, that utilizes agroecological analyses as an element of national agricultural agenda planning and policy implementation at the local level. Until we do, our approach to agricultural sustainability will remain unproductive.

Concepts of Biological Structuring

As we move to the farm level of systems research, our ecological tools have theoretical application, yet the understanding of interactions among systems is still limited. The concept of biological structuring has been outlined but lacks measurement and quantification.[8]

For example, crop rotations affect the shifting of weed species, stabilizing pest populations, and the vertical movement of nutrients in the soil.[9] If they are properly used, crop rotations can reduce production costs. Mixtures of annual crops and perennials are especially well suited to low soil and water resource environments in which soil erosion, seasonal drought, or other factors favor perennials. The integration of animals into intensive crop systems increases farm production. These integrative factors are important particularly in small farm systems in low-resource areas. These concepts are understood by traditional farmers but as yet poorly quantified in scientific study.

Less recognized is the fact that crop nutrient flow should be focused on movement into and out of the soil organic matter rather than along the lines of conventional strategy in placing needed crop nutrients directly into the soil-water solution through use of highly soluble fertilizers. This approach fosters better soil structure and minimizes nutrient loss from the soil by runoff or leaching. There is widespread evidence to support this approach but as yet little scientific evidence.[10]

Benefits of biological structuring, with the crop diversity over space and time in the form of varied rotations on different farm fields, seem to include increased stability over short-term fluctuations in rainfall, increased efficiency of nutrient flow, and more effective pest management. Several of these concepts, including flow efficiency, have been researched,[11] but few have been applied in the form of new technologies. Aside from having a range of crops, each with a different climatological response, there is some evidence that the rotation effect on the soil leads to better water infiltration and holding capacity, which in turn leads to better crop drought tolerance.

Lessons from Green Revolution Successes

The Green Revolution in Asia was successful in increasing production during the 1960s and 1970s when the following conditions were met:

1. New technologies were made available to farmers who were highly skilled at using the technologies and resources; little change occurred in the absence of new technologies.

2. Local institutions, scientists, and development workers were available to provide the momentum for change—a key condition for success.

3. New technologies were effective only in agroclimatic areas of adaptation. These technologies, such as a particular crop variety, an herbicide, or fertilizer intervention, when assembled in an "improved package," tended to have rather narrow limits of soil, rainfall, or temperature in terms of optimal adaptation and economic response.

4. Crop technologies requiring high soil nutrient levels were productive only in areas with good soil and water resources. Food production was significantly increased, yet the gap widened between low- and high-resource farming. Alternative technologies were needed for low-resource areas.

5. Maximum progress was made when development efforts were narrowly focused; a broad development agenda seems to dilute effort.

6. The food grain technologies have not favored larger farms. Small farms have benefited equally. In Asia at least, attempts to industrialize food grain production on capital-intensive mechanized farms failed for the most part. In high capital cost, high-risk areas, small farms tend to be more efficient.

New Imperatives for the 1990s

Most national agendas for agricultural development will continue to emphasize production but will provide for a broader range of high market value vegetable, fruit, and animal products to meet market demand in urban centers. Farm employment and incomes will be a close second. So far, international agricultural development institutions such as USAID, the World Bank, and the international agricultural research centers have focused on stabilizing and broadening production in high-resource areas. Increasingly, they will have to examine the effects of their technologies on incomes. Production systems will have to reflect the growing need for information-intensive rather than input-intensive systems.[12]

Other segments of the international community, aside from the commodity-specific institutions, must provide technologies for low-resource areas. These would include improved varieties and species of fodder grasses for livestock feed, improved varieties of high-value perennial species and fruit crops, and better species of legumes to improve the nitrogen balance in intensive crop systems. Most importantly, scientists at the international and national levels who furnish these technologies must become sensitive to national needs, especially the need to interact with development workers at the field level who work with farmers to integrate the new technologies into local systems. Consideration also must be given to environmental impact, farm worker safety, the role of women in agriculture and food distribution, and other social issues, as these interface with technology development and application. The Green Revolution's lessons about assessing measurable output should not be forgotten.

Is all of this possible? And will it work to alleviate hunger? One solution to hunger clearly will not work: the conversion of cellulose and other woody materials into foodstuffs by means of research on the chemistry of raw materials produced from perennial crops. Farmers in low-resource areas would be expected to produce these raw products with industrial techniques that are used to process and produce acceptable types of food.[13] Although this approach may meet the need for food, it is counterproductive to the goal of raising rural income and reducing capital costs of farming. Small farmers would be led deeper into poverty if they had to produce raw products for industrial use on small, resource-poor farms.

The model that best meets social needs in developing countries is one that produces finished food products as close as possible to the farm, rather than extending food production through a long industrial chain. Poor people can ill afford the service costs of industrial production. This point deserves considerable analysis, debate, and resolution, since it is pivotal to the direction of Third World agricultural development.

An ongoing development program conducted by the Philippine Department of Agriculture in the southern Bicol region of Luzon is a better example to follow. It has shown that incomes of resource-poor small farmers can be more than doubled by incorporating high market value crops such as pineapple, coffee, black pepper, and vegetables, and livestock such as goats into traditional, environmentally stable farming systems.[14] Farmers themselves chose this approach, working in collaboration with researchers and extension specialists. The project area, now being broadened, exemplifies the conscious harmonizing of development agendas at the national and local level, along with support of an international donor, the U.S. Agency for International Development. Farmers themselves determined the technologies to test, utilizing crop and animal technologies from international sources. Farmers and researchers collaborated on testing and on local adaptation. This model should be replicated widely.

It is clear that new technologies will be needed to achieve dramatic increases in food production to satisfy population growth in developing countries. These technologies must also succeed at expanding employment and increasing incomes among the rural poor. They must stabilize soils while minimizing adverse effects on the environment. They will probably arise through research at the national and international levels. These technologies increasingly will be adapted to specific farming systems by means of on-farm testing. This will require agricultural development scientists and extension workers to become more aware of national development agendas as well as the environmental conditions of actual farming systems. The tools and concepts of agroecology must be integrated with science if nations are to succeed in alleviating hunger and malnutrition on a sustained basis.

Notes

1. Low-resource areas are those that have poor soils, limited water due to low-level or erratic rainfall, or lack of irrigation, or that are remote from or hard to reach in relation to markets. Any one factor or a combination of them will limit production potential.

2. *Report of the Indian Council of Agricultural Research Review Committee* (New Delhi: ICAR, 1988), 14–15.

3. Ibid.

4. R. R. Harwood, *Small Farm Development: Understanding and Improving Farming Systems in the Humid Tropics* (Boulder, Colo.: Westview Press, 1979).

5. D. Byerlee, M. P. Collinson, R. K. Perrin, D. L. Winkelmann, S. Biggs, E. R. Moscardi, J. C. Martinez, L. Harrington, and A. Benjamin, *Planning Technologies Appropriate to Farmers: Concepts and Procedures* (El Batan, Mexico: CIMMYT, 1980).

6. M. Dever and S. M. Talbot, *To Feed the Earth: Agroecology for Sustainable Development* (Washington, D.C.: World Resources Institute, 1987), 7.

7. M. Altieri, *Agroecology: The Scientific Basis of Alternative Agriculture* (Boulder, Colo.: Westview Press, 1987), 6.

8. This refers to the types and amount of complementary or even symbiotic interaction between crops in rotation, sometimes expressed as their combined effect on noncrop organisms. See C. Francis and R. Harwood, *Enough Food: Achieving Food Security through Regenerative Agriculture* (Emmaus, Pa.: Rodale Institute, 1985), and C. A. Francis, R. R. Harwood, and J. F. Parr, "The Potential for Regenerative Agriculture in the Developing World," *American Journal of Alternative Agriculture* 1, no. 2:65–74.

9. Vertical movement is the result of complex processes in the soil whereby nutrients are moved upward through the roots and stems of roots by means of soil insect activity or are carried downward with the movement of water.

10. R. R. Harwood, "History of Sustainable Agriculture: U.S. and International Perspective" (Paper presented at the International Conference on Sustainable Agricultural Systems, Ohio State University, Columbus, September 19, 1988. In press.).

11. *Maximizing Fertilizer Use Efficiency*. FAO Fertilizer and Plant Nutrition Bulletin No. 6 (Rome: FAO, 1983).

12. *Report of the ICAR Review Committee.*

13. M. H. Rogoff and S. L. Rawlins, "Food Security: A Technological Alternative," *Bioscience* (1987):800–807.

14. F. C. Byrnes, *No Turning Back: Small Steps Lead Filipino Farmers toward Self-Reliance and Increased Income* (Quezon City, Philippines: Department of Agriculture, Republic of the Philippines, 1988).

CHAPTER 12

Food and Culture

An Anthropological View

Sidney W. Mintz
William L. Straus, Jr., Professor of Anthropology, The Johns Hopkins University, Baltimore, Maryland, United States

More than fifty years ago, Professor Sir Raymond Firth, the dean of world anthropology, called for a series of careful ethnographic studies of the food habits of native peoples. His own paper on the study of food habits, which he modestly described as "a few reflections on a possible systematic field approach to the situation,"[1] addresses issues which no student of the anthropology of food can afford to ignore.

Unfortunately, Firth's initiative did not lead to the systematic ethnographic research the subject warranted. The brilliant investigations of Audrey Richards in the 1930s[2] have not been matched; and the work of Rosemary Firth[3] never attracted the attention it deserved. Margaret Mead made some useful programmatic statements on food habits during World War II and produced a book on how cultural change might affect such habits;[4] but that work did not result in much additional ethnographic research. Anthropologists today continue to examine food habits and offer insights on the role of culture in shaping or preserving them. But large-scale ethnographic research on food habits, to provide the detail that questionnaires cannot supply, remains relatively rare.

Perhaps no statement about the anthropology of food has received as much public attention as Claude Lévi-Strauss's provocative comment that foods must be "good to think" before they can be "good to eat." The emphasis on the social and symbolic nature of human acts, including food-consuming behavior, the idea that socially learned behavior (culture) always determines the relationship between bodily needs and their satisfaction, is probably the single most important assertion anthropology has to offer on this subject. Biology may eventually tell us everything that we need to know about what we need to eat. However, it tells us little about why we eat what we eat, and next to nothing about how to change food habits. Human beings are animals, to be sure; but they are more different from any other kind of animal than any other two kinds of animals are from each other. The Bible tells us as much; but it is not for Biblical reasons that we are led to accept our human uniqueness. When we talk about how we may differ from other animals in what we eat and the ways we eat—mashed potatoes or raw clams, eaten sitting or standing, five times daily or three, each and all such specific social habits entirely unrelated to our biological nature—we have in mind the activities and meanings that set us clearly apart from all other forms of life.

Humans have natures, although nobody is able to say just what they are. From the moment of birth onward, and very likely even before, each of us is raised in a specific cultural, rather than natural, context. Individuals learn a particular language, eat particular foods at particular times, are rewarded and punished for particular behaviors, and all of this is done in culturally specific ways. "Eat your spinach! Stop fidgeting! Wipe your mouth on your napkin! Leave the table and go to your room! No dessert today!" are culturally specific forms that persist throughout one's life, and, indeed, are often imposed on one's offspring. But of course the more unthinkingly one lives one's life, the more "natural" these forms seem to be. An imaginative dialogue, "I'm so hungry I could eat a horse." "A *horse*? Are you French? . . ." captures the idea that from the very beginning, human "nature" is molded and transfigured by "culture."

Food and eating comprise an enormously valuable index of our humanity and the variability of culture and its power over us. Food taboos are probably the most dramatic evidence. But almost everything about how we eat, what we eat, when we eat, and with whom we eat exemplifies human variability from one culture to another, and the way we confuse the natural with the socially learned. Regardless of whether we eat with our hands, chopsticks, or flatware, there is always an etiquette, a right and a wrong way. People rarely eat everything available to them; they always eat something some other people find repulsive. They always eat at the end of a recognized social process of some kind; they never "just dig in." The fact that we often urge people to "just dig in" is evidence that there always is an etiquette.

Human beings have been seeking and successfully finding their food for perhaps three million years, yet only in the last 12,000 years or so have they learned to domesticate plants and animals in order to control their food supply. Domestication really means controlling the reproduction of some other living thing, a process that human beings have been able to effectuate with animals and plants not just once, but at many different times and with different living things: rice, soybeans, and pigs in Asia; potatoes, llamas, and guinea pigs in the Andes; tomatoes, chocolate, chili, and turkeys in Meso-America; millet, okra, and one species of rice in Africa; olives and cabbage in Europe. Each was domesticated by nameless ordinary people and bequeathed to us by cultural inheritance. While we learn about Galileo and Copernicus, Edison and Burbank, we know little about those anonymous but ingenious men and women who learned how to domesticate. Domestication is probably the single greatest technical achievement in the human record, more important than the internal combustion engine or nuclear energy. It was, from the beginning and long before these other triumphs, a remarkable way to capture and control energy.

To be sure, domestication was not a single event, but a lengthy and complex process, originating in many different world areas and realized through the mastery of many different skills, and with hundreds of different plant and animal species. Like the internal combustion engine or nuclear energy, though it can be treated as a unitary phenomenon, it really represents numerous small discoveries, combined and perfected over time. The scientific achievements we have recorded since the dawn of modern civilization, including the internal combustion engine, were the culminations of millennia of prior technical progress, largely underwritten by the control of the food supply, beginning with domestication. Furthermore, domestication was a remarkably economical and relatively nondestructive way to capture and conserve energy, as compared to the uses we have made so far of fossil and nuclear fuels.

Yet in spite of the domestication of a huge variety of plants and animals, a relatively small number has become the subsistence mainstay of our species. (Important though they are, domesticated animals will be left aside in this account. They are so high up on the food chain that expansion of their production in the future raises thorny ethical questions. Very crudely stated, every single animal fed on food that human beings could eat—such as a cereal grain—represents some sort of tradeoff in energy terms: less for one human being, so that some other human can enjoy a "richer" diet. We cannot deal with the implications of that problem here.)

A dozen or so grasses and perhaps an equal number of rhizomes or tubers were among the plants upon which our species gradually became dependent. The grasses include wheat, barley, oats, rye, maize, rice, and the millets; not many more ever became truly important. The tubers include manioc (cassava), sweet potatoes, potatoes, taro, and yams. Around these dozen plants most of the major societies in world history built their food supply. Moreover, the increase in human population during the period when domestication was mastered makes it likely that the majority of human beings in all of history subsisted on this rather small number of foods. Naturally, there was considerable localization:

rice, sweet potatoes, and taro were important in Asia; maize, potatoes, sweet potatoes, and manioc in the New World; and wheat, rye, barley, and oats in the Middle East.

Notably, everywhere that one finds these grasses and rhizomes, plants with abundant "starch" or complex carbohydrates, one also finds one or more legumes or pulses that carry protein (e.g., beans, chickpeas, peas, and peanuts). A Mexican tortilla "goes with" red beans; in the Caribbean islands, red or black beans go with the rice; in Asia, soybean extracts accompany rice; in the Middle East, chickpeas commonly go with wheaten products. Why a legume always seems to accompany a complex carbohydrate is not so easy to explain, though from the point of view of human diet, it is certainly a healthy combination, especially in areas lacking adequate sources of animal protein.

Everywhere that people eat one or more complex carbohydrates along with one or more legumes, they also use certain preferred flavors with their food. Elisabeth Rozin has invented the term "flavour-principle" to describe such preferences.[5] But the flavors form a kind of set or aggregate of tastes, a fringe of foods which accompany the starches and the legumes. To explain what I mean by calling them a "fringe," I will cite the work of a brilliant food anthropologist, Audrey Richards. She discusses the Bemba, an African agricultural people, whose principal food is a grain that is made into a gruel. According to Richards:

> To the Bemba each meal, to be satisfactory, must be composed of two constituents: a thick porridge (*ubwali*) made of millet and the relish (*umunani*) of vegetables, meat or fish, which is eaten with it. . . . *Ubwali* is commonly translated by "porridge" but this is misleading. The hot water and meal are mixed in proportion of 3 to 2 to make *ubwali* and this produces a solid mass of the consistency of plasticine and quite unlike what we know as porridge. *Ubwali* is eaten in hunks torn off in the hand, rolled into balls, dipped in relish, and bolted whole.
>
> Millet has already been described as the main constituent of Bemba diet, but it is difficult for the European, accustomed as he is to a large variety of foodstuffs, to realize fully what a "staple crop" can mean to a primitive people. To the Bemba, millet porridge is not only necessary, but it is the only constituent of his diet which actually ranks as food. . . . I have watched natives eating the roasted grains off four or five maize cobs under my very eyes, only to hear them shouting to their fellows later, "Alas, we are dying of hunger. We have not had a bite to eat all day. . . ."
>
> The importance of millet porridge in native eyes is constantly reflected in traditional utterance and ritual. In proverb and folktale the *ubwali* stands for food itself. When discussing his kinship obligations, a native will say, "How can a man refuse to help his mother's brother who has given him *ubwali* all these years?" or, "Is he not her son? How should she refuse to make him *ubwali*? . . ."

> But the native, while he declares he cannot live without *ubwali*, is equally emphatic that he cannot eat porridge without a relish (*umunani*), usually in the form of a liquid stew. . . .
>
> The term *umunani* is applied to stews—meat, fish, caterpillars, locusts, ants, vegetables (wild and cultivated), mushrooms, etc.—prepared to eat with porridge. The functions of the relish are two: first to make the *ubwali* easier to swallow, and second to give it taste. . . . The Bemba himself explains that the sauce is not food. . . . Meat and vegetable stews are cooked with salt whenever possible, and there is no doubt that an additional function of the relish in native eyes is to give the porridge taste and to lessen the monotony of the diet.[6]

What Richards dubs "relish" and Rozin "flavor principle," I call "fringe." Every agrarian cuisine has a fringe; these flavoring additions "help the food go down." They differ in many ways from the basic starchy food, and some of those differences—such as color, texture, solidity, and of course taste—play a part in the total meal. But it is important to view these three types of food as categories, not as particular food items. The starchy center of the cuisine I call the "core"; the flavor-giving foods, the "fringe"; and the protein-giving food, the "legume." Together they form a pattern that I call the "core-fringe-legume" (CFLP). I refer to this as a dietary pattern because it recurs in many different cultural instances. In each the particular food is not as important as the category it exemplifies. Each category has a structural relation to the other categories in each cultural instance.

The CFLP is the outcome of a long process that began with the domestication of plants and that has never ended. Cereals, the most important item in the core, still provide more than half of the world's calories, almost half of the world's plant protein, and take up more than 70 percent of the cultivated land on the earth's surface. In India, cereals provide 70 percent of all calories; in China, 80 percent. Together with the legumes, the cereals provide more than two-thirds of the dietary protein consumed by human beings,[7] and probably most of their calories. It would be difficult to overestimate the importance of the core and the legumes in assessing world food behavior.

In many cuisines, of course, the place of the legume is taken wholly or partly by other protein sources, such as eggs, fish, fowl, and meat. But the common label for legumes—"poor man's meat"—underscores their importance in diets of the world. The "fringe," which covers a wide variety of foods, is particularly important for its role in endowing the basic food with a special character, so that more of it can be eaten with enjoyment. Completely unflavored pasta, potatoes, or gruel is difficult to eat in large quantities, even when one is hungry and/or undernourished. The fringe makes it possible to eat more of the food that is most available.

I have noted that the CFLP represents the food categories that have been eaten by probably the majority of humans who have ever lived—even though such patterns are no more than 12,000 years old. Yet it is equally important to note that, in the last five centuries, the dietary pattern that CFLP represents has begun to crumble worldwide. Many different forces are at work, among them the vastly increased movement of foods, including basic foods, over great distances, and the rapid decrease in the number of primary producers as a proportion of the world population. As foods are increasingly produced by others, control over what we eat declines. A food substitution process take shape.

Though preferences for particular foods are still exercised, choices are now made within a narrower range of available alternatives, within which imported and different foods will probably figure importantly. In addition, calamitous conditions, such as famine, drought, and war, can drive people away from their traditional cuisines and toward substitutes over which they have little control. There is relatively scanty ethnographic study of the food substitution process. In the cases where some choice is exercised, as distinguished from calamities, yet where there is little control over the circumstances under which the choices are made, further study would be particularly useful. In a series of important papers, Mary Weismantel has demonstrated how need and desire change under the pressure of labor migration and family disruption, such that new "luxury" foods begin to displace cheaper, more traditional and probably more nutritious items.[8] More such research is badly needed.

It is clear that some people can be tenacious in their food preferences, clinging to traditional foods with astonishing loyalty. Others may demonstrate more passive attitudes toward new foods, consuming them without protest or even with unexpected enthusiasm. Indeed, both reactions may turn up among the same people reacting to pressure, in their responses to different food novelties. These seemingly contradictory tendencies need to be carefully examined if we are to influence future eating habits in ways other than by sheer compulsion.

In recent work,[9] I have emphasized the rise of sucrose-eating in Europe, beginning around the mid-seventeenth century. Sweetness apparently is a universally sought-after taste, and increasing processed sugar consumption may be no more than a natural tendency working itself out. However, this explanation is insufficient, since many different factors have played a part in the rise and intensification of sucrose consumption.[10] Processed sugar consumption in the West apparently has leveled off of late, though at a high level—as much as 20 percent of caloric intake in some countries and probably even more for certain population groups such as the young. In many developing nations, sugar consumption as a proportion of calories continues to rise.

Another growing source of calories is fats; again, there is some leveling off in the industrialized countries, together with continuing increases in developing countries. Sugars and fats are of special interest because both are the staples of "fast foods"; their consumption in non-Western countries may be correlated with the diffusion of fast food eating habits. The best example of this is the effervescent, heavily sweetened soft drink, the present consumption of which in the United States now exceeds that of water. The popularity of these drinks is growing in much of the non-Western world, among both poor wage earners and among the more Westernized segments of the middle and upper classes.

A parallel growth in the consumption of fats in the form of broiled or deep-fried meats, fowl, or fish, often heavily salted, flavored, and breaded, is also evident. When advertised in a culturally appropriate way with appealing symbols, the public consumption of such foods and soft drinks turns out to be a principal form of identification with Western lifestyles and power. However, viewed from the perspective of energy input and output (the number of calories used to place one calorie on the table), these swiftly spreading food habits are retrograde in the extreme. Their long-term negative consequences are not fully assessed, but it is highly probable that they will progressively undermine the older CFLPs of poor agrarian societies.

It is not possible to assert with assurance that each such shift represents a decline in nutrition. But it is clear that, in energy terms, these trends bode ill for the future. At the same time that fats and sugars figure more importantly in the changing food habits of the developing countries, nutritionists in the West have been pressing for decreases in their consumption in the developed countries.

People in developing nations who are open to change are, on the one hand, those who have been pulled loose from their agrarian roots by poverty, land loss, famine, or unemployment, and who have not yet been able to reestablish a stable home life with traditional meal patterns. The food habits of such people reveal the apparently paradoxical countertrends of tradition and change, and their difficulties in trying to go on as they were before.

At the same time, middle-class persons in the developing nations are often attracted to such novelties as soft drinks and fast foods because of their symbolic significance as emblems of modernization and sophistication. They, too, are impelled to move toward new dietary habits, though their cuisines are probably less representative of the traditional CFLP in any case.

In sum, anthropologists are able to say a good deal about the role of cultural factors in food habits, yet they lack the corpus of solid ethnographic observation necessary to draw firm conclusions about culturally specific persistence versus modification in food habits. Both resistance to change and readiness to change can occur within the same population, and I can only guess that these tendencies may actually be consistent, though they appear contradictory. Without substantial additional ethnographic detail, the effort to interpret food habit changes or to effect change in food habits will remain fragmentary and tentative.

Notes

1. Raymond Firth, "The Sociological Study of Native Diet," *Africa* 7, no. 4:402.

2. Audrey Richards, *Hunger and Work in a Savage Tribe* (London: George Routledge and Sons, 1934); and *Land, Labour, and Diet in Northern Rhodesia* (London: Oxford University Press, 1939).

3. Rosemary Firth, *Housekeeping among Malay Peasants* (London: London School of Economics Monographs, 1943).

4. Margaret Mead, "Dietary Patterns and Food Habits," *Journal of the American Dietetic Association* 19 (1943):1–5; and *Cultural Patterns and Technological Change* (Paris: UNESCO, 1953).

5. Elisabeth Rozin, *The Flavour-Principle Cookbook* (New York: Hawthorn, 1973).

6. Richards, *Land, Labour, and Diet*, 46–49.

7. Harold McGee, *On Food and Cooking* (New York: Charles Scribner's Sons, 1984), 226.

8. Mary Weismantel, "*Wanlla:* Desire and Demand in the Northern Andes" (unpublished manuscript, 1986); and "The Children Cry for Bread: Hegemony and the Transformation of Consumption," in *The Social Economy of Consumption*, ed. Benjamin S. Orlove and Henry J. Rutz (Lanham, Md.: University Press of America, in press).

9. Sidney Mintz, *Sweetness and Power* (New York: Viking-Penguin, 1985).

10. Sidney Mintz, "The Power of Sweetness and the Sweetness of Power," The Eighth Duijker Lecture (Amsterdam: Van Loghum Slaterus, 1988).

CHAPTER 13

Economic Perspectives on Combating Hunger

Beatrice Lorge Rogers
Associate Professor of Food Policy, School of Nutrition, Tufts University, Medford, Massachusetts, United States

Economic thought has led to a better understanding of the food chain—the processes from food production through consumption that determine the prevalence of hunger and malnutrition in the world. At the most fundamental level, economic analysis has demonstrated that world hunger (excluding famines caused by war, drought, or natural disaster) is first and foremost a poverty problem.

An adequate national food supply is, of course, a prerequisite to achieving food security for all households. But even in countries with fully adequate food supplies at the national level, maldistribution of income results in high percentages of food-poor households. One reason for this is that each country is part of the world economy. If there is no effective demand among low-income households within a given country—that is, demand backed by the money to pay—then the food produced there may be exported to markets where effective demand is high, with the result that food is withdrawn from poor households, regardless of their need for it. Food supplies in some forty-five countries, mostly in Africa, it is estimated, are inadequate to meet the needs of their populations.[1] Yet even in these food-scarce countries, malnutrition is not a widespread problem among the well off.

Economists view the elimination of world hunger as largely a question of solving the world's poverty problem. Yet it is now well understood that improvements in national income, like aggregate increases in food supply, are not sufficient to improve the welfare of poor households.[2] A healthy and growing national economy offers more opportunities for the poor, yet growth-oriented economic policies vary with respect to their effects on income distribution and on poor households.

The implication for policy is that antihunger efforts need to focus on the poor, wherever they are: the urban underemployed and unemployed, the rural landless, and rural farmers with inadequate land or other resources. Targeted efforts to alleviate hunger have to focus on poverty, rather than on a particular sector of the economy or region of the country. Similarly, the objective should be the alleviation of poverty, rather than the enhancement of any one particular income stream.

For example, a government may encourage economic growth in the agricultural sector either by investing in an irrigation system that would benefit large rice growers, or else by constructing a network of roads that would permit small vegetable producers to market their perishable products in nearby urban areas. The first approach might increase overall income and agricultural production as much as the second, but the second would be more effective in raising the incomes of poor households and alleviating hunger.

Income interventions to benefit the poor, even poor rural farm households, do not necessarily have to focus on farm prices or markets. Most farm households have multiple sources of income, so that other types of income- and employment-generating programs may be just as effective. In the Dominican Republic, for example, a recent study found that only 3 percent of farm households depended on farming for more than 90 percent of their incomes.[3]

The role of food prices in determining the prevalence of hunger and malnutrition has received much attention from food economists. The so-called food price dilemma[4] refers to the tension between efforts to encourage agricultural production by keeping prices high and to protect the food consumption levels of the poor by keeping prices low. The resolution of this dilemma may lie in focusing specifically on the foods (or other commodities) produced and consumed by the poor. To continue with an earlier example, a policy that keeps the price of rice high might be of no benefit to poor farmers (if rice tends to be grown by wealthy farmers) nor of particular harm to poor consumers (if rice tends to be a rich person's food).

In the Dominican Republic study, in fact, we found that a policy to lower the price of chicken (a middle-class food) actually reduced the caloric and protein intake of the poorest households. When chicken was relatively expensive, low-income households apparently felt they simply could not afford it; when the price was reduced, these households decided to substitute small amounts of the luxury food for some of their normal quantities of rice, beans, oil, and plantain. This resulted in a net nutritional loss to the diet.[5]

Efforts to alleviate hunger, therefore, must take into account the distinctive consumption and production patterns of the poor. Otherwise, they may succeed in achieving short-term objectives (such as increasing crop yields) while failing to achieve the long-term goal of abating hunger. One well-known example of this is in India, a country that has gone from food deficits to surpluses in less than two decades, largely due to the astonishingly successful work of the agricultural research community. At the same time, the prevalence of malnutrition, as measured by infant mortality, has not shown comparable improvement. In some regions, the introduction of high-yielding varieties of rice disrupted the economic system, undermining the status of the poor; land values rose and poor tenant-farmers were displaced, losing their main source of subsistence.

This example reveals the critical importance of understanding the interaction between economic and other factors affecting household access to food. In an economic setting in which the poor have ownership or at least guaranteed rights to use their land, for example, a new technology might have unequivocally positive effects on the poor. In certain regions in India, a more complete understanding of the economic situation of the poor might have led to the introduction of a complementary intervention to protect their incomes and access to food, as new food technologies were introduced.

Greater understanding of the economic forces accompanying the introduction of new agricultural technologies has contributed to a heightened research focus on the crops of the poor, such as sorghum, millet, and cassava, and on methods of cultivation that take into account the constraints facing poor farmers, such as unpredictable rainfall and lack of access to irrigation. Farming systems research provides valuable guidance on the applicability of new technology in field situations.

The development of new agricultural technology—new crop varieties, methods of cultivation, and systems for food processing and storage—greatly expands the possibilities for households as well as nations to achieve food security. But economic forces largely determine whether these enhanced possibilities are translated into improved welfare for poor households. Research into agricultural and food technology can be made more relevant to the struggle to end hunger if economic factors play a role in determining research priorities.

For example, a current study in urban areas of Mali has found, contrary to expectations, that rice consumption is not limited to well-off households. Households at all income levels derive about the same proportion of their diets (in calories and protein) from rice and from the coarse grains such as millet and sorghum.[6] Since much of the rice consumed in Mali is imported, while millet and sorghum are locally produced and less expensive than rice, real economic advantages in household income can be gained by promoting consumption of coarse grains. However, the far greater time and labor costs of preparing the coarse grains constitute a barrier to increasing their consumption. A simple, inexpensive method of processing these grains could remove this barrier, thereby providing poor households with a substantial improvement in their diets. Increasing the production of millet and sorghum alone would have a less positive effect if barriers to consumption were not also eliminated.

One conclusion drawn from this example is that the task of eliminating hunger requires a detailed understanding of its multiple determinants in each unique setting, and that the simple or apparently obvious approach may not be the best one. This applies to interventions that target household income as well as to strategies that enhance food production.

Despite the well-established association between household income and nutritional adequacy, recent studies have indicated that marginal increases in household income may not automatically result in improved nutritional status for all members.[7] These studies have led to a new research focus on the dynamics of resource allocation and exchange within households. Just as communities are made up of many households, who may or may not benefit from new agricultural or economic approaches, so, too, are households made up of individuals, each of whom may be affected differently by a given approach. Numerous studies have indicated that alternatives for increasing household income differ with respect to the nutritional outcomes for each member of a household, particularly women and children.[8] An individual's access to food may be determined by his or her current or future economic contribution to the household. One earner's control over income may affect whether additional income will be used for food or for other goods.

This relatively new area of economics—focusing on the household level—represents an important advance that can strengthen the understanding of hunger and approaches to combating it. Household analysis does not negate earlier analyses, which considered the household as a single unit; rather, it takes advantage of new information derived from farming systems, anthropological, and economic research to extend the gains of the earlier work. This is one more example of the synergy achieved when scientific disciplines together address a problem like hunger.

The food chain starts with crops growing in the field. It continues through harvesting, processing, storage, marketing, and distribution, and ends with the purchase and consumption of food by humans and their metabolism of the nutrients. Economic factors affect every link in the chain. Research on the economic determinants of crop production and marketing has been enriched by the recent focus on economic factors affecting household and individual food consumption choices.

In recent years, an increasing emphasis has been given to the macroeconomic factors affecting food consumption. This has resulted, in part, from the accumulating experiences of high-debt countries that have had to adopt belt-tightening macroeconomic policies known as "structural adjustment." Empirical investigation has failed to support certain intuitively held views about the consequences of such policies. For example, governments constrained to reduce their own spending typically cut social programs, such as health care, less significantly than infrastructure development projects, such as roads and electric generating stations.[9] Understanding how these decisions affect the determination of food prices and household incomes (e.g., roads facilitate food marketing, pricing, and access) is important in predicting the food and nutritional effects of structural adjustment policies on the poor.

Finding the solution to world hunger requires the application of economic analysis, along with the knowledge gained from many other disciplines. No single discipline, nor even the whole range of disciplines working separately, can accomplish what can be achieved when specialists from many disciplines work together and build upon each other's insights.

Notes

1. Robert W. Kates, R. S. Chen, T. E. Downing, Jeanne Kasparian, and Ellen Messer, *The Hunger Report 1988* (Providence, R.I.: Alan Shawn Feinstein World Hunger Program, Brown University, 1988).
2. Judith McGuire, *Malnutrition: Opportunities and Challenges for A.I.D.* (Washington, D.C.: National Center for Food and Agriculture Policy, Resources for the Future, 1988).
3. B. L. Rogers and Anne Swindale, *Determinants of Food Consumption in the Dominican Republic.* Report prepared for U.S. Agency for International Development Office of Nutrition, April 1988.
4. Peter Timmer, W. P. Falcon, and S. R. Pearson, *Food Policy Analysis* (Baltimore: Johns Hopkins University Press, 1983).
5. Rogers and Swindale, *Determinants of Food Consumption.*
6. B. L. Rogers and Melanee Lowdermilk, *Determinants of Food Consumption in Urban Mali.* Report prepared for U.S. Agency for International Development Office of Nutrition, October 1988.
7. Eileen Kennedy and B. Cogill, *Income and Nutritional Effects of the Commercialization of Agriculture in Southwestern Kenya,* Research Report no. 63 (Washington, D.C.: International Food Policy Research Institute, 1987).
8. Shubh Kumar, *Impact of Subsidized Rice on Food Consumption and Nutrition in Kerala,* Research Report no. 5 (Washington, D.C.: International Food Policy Research Institute, 1979). Jane Guyer, *Household Budgets and Women's Incomes,* Working Paper no. 28 (Boston: African Studies Center, Boston University, 1980). Angelique Haugerud, *Development and Household Economy in Two Eco-Zones of Embu District,* Working Paper no. 382 (Nairobi: Institute for Development Studies, University of Nairobi, July 1981).
9. Jere Behrman, "The Impact of Economic Adjustment Programs," in *Health, Nutrition, and Economic Crisis,* ed. D. E. Bell and M. R. Reich (Dover, Mass.: Auburn House Publishing Company, 1988).

CHAPTER 14

Confronting the "Nuts and Bolts" in the Food Chain

A Colloquium Summation

Gelia T. Castillo
University Professor, Department of Agricultural Education and Rural Studies, University of the Philippines at Los Baños, College, Laguna, Philippines

I must have had a hole in my head for accepting this assignment, which requires either full concentration on today's proceedings in order to produce a reasonable summation or a calculated anticipation of what all the brilliant minds will say. What I will present is an extrapolated summary of anticipated as well as actual discussions. Any omission is accidental; all additions and misinterpretations are intentional. After all, I did not take the twenty-four-hour trip to Washington and the equally arduous trek home just to say "*Amen.*" It will be a waste of your air ticket, my time and energy to do that. You can afford to waste your resources, I cannot.

Let me say, however, that because Dr. Chandler is the honoree, my husband insisted that I not only accept the invitation but also fulfill the assignment with some dignity. Furthermore, because Nevin Scrimshaw has always personified the "food chain" in whatever he does, he deserves full support in his call for action to *complete the food chain.* This call for action becomes all the more significant in the light of two glaring realities: (1) there is a great deal which can be done but which is not being done; and (2) so much more is being said than being done, as if saying it does it.

However, through the years that we have known Dr. Chandler, he cannot be accused of talking much and doing little. That's why I'm here.

Fortunately for me, the keynote paper is, in many ways, already a comprehensive summary of the kinks in the food chain manifested in such phenomena as: food surpluses in the North and shortages in the South; food losses in food-short countries; a great deal of knowledge generated about nutrition and yet general ignorance prevailing; nutritional deficiencies persisting despite cheap and effective means of preventing such; continuing gaps between potential and actual yields; famines even when national food supplies are adequate; population continuing to increase while forests disappear and desertification rapidly proceeds.

The Scrimshaw message is that "*achieving food security and overcoming world hunger requires the cooperation of a variety of disciplines. . . . Every step in the food chain requires attention.*"

In this "holistic" approach to food security, actions are required to *maintain food production*; to *reduce food losses*; to *improve food utilization*; to *improve international food-related policies*; to *provide for disasters* and to *develop in the developing countries themselves the capacity to deal with their own problems* in a *multidisciplinary and multisectorial fashion.*

The major themes in the six papers on regional perspectives and five on disciplinary perspectives center on the following:

1. Practically everyone argues for investment in the development of human and institutional capacity not only for science and technology but for development planning and implementation. Needless to say, it is not only the development but also the *maintenance* of such capacity that is crucial. In keeping with the theme of the colloquium, all the papers seem to support the call for multisectoriality and multidisciplinarity in the development of this essential capacity.

2. The differences within regions and within countries with respect to the configuration and the components of the food chain were repeatedly highlighted in the papers to underscore the importance of each country developing its own human capital. As they said in various ways:

Solution for each country must be found in the country itself.

Local people—local solutions.

It is unsustainable to rely on expatriate agricultural scientists, planners, policy makers.

Target technologies to specific environments.

Use traditional food profile as starting point for developing food policy strategy.

Regional and local factors must be analyzed and the most adequate multisectorial solution for a specific country should be designed.

In addition, the importance of community and farmer participation in the implementation of the food chain has been underscored.

3. The papers on the Arab world and the West African Sahel argue that there is a potential to increase food availability, local food production, and productivity as well as food security through proper use of resources, and in the case of the Sahel directing efforts to small farmers, locale-specific food research, and to rainfed agriculture, which has not been done so far. The need for a code of good conduct in food aid which

would make a distinction between increasing dependence and providing security in the Sahel was put forth.

4. Countertrends of tradition and change mentioned by Sidney Mintz are very much in evidence in the consumption patterns of West Africa, where urban consumers are constantly increasing their demand for rice and wheat while local farmers continue to grow traditional crops of millet and sorghum.

5. Thailand's experience in completing the food chain is instructive in this era of the Green Revolution because Thailand has not adopted new rice varieties. Local varieties, despite low yields, have persisted. In tackling malnutrition, curative health care was an effective entry point, and the northeast was its region of focus.

6. Increasing food crop quality and the role of food science and technology in food systems improvement through agroindustries were illustrated convincingly in one of the food chain models.

7. One question asked, which brings the nutritional physiologist and the development planner together despite the author's skepticism about multidisciplinarity, is: "Are you planning for survival or planning for improvement?" Answers to biological questions are very important for rational planning, the paper argues.

8. The potentials of agricultural biotechnology and the unfounded fears associated with it leave a lot of room for exciting prospects even at the village level, when the technology is demystified.

For example, in Dalat, Vietnam, a few selected farmers produce large quantities of in vitro plantlets using rustic facilities in their homes. From these, nodal cuttings are rooted in nursery beds at high densities to become first-generation mother plants. Apical cuttings are made from these to produce a larger generation of mother plants. From all these mother plants, apical cuttings are then taken and rooted in small bamboo or banana-leaf pots and sold to farmers who transplant them directly to the field. Materials are used up to four generations before they are replaced by new rooted apical cuttings.

In the Red River Delta, seed storage is difficult during the nine months of hot weather. National research proved that sprout cuttings from tubers stored 7–9 months rooted well and when transplanted to the fields gave yields of up to 20 tons per hectare. By using tubers and sprouts, investment in seed tubers is only 15 percent of the cost of planting tubers alone. In 1986, 100 hectares of potatoes were grown using this system.[1]

9. Only two papers, one on the Arab world and the other on the importance of female education in South Asia, referred to the role of women in the food chain.

One wonders at this point whether the international development community is not suffering from WID-weariness (women in development). There are hundreds of studies and lots of WID consultancies, but real women who need development are still waiting for WID benefits.

10. The role of health in the food chain or the role of food in the health chain is so obvious that it is surprising that these two sectors hardly intersect even when they are both concerned about the welfare of the same group of people. It is encouraging, therefore, that in this colloquium, several of the papers pointed out these connections. It must be said, however, that for some reason, in general, the nutritionists seem to have a broader view of the food chain than the agriculturists, although we would like to think that change is taking place among the latter.

11. In completing the food chain, at least one paper reminded us that the food situation at the global and national level does not necessarily depict the situation in poor households. There are insights to be gained from household-level analysis where the dynamics of human survival are in evidence.

But to do justice to the keynote paper and the regional and disciplinary perspectives, we have to take the food chain beyond a summary. Although the required actions together make up a chain, each one of these actions requires the pursuit of a chain and attention to its "nuts and bolts." For example, the Green Revolution has had its share of critics, awards, and glorifiers, including Michael Lipton, who recently came to the conclusion that the new rice technologies are "small-farmer friendly." However, its less heralded value is the fact that the Green Revolution enabled the products of science to intrude into farmers' heads, thus opening up new horizons, hitherto not part of their traditional world. Now they are constantly experimenting with new ways, although some of them come to it later than others.

Millions of dollars have been spent researching postharvest technologies—driers, for example—to reduce food losses. So far, most of these driers have not been adopted. On the other hand, multipurpose pavements continue to be the most popular solar driers by day and dance floors by night.

Studies of vegetable farmers who are heavy users of pesticides have shown that they are all aware of the bad effects of the chemicals on their own health and on the environment but will still continue using them despite ill effects. They believe that using fewer or no pesticides at all will contribute to a decline in profits. To escape the consequences, farmers who can afford it hire somebody else to apply the insecticides—thus passing on the ill effects to those lower on the totem pole.[2]

From sustainability analysis and impact evaluation studies done by the World Bank, it was established empirically that in the projects which failed to achieve sustainability, institutional development objectives were notably lacking from the outset of the project design. Conversely, it was found that the successful projects had in common a clear attempt by design to enhance the institutional capacity in some form. Furthermore, considering the heavy debt burden many of us suffer from, we concur with Michael Cernea's assessment that "in part, the international debt crisis is a product of repeated investments in non-sustainable development programs."[3]

A review of farm-household connections in everyday life for resource-poor households highlights the fact that *household food security* is their major preoccupation. It is not rice; it is not corn; it is not root crops; it is not beans; it is not vegetables; it is not livestock; it is not wage labor; it is not remittances but all of the above, sometimes in minuscule amounts but in unimaginable combinations. It is not just field agriculture but also household gardens; not just men, not just adults but also women and children who participate in the production and management process. While commercialization of production is an implicit objective in many agricultural development programs, we have seen that those who sell and even sell much are not necessarily better nourished than those who produce enough to eat and sell little.

But for those who have no access to land, the bottomline indicator for food security is access to a job. As villagers explain: "Some households obviously belong to the lowest rung of the ladder because upon waking up in the morning, they do not know where they will work."[4]

An International Food Policy Research Institute (IFPRI) report says that "in developing countries agricultural prices have enormous human and political implications. The cost of food, of course, is of elemental importance to the poor, but agricultural prices have profound effects on growth, equity, and stability throughout a developing economy."[5] Results of recent studies, however, suggest that there is a chink in the armor of food price policy. For example, the report on Thailand found that only 13 percent of extra margins generated by price support programs were received by farmers (mainly large commercial ones in the central plain). Only 30–50 percent of total production is marketed. Fifty percent of paddy farmers sell less than 10 percent of their rice production and many of them are net purchasers of rice. It was also observed that "when the price of rice rises, small farmers sell more and eat less without substituting other foods for rice, thus experiencing a decline in calorie intake and nutritional status."[6]

Another study on rice market intervention policies in Asia admonished "external advisors to accept with humility the conclusion that food prices are too important to leave to economists."[7]

I believe there are not very many humble economists in Washington, and so this admonition is not likely to be heeded.

The Winrock International 1987 Annual Report says that 90 percent of all the crops grown in developing countries are sown from seeds selected and stored by farmers. The 1987 Report of the Centro Internacional de Agricultura Tropical (CIAT) mentions that their bean program and national programs have developed many superior varieties of beans, and 100 or more have been released by the national programs. Even so, getting the seeds of these improved varieties into the hands of small farmers has proven to be a weak link in the technology chain. In Colombia, a country with a relatively advanced seed sector for Latin America, seed producers provide only an estimated 15–20 percent of all maize seeds used by farmers. For beans, the estimate is less than 3 percent. Small farmers, therefore, tend to save their own seeds.

In the Philippines, where 90 percent of rice production comes from new varieties, about three-fourths of farmers use seeds from their own stock. It is surprising that seed management is not always part of what is taught in extension, considering that estimates of yield reduction attributable to poor seed ranges from 12 to 20 percent.[8]

But my favorite nuts and bolts kink in the food chain is the vitamin A, iron, and iodine trilogy. Why, why haven't we done more—when the problem seems to be well defined, the solutions well researched, and the actions required seem to be so obviously doable?

All these examples were cited in this extrapolated summary in order to support the argument that the food chain must be applied not only across sectors and across disciplines but from macro to micro, from the doable to the impossible. The chain can run from global, regional, national, community to household and vice versa. Insights from the household and community level must feed into institutional policies and perceptions at the global level. There are also South-South chains in addition to the usual North-South ones.

Given all that has been said, let us locate the food chain in time and space. *The time is now* and *the place could be Bangladesh.* What do we do now that will make a difference to nutrition security tomorrow? Let us do what is doable now. The impossible we can return to tomorrow.

As one of the speakers said, "We should stop talking about hunger without more positive and practical action."

As another paper asserts, "Multidisciplinarity is seldom really successful except when people are actually working together on a practical project for a reasonable length of time."

How about putting this food chain into action so that we can put it to a test in real life?

Notes

1. International Potato Center, *CIP Annual Report, 1986–87* (Lima, Peru: CIP, 1987), 189.

2. Agnes C. Rola, "Pesticides, Health Risk, and Farm Productivity: A Philippine Experience," University of the Philippines at Los Baños, Center for Policy and Development Studies, July 1988.

3. Michael M. Cernea, *Farmer Organizations and Institution Building for Sustainable Development,* World Bank Reprint Series No. 414 (reprinted from *Regional Development Dialogue,* vol. 8, no. 2 (Summer 1987): 1–24.

4. Gelia T. Castillo, "Finding Connections between Farm and Household" (Paper prepared for the Ninth Meeting of the Technical Advisory Committee, Food and Fertilizer Technology Center, Taipei, Taiwan, May 16–21 1988).

5. *International Food Policy Research Institute Report,* vol. 10, no. 3 (Washington, D.C.: IFPRI, July 1988).

6. Theodore Panayotou, "Food Price Policy in Thailand" (Paper presented at the Conference on Comparative Food Price Policy in Asia, sponsored by the Food Research Institute, Stanford University, International Rice Research Institute, and Rockefeller Brothers Fund, January 26–27,1987, IRRI, College, Laguna, Philippines).

7. J. Keith Johnson, "Overview," in *Evaluating Rice Market Intervention Policies* (Manila: Asian Development Bank, 1988), 21.

8. Gelia T. Castillo, "Social Science Research and Agricultural Development Policy: Pedestrian Views of a Non-Economist" (Paper presented for workshop on Policy Considerations for Structural Changes and Development in Philippines Agriculture, University of the Philippines at Los Baños, College, Laguna, Philippines, April 1988).

CHAPTER 15

Toward a Sustained Agricultural Economy

Remarks of the Laureate of the 1988 General Foods World Food Prize

Robert F. Chandler, Jr.
Founding Director, International Rice Research Institute, The Philippines

I have never felt more deeply honored, nor so generously rewarded, than as the fortunate recipient in 1988 of the General Foods World Food Prize. My lasting gratitude extends not only to those directly responsible for my selection but also to the host of others, men and women alike, who over the years have supported and strengthened whatever role I have played in international development. As this audience well knows, I was awarded the prize primarily as the founding director of the International Rice Research Institute (IRRI) in the Philippines—the institution that spearheaded the Green Revolution in rice, especially in Asia, where 90 percent of the world's rice is grown and consumed.

I was fortunate to have been selected as the first leader of IRRI's research and training program and to have played a role in its planning, organization, and implementation. The almost thirteen years that my wife, Sunny, and I spent in the Philippines were among the most satisfying and rewarding of our lives. Obviously, credit for the success of IRRI should be shared with many people and organizations, especially the Rockefeller and Ford foundations, the Government of the Philippines, and the young, capable, international staff that got it off to such a good start.

I am not going to attempt to match the eloquence and wisdom of my friend of long acquaintance, Dr. M. S. Swaminathan, who in 1987, as the first and highly deserving recipient of the World Food Prize, described so memorably the interrelation of ecological, social, economic, and agricultural elements in any lasting solution to world poverty and hunger. Instead, I shall deal more with facts and figures that reveal current progress as well as problems that face us on the food and population front.

As news commentators say, "There is good news today and there is bad news." So it is with food and population. There are developments to cheer and developments to deplore. Let us look first at the good news about the production of rice and wheat, the world's two most important food crops.

In 1965, just before the wide distribution of modern rice varieties with high-yield potential, production in the eighteen Asian countries that grow and consume most of the world's rice was 233 million metric tons. By 1986, twenty-one years later, that figure had jumped to 432 million tons, an increase of 85 percent. Eight of those countries had more than doubled their production.

Moreover, during the same period, the human population in the eighteen countries had advanced from 1.7 to 2.7 billion, an increase of 59 percent. For the first time in modern history, Asian per capita rice production had markedly increased. In previous decades, harvests had either kept pace with population growth or had fallen behind.

The 85 percent increase in production in Asia was due more to augmented yields than to increases in area devoted to rice. The gain in yield was 60 percent, while the land area planted to rice expanded by only 14 percent. Moreover, since 1977 neither China nor India, the world's two largest rice-growing countries, has shown any increase in area planted to rice. This means that additional land suitable for rice is no longer available and that future gains in harvest will have to come from increased yields on land already devoted to that crop.

In Africa, the situation is quite the opposite. During the twenty-year period from 1965 to 1985, rice yields on that continent rose only from 1.68 to 1.80 metric tons per hectare, a gain of a mere 7 percent, whereas the land area planted to rice expanded by 60 percent. Although Africa produces only 10 million metric tons of rice annually (compared to over 430 million in Asia), rice is the cereal grain that is growing the fastest in production—faster than sorghum, millet, or maize, Africa's traditional cereal crops. Indeed, rice is so popular in most African countries that large quantities are imported, mainly to satisfy the demands of urban populations.

Even greater strides have been made with wheat. In the first five years after the semidwarf wheats were widely planted in India and Pakistan, for example, production doubled. The Green Revolution in wheat was sparked by Nobel laureate Dr. Norman Borlaug of the Centro Internacional de Mejoramiento de Maíz y Trigo (CIMMYT), whose capable, devoted, untiring efforts influenced many governments to realize the potential for greatly increasing production of that crop.

The principal reason for the improved production of both rice and wheat was the revolutionary development of varieties that were short, stiff strawed, nonlodging, heavy tillering, and fertilizer responsive, and in addition, resistant to most major insect pests and diseases. Since the introduction of these new varieties, there has been a substantial increase in the use of chemical fertilizer and in the development of new irrigation systems. In every country that was able to increase markedly its production of either rice or wheat, the political leaders not only had gained an understanding of the importance of agricultural development but had become highly committed to an action program.

In fact, enough cereal grain is being produced to feed the world (at current inadequate levels of nutrition), but national and individual poverty and food distribution problems continue to cause about 500 million people to suffer from malnutrition. The situation, however, would be much more critical were it not for the creation and widespread adoption of modern varieties of rice and wheat.

Although further progress will be made in alleviating the closely related scourges of hunger and poverty through increased food production, there are limits to what can be done unless human beings are able to control their numbers.

The population problem, more than any other element, threatens the well-being of the human race. World population has passed the 5 billion mark. Each year adds more than 80 million people to the total, more than 60 million of whom will be living in Africa, Asia, and Latin America, the regions least able to accommodate them.

The only "good news" on the population front is that the growth rate has been declining since 1970, a reversal of all previous trends since record keeping began. Other than in the prosperous, industrialized nations that have essentially stabilized their populations, the decreases have occurred mostly in Asia—primarily China, Korea, Singapore, and Taiwan. China, with one-third of Asia's inhabitants, has reduced its population growth rate to 1.2 percent annually, an almost incredible achievement. Offsetting that historic advance is the fact that, on the average, African populations are still growing at the rate of 2.8 percent and Latin American populations at 2.4 percent.

United Nations experts predict that by the year 2000 the population growth rate will be reduced from the current 1.7 percent to 1.5 percent. However, because population expands exponentially, rather than arithmetically, the number of people to be added in the year 2000 will be 92 million, in contrast to the 80-million addition in 1988. This forecast is based on the United Nations estimate that the earth will harbor 6.15 billion at the end of this century.

In 1945, the eminent demographer Dr. Frank Notestein propounded the theory that there are three stages of population growth as countries develop socially and economically. The first stage is high birth rate and high death rate, during which populations increase very slowly. For example, world population grew only from 510 to 625 million between the years 1650 and 1700, an average of but 230,000 per year.

The second is high birth rate and low death rate, the stage that much of the Third World is in today. The control of such diseases as malaria, yellow fever, and polio, and the improvement in nutrition have greatly increased human survival in the poorer countries, but birth rates remain high.

Low birth rate and low death rate is the final stage in the transition, the one that the United States, Canada, and Western Europe are in today and the one that we hope the entire globe will reach eventually.

The fear of population watchers today is that many Third World countries will not be able to move from stage two to stage three but will be caught in what Lester Brown of the Worldwatch Institute calls the "demographic trap." Unable to achieve the social and economic gains that usually reduce birth rates, the population expands to the point at which demand exceeds the sustainable yield of cropland, forests, grassland, and even aquifers supplying fresh water. Finally, death rates rise again and conditions revert to stage one, when life becomes intolerable, dominated by chronic hunger, frequent famine, and social conflict—even civil war.

There are those who contend that population control is not important, that people are a resource and that to limit their numbers is to reduce the opportunities for human development. Others claim that there is an ample supply of uncultivated land and other natural resources and all that is needed is to exploit them. It is difficult to understand how such a view of seemingly infinite reserves can long be held in this finite world.

There are limits to the available quantities of arable land, of fresh water supplies for irrigation, of areas that can be devoted to forests, and of food resources from the oceans. Furthermore, solar radiation and average world precipitation cannot be increased by human beings, and, despite the advances made in augmenting the yield potential of food crops, there are limits to the genetic improvement of both plants and animals.

Notwithstanding these inevitable restrictions, we must continue to intensify our struggle to bring a better life to the poverty-stricken people of the Third World. It must be said, however, that the job cannot be done by the richer nations alone. The afflicted countries must come to realize that their survival depends upon their own national efforts. They must fully and wisely utilize not only foreign financial and professional assistance but their own resources, both human and natural.

Development, as we know too well, is a slow and complex process. Nevertheless, we have available today, as never before, the technology and know-how to increase food production. We can all agree that what is needed is less rhetoric and more action.

Yet I must rely on even more words to list here what many in international agriculture have long seen as some of the most essential actions that food-deficient nations must take to develop a sustained agricultural economy. With foreign assistance and their own resources, they must make maximum use of available water resources for irrigation; improve and extend farm-to-market roads; build schools and strengthen institutions of higher education; provide rural credit for qualifying farmers; establish production incentives, such as price supports and subsidized inputs; improve the chain of communication from agricultural researcher to extension specialist to farmer; provide adequate financial support for both agricultural research and extension; and, finally, develop a widespread system of on-farm applied research and demonstration plots with improved varieties and technology.

Permit me to elaborate further on some of these needed actions. Among the most important is education. In some African countries, where 90 percent of the people cannot read or write, it is extremely difficult to introduce new technology or involve the population as a whole in national development programs. In Asia, on the other hand, it is evident that the countries with the highest literacy rates have adopted new technology fastest and have shown marked increases in both rural and urban incomes.

In addition, agricultural research findings must be extended to the farmer. Especially in Africa, many results from experiment stations and agricultural colleges never reach the farmer. In my view, there are two principal reasons for this. One is that the scientists themselves are not as much concerned about the plight of the farmer as they are about promoting their own reputations among colleagues and peers. The other is that, in many instances, the agricultural extension programs are poorly supported. Often, extension agents have no transportation and can only wait in their offices for the farmers to come to them.

Sustained farming systems must replace slash-and-burn cultivation. It is estimated that over 250 million people eke out a living from a system of shifting cultivation. Crop yields are pitifully low and farmers and their families are always poor. Foresters, agroforesters, and agronomists urgently need to work together to develop farming systems that will permit farmers to cultivate a given plot of land continuously and yet maintain the fertility and productivity of the soil.

Food shipments are not the answer to rural development. There are those who argue that since the United States, Canada, and Australia, for example, produce a surplus of food grains, we should simply make huge shipments to the food-deficient nations to alleviate the problem. In my opinion, this is counterproductive to development, because it removes the incentive for countries to increase their food production. There is the old adage, "Give a man a fish and he eats for a day. Teach him to fish and he eats forever." In cases of severe famine, of course, there is no question that food must be shipped until the disaster is over.

Dedicated leaders with a national will for development are also urgently needed. It has been my observation that the countries that have made the most progress in combating food deficits and malnutrition are those in which the top government officials (including presidents and prime ministers) have been truly concerned about the welfare of their citizens and have supported strong programs to improve their condition. When the leaders of a country are more concerned about their own prestige and power than about their people, a lack of confidence arises among the population, which then tends to impede the national will that is necessary for development.

From my experience in Asia and Africa, I am convinced that farmers will use new varieties and crop management methods if they can see for themselves a 50 to 100 percent gain in yield on their own fields or on those of a neighbor. Many development specialists maintain too conservative a view and are overly reluctant to expose farmers to modern techniques, thinking that they cannot afford to use them. In reality, if they are not to be mired in a succession of inadequate harvests, farmers cannot afford not to use them.

Although I favor maximum use of organic plant residues and compost, I contend that in the long run, Africa, for example, cannot feed its ever-expanding population without the use of abundant quantities of chemical fertilizer, nor without making much better use of its water resources. We need only look at pragmatic China to support this contention. Furthermore, prosperity will continue to elude the average African farmer until we find a substitute for the hand hoe, the labor-intensive tool that is still the principal implement for land preparation.

In addition, relief must be found for the estimated 250 million people in the tropics and subtropics who are barely eking out a living from shifting cultivation. Research must be accelerated to develop a sustained crop-and-tree production system that will eliminate the terrible destruction of forest resources now occurring under slash-and-burn agriculture.

Considering the rate at which the population is still expanding in the poorer countries and the knowledge that the number of people who are added to the world in the early part of the next century will be even larger than it is today, I predict that world population will at least double before it stabilizes. If this forecast is true, it will require a herculean effort, with an enormous commitment of financial and human resources, to maintain this planet as an acceptable place on which to live.

We are meeting the challenge of outer space; we commit huge sums for national defense. We can meet, I feel certain, the challenges of our planet.

CHAPTER 16

Excerpts of the Discussions following the Morning and Afternoon Panels

[*Editors' Note: The speakers in the colloquium presented their papers in two panel discussions: a morning panel exploring regional and international perspectives on agricultural, food, and nutrition issues; and an afternoon panel that explored these issues from the perspective of several academic disciplines and professions. After each set of presentations, the panel moderators elicited additional comments from the speakers and comments and questions from the audience. The following are excerpts from these discussions. Anne de Lattre chaired the morning panel; Beatrice Lorge Rogers chaired the afternoon panel.*]

Excerpts of the Discussion following the Morning Panel

Anne de Lattre (moderator): The floor is now open to questions. You can address your questions to the panel as a whole or to individuals, as you like.

John Waterlow: I'd like to start off with a question to you, Madame de Lattre. I find it extraordinary, as you say in your paper, that food aid needs generally are not carefully scrutinized and evaluated. The results of development projects in agriculture and food assistance are not always evaluated properly. When I was adviser on nutrition to my overseas development ministry [in Great Britain], I urged them to raise with the development assistance committee the possibility that 5 percent of world food program funds might go to evaluation. Of course, it didn't go through. But why has there not been an emphasis on evaluation from the very beginning of overseas food aid or development aid programs?

Anne de Lattre: Well, with respect to food aid I would say that food aid has become a profitable convenience for both parties. In a situation where the recipient government draws large benefits from food aid and where the donors can improve their aid record, and draw on their surplus, there is a built-in situation to avoid evaluation. I think that this is what happened for a very long time, although I would say that the situation is changing. At last, some donors are trying to be much more careful about aid requests; they are trying not to overrespond, so that I think we are beginning to see the end of a tunnel. As far as the evaluation of projects, I think I would like to turn to Uma Lele, who is doing an evaluation, to answer this question.

Uma Lele: Before I answer a question about the evaluation of projects, I want to say there is probably only one side of the food aid picture that has been presented here today, and I'd like to present another side. If one takes the example of the Indian subcontinent where, in the late 1960s, food aid had come into much disrepute, I think one has to recognize that if it weren't for food aid, many more people in South Asia would have died. At that time the new technology—the Green Revolution in rice and wheat—was not yet known to scientists. The difference I see between South Asia and many parts of Africa is this: in the mid-1960s when countries like India had a really severe food crisis and recurring droughts, as a result of food aid a large number of people did not die, and I think we must recognize that that was a very important role that food aid played in those days. But I think the main difference which has probably come out somewhat implicitly in what we have been saying is that in the mid-1960s, when India had a major food crisis, there was a strategy for developing agriculture. Norman Borlaug and others who were advising India had in their minds a strategy, and they were able to convince policy makers in South Asia that if only they did A, B, and C, they could increase their wheat production by a hundred percent in five years. And there were very clear directions. When I look at the problem in Africa at the present time, there is not a clear set of solutions which are available on a country basis. Just to say that food aid is bad without providing any positive solutions is not terribly helpful. I would say that if hunger and malnourishment in South Asia are going to be addressed in the next ten or fifteen years, food aid can play a very substantial role in addressing that problem, provided it is done in the context of a sensible development policy. I feel that large numbers of South Asian countries now are in a position to adopt a sensible developmental policy so that food aid doesn't become counterproductive. I think, however, if that is going to materialize, then food aid has to become much more reliable and consistent, and not something which becomes a political tool that's available one year and not available in the subsequent years. Governments have to count on it from year to year and to build their long-term strategy for developing their agricultural sector.

With regard to evaluations, I want to emphasize that at the World Bank we normally undertake evaluations of development projects. In fact, I think every project that is financed by the Bank is legally required to perform an audit; there are very elaborate evaluations that have taken place. I think there are two kinds of questions that we need to ask ourselves. First, have the evaluations always been reflected in the subsequent policies that have been adopted—the lessons reflected in policy decisions? In many cases they have not been. So I think if we said that there are no evaluations, we would be wrong, because there are many evaluations. The question is, how do they influence policy? Secondly, it's one thing to do project evaluations; it's another thing to develop an agricultural strategy that would lead to growth in the long run. That's where I think the difference between South Asia, East Asia, and Africa is very evident—namely, in terms of developing agriculture from a long-term point of view. There are many project evaluations at the World Bank showing that rates of return to projects in Africa are lower than they are in the case of South Asia.

J. E. Dutra de Oliveira: I'd like just to say a few words about food aid in Brazil. We tried to stop it because we thought it was bad for food production in the country. But it's interesting that although we stopped foreign food aid, we have a food aid program inside Brazil, and we are doing exactly the same thing that foreign countries did for Brazil in an earlier period. We are taking food from the best parts of the country and sending it to the Amazon region, for example. In these areas they have fish, but they also could obtain buffalo milk or milk from cows from the south of the country. I think that we didn't learn the lesson. Another aspect is that because most of the food programs in Brazil are done by the government, and there are political criteria involved, there is less interest in evaluation.

Norman Borlaug: I think we have some outstanding examples of how food aid can be used to turn a country around in its agricultural production. India is exhibit A. At the right time the decision was made in India—the leaders and the farmers concluded they were going to walk on their own feet. The technology was there, and it had been demonstrated. The grassroots were afire and policy had to change. So there's a time and place when you change from a Dr. Jekyll to a Mr. Hyde, if you're working in the area of overseas technical assistance. The technology has to be there first, and it has to be demonstrated in its applications—not on a few small plots but initially on dozens, then hundreds, and then thousands of plots, on farmers' fields, under practical, realistic conditions. And eventually 400,000 farmers in India, or perhaps that was closer to a million, knew and understood what was possible with the technology and the technical aid. Those grassroots fires sort of singed the feet of the political leaders, and then they were willing to make drastic policy changes. And there's another example of how to use food aid. It came later in India, and this concerns the milk revolution. Unlike the case of wheat and rice, we could never get transferred funds from the resale of P.L. 480 wheat or of other types of foreign aid grains into a fund to support research and extension. But one leader was smart enough to do this from the resale of a type of milk powder. He had a certain percentage of the funds set aside, and he created an independent agency to support the development of the milk industry. Today, the development of milk production in India is another major example of how these funds should be used.

Excerpts of the Discussion following the Afternoon Panel

Beatrice Lorge Rogers (moderator): I would like to entertain questions and comments.

Patricia Kutzner: Last year's food symposium had a very strong ethical focus. This year the focus is more scientific, and I would like to ask the panel to do a little blending. I would simply like to ask one question and ask each of the panelists to reflect briefly on the question from his or her own experience. In your work, what do you find to be the greatest ethical dilemma or challenge?

John Waterlow: Well, for me as a pediatric physician doing research on malnourished children, the ethical dilemma is: what is it legitimate to do from the point of view of research on a sick child in order to get that child better, or other children better? Ethical problems inevitably arise.

Pablo Scolnik: I could go on for a couple of hours on that question. It's a very tough one. I like to call myself a scientist with social responsibility, and I ask myself that question many times. Two issues come to mind; one involves the environment. We want to improve food quality and quantity, and yet we don't want to damage the environment. It used to be that we worked on the assumption that all the things that were toxic or were carcinogens were actually produced by man; all we had to do was keep an eye on the chemical companies to see what kind of products they were developing. Now we have learned that plants themselves produce toxins and produce chemicals that are powerful carcinogens. And what we have to understand is the biology of the system, of both natural and man-made substances. That's a very tough question from the technical point of view. That's one concern about the safety of the foods we produce. And the second is that for all these new technologies we work on, the price of development is just staggering, and companies and even governments have to recover those investment costs before they can think about providing the new technologies free or inexpensively to Third World countries. So the question arises, how are we going to transfer that technology to the Third World in a timely and productive fashion?

Ricardo Bressani: Right now I am getting involved in a project involving a cooperative and that deals with the development of a number of technologies. In order to get the program going I met with this cooperative, maybe eight to ten times. The women and men have asked me for about seven different activities to be done at the cooperative. And they are very strong about what they ask. My problem is that I have only three years or so in which to do whatever they want me to do, and I cannot do all seven things in three years' time. So my dilemma, my problem is how can I choose the best of the seven things and at the same time satisfy the needs of the others.

Richard Harwood: I've been weighing an issue that has been bothering me. It is an equity issue. In our Western concept of agricultural development for the last fifty years or so, we've focused on efficiency of use of labor, of the individual productivity of workers. Our goal has been to get people out of agriculture as much as possible and into higher-paying kinds of jobs, into industry. Yet as we heard from Dr. Lele this morning about the massive population increases in India alone, for instance, the two or three hundred million new people who are going to be depending on agriculture for their livelihood—we're going to have to look at agriculture not just as a means of producing food but as a vehicle for providing employment. It's cheaper to generate jobs in agriculture than it is in industry by severalfold, and we haven't adjusted our thinking to that. We tend to think, well, we'll increase labor productivity with whatever technologies happen to come along, and let the people migrate to urban areas where someone else will take care of them. To me that is a very basic problem, with ethical and equity implications, for many countries.

Sidney Mintz: The ethical problems I confront in my profession are of two quite different kinds. The first is the obvious problem that faces a fieldworker, an anthropologist, who works with people and who tries hard to win their trust and to find out from them how they see the world. Every piece of information I elicit from an informant who belongs to a different culture—I get that information for nothing and that person has taken me into his confidence—weighs on me, because I never know how it might be used against him. That's the first thing—the right to knowledge, which I think is an agonizing ethical question at least for anthropologists. That's related to a different kind of problem. It's the right to tamper with the information, and I think that's a real ethical question that faces many of us even though we don't know it—our underlying faith that we do really know more than the people we are trying to help. The assumption we make about our society is that because it's technically superior, it must be morally superior. And I think we do make that assumption, though we hate to admit it and rarely confront it.

Beatrice Lorge Rogers: For economists making economic policy recommendations, maybe we couldn't do anything if we ever let ourselves think too hard about the fact that we're dealing with very powerful forces that affect people's lives. The fact is that we are dealing with very fundamental determinants of a people's well-being, their access to their livelihoods, and so on. I feel safe in saying that none of us would claim to be able to predict all of the effects and consequences of our efforts. Often, there are unforeseen effects, some of them very negative. Some of them are very negative even in projects that are quite positive and quite successful. Another dilemma in the discipline of economics is the equity versus growth question, broadly stated. When you look at the movements toward free-market systems, you can see growth but also an increase in people left by the wayside. If you insist in policy terms and have the power to insist on equity, there's no question you sacrifice growth. Everybody can wind up worse off, and yet there is an ethical question involved. Perhaps, one way out of that dilemma is to target vulnerable groups, just accepting the need to protect vulnerable groups while implementing policy interventions.

Martha Lewis: This is about your [Rogers's] comment earlier, that it mattered a great deal whether it was a woman or a man in the family household who got the income, that there was a positive correlation with a family's nutrition if the increased income went to the woman in the household. Can you comment further on this?

Beatrice Lorge Rogers: I'm delighted that you brought up that issue. It happens to be one that's of great interest to me. There are a lot of studies that have shown a difference—namely, that show that the source of income and particularly the earner of income is one of the factors determining how the income is used. We've compared households of equal income with women working and not working and found that women tend to spend more money on food. There's a lot of suggestive evidence in that direction, but it's not "the good moms, the bad dads" theory of development. And I think that's a real concern. There seems to be strong evidence that income channeled through the woman in the household tends to be translated into increased food spending. But the studies represent a research frontier. I think it's an area where there's a great deal to be learned. Certainly, however, there is an equity question in terms of who gets the income resulting from labor. There are several examples of big agricultural development schemes that found it easier to channel income to the head of the household upon harvest, rather than providing returns to labor on a person-by-person basis. That was perceived as being very inequitable, not surprisingly, by the people who lost control over that income because it wasn't channeled to them.

Miguel Jimenez: I'd like to make reference to Dr. Scolnik's closing remarks today. He mentioned that many of the people who come to this country under scholarships offered by international organizations are then sent back to their countries with a lot of knowledge, with a diploma, but with few resources with which to carry on their work. I think Dr. Scolnik held out a challenge to international organizations to provide overseas students with resources when they return to their countries so they can apply the knowledge they received here. Otherwise, there will be tremendous frustration.

Beatrice Lorge Rogers: You mean, to see that technology and training gets transferred back, gets diffused in many countries.

Pablo Scolnik: You interpreted my remarks in the correct way, and the problem is the lack of international programs that actually support that sort of thing. It's very easy to complain as the head of a lab in this country, because a graduate student or postgraduate student is very inexpensive labor. The fellow will really work very hard to finish his Ph.D. and produce a lot, but there is no incentive to keep in touch with that person when he or she returns to the country, or to bring that person back for short periods of time. There is reason to argue that a training program that doesn't take into consideration a long-term association with students is lacking in certain value over the long run.

CHAPTER 17

Directions for Research on Completing the Food Chain

A Discussion at the International Food Policy Research Institute

[*Editors' Note: In cooperation with the International Food Policy Research Institute (IFPRI) in Washington, D.C., a two-hour discussion was held at IFPRI headquarters on the morning following the colloquium (October 5, 1989) to examine the research implications of the papers presented the previous day. The discussion, titled "Directions for Research on Completing the Food Chain," was chaired by John W. Mellor, director of IFPRI. The discussion was taped, transcribed, and edited for clarity. Participants included the colloquium speakers and other scholars and policy leaders in the fields of food policy, agriculture, and nutrition. Among the participants were Norman E. Borlaug, Distinguished Professor of International Agriculture at Texas A&M University and laureate of the Nobel Peace Prize in 1970 for his work in agriculture; Robert F. Chandler, Jr., laureate of the 1988 General Foods World Food Prize; and A. S. Clausi, chairman, Council of Advisors, General Foods World Food Prize. Other speakers included Richard H. Sabot, professor of economics, Williams College, Massachusetts; Eileen Kennedy, deputy director, Food and Nutrition Policy Program, Cornell University, New York; Ronald C. Duncan, International Commodity Markets Division, World Bank; Peter Temu, UN World Food Council; Alan Berg, senior nutrition advisor, World Bank; and Curtis Farrar, executive secretary, Consultative Group on International Agricultural Research, Washington, D.C.*]

John Mellor: It is a great pleasure to welcome this distinguished group of individuals in the fields of agriculture, food policy, biotechnology, and nutrition to IFPRI (the International Food Policy Research Institute). I am hoping that we can focus this morning's discussion on issues in agriculture and food policy for which we lack answers—and relate it to yesterday's colloquium. I have a vested interest at IFPRI in seeking out gaps in our knowledge since we are always worrying about whether we are on the right track in terms of allocating IFPRI's research capabilities. I see this as a wonderful opportunity to examine where research should be going in this very difficult area. It also makes sense to focus on food and poverty since, from our point of view, the gaps in the food chain relate mainly to low-income people.

Two substantive comments come to mind after reading the colloquium papers. I wish to introduce our discussion by drawing attention to these two issues. I will state each as an assertion and then elaborate briefly. First, the pressing equity concern in poor countries is raising large numbers of people above a minimal, absolute level of poverty. Two, to achieve this objective requires broad participation in increasing food and agricultural production.

When economists deal with the problems of poor people in poor countries, we have a fairly solid rationale for emphasizing the ways people can be lifted above some absolute poverty line. On the other hand, when economists look at the problems of the poor in rich countries, we tend to focus not on an absolute poverty line but on the distribution of income. We raise moral and equity questions about the fact that some people have incomes that are so much higher than others. In relation to developing nations, we put the emphasis much less on income distribution and much more on the fact that we are dealing with countries in which 30 to 40 percent of the people are below an absolute poverty line, so we tend to be less bothered if, in the process of lifting ten people above that line, one person happens to double his income. Note the distinction I am making. We obviously do not have complete agreement on the distinction, but we do have fairly solid philosophical grounds for it, which the economist-philosopher Amartya Sen has spelled out.

There are, of course, very profound problems connected with the idea of an absolute poverty line: as soon as you have an absolute poverty line, then there is an absolute posited. As economists, we always have been grateful that nutritionists could give us this absolute measure; that is, if an individual had fewer than 2,164 calories, let's say, that was really disastrous to his or her health, and if you could just bring people three calories above that line, then you were into a different ball game. What we economists have discovered recently is that there really is not a nice rigid line there. Unfortunately, the fact that nutritionists seem to be unable to give us a nice neat line does not abrogate the underlying principle: that if there are massive numbers of people who live in circumstances that by some definition we find morally unacceptable, we need to concentrate on improving their situation. Since quite a number of you have backgrounds in nutrition and the biological sciences, I would like to see what you have to say on that, including perhaps telling me that I'm talking nonsense.

Another issue I want to put on the table is a shortcoming that I found as I went through the papers that creates a problem for those of us who work on the policy side. We now have quite a sizeable body of research at IFPRI and at other research institutions that shows that with a mass of people below some absolute poverty line in the rural areas of developing countries, it really is virtually impossible and certainly impractical to lift them above that poverty line without taking action to increase agricultural production. While it is true that the problem of those poor people is the lack of food entitlements, or the means to acquire food, one cannot argue that there is no production problem. To put it in more positive terms, if you're going to increase the entitlements or access to food of the rural poor, you have to increase agricultural production. This has to happen not only for the direct effects insofar as many people make their living producing food; but, in addition, for the much more substantial indirect effects, the latter being perhaps two, three, and even five times as important as the direct ones.

So it's quite counterproductive to try to say the problem is an entitlement problem alone and, therefore, not a production problem. We can make that distinction in the United States, where agriculture is such a small part of the society, but that distinction distracts us from very critical problems that have to be solved if the food chain is to be completed for poor people in rural areas of developing nations.

Let's proceed by asking the moderators of the two panel discussions at the colloquium to briefly summarize the highlights of the panels, and then open the floor to general discussion.

Anne de Lattre: I can't pretend to do justice to the contributions that were made at the Smithsonian colloquium by scientists and scholars and policy advisers, all of them with such great sensitivity and perception. I would hope they would comment themselves where I have failed to convey what they actually wanted to get across. There was one sobering thought that many participants expressed, which is that the work of economists has not facilitated the development process as much as it could have. Poor advice and insensitivity to the social issues of alleviating poverty have led to a lot of blind alleys. Another view that was shared by panelists was that national policies leading to increasing self-reliance and sustainable development are essential to the development process and, perhaps more importantly, to human dignity and pride. There was a feeling that as long as governments fail to get their priorities straight, the role of scholars, scientists, foreign advisers, and of external assistance will have only a limited impact. I think the panelists will agree that this point should be pushed and perhaps researched more. There is a sharing of experience within and between countries, and perhaps we can bring to the forefront successful cases as explained by Dr. Aree Valyasevi. Uma Lele reminded us of the enormous problem that South Asia will be confronting during the next thirty years or so. She raised the issue of the need to improve rural infrastructure, fight land erosion, and increase cropping intensity and crop yields.

Regarding the African situation, perceptions are mixed. On the one hand, there is the feeling that African populations are resilient and dynamic, that they have a capacity to adapt and innovate. On the other hand, there is also evidence that governmental awareness of new risks in food policies is quite low, although this is not true everywhere. IFPRI would do a great service by carrying out more country-specific food analysis, more country-specific analysis of institutions, more country-specific research on what is being done to assist women in the agricultural sector with the objective of sustainability. Dr. Thomas Odhiambo reminded us that the present consumption profile of many African countries is unsustainable. What can be done? We heard Dr. Borlaug speak on possible breakthroughs in maize and sorghum development in Ghana. Is it possible to research what is going on and disseminate the results for the benefit of other African countries? Breaking the famine cycle was also raised as a theme for research. I believe this type of research would furnish evidence of the inadequacy of existing organizational structures to deal with disasters such as famines. Why do we have plans in our countries, in the United States and certainly in France, to deal with any kind of disaster in a hurry? Can we study whether we could have that sort of preparation very soon in African and Asian countries?

Beatrice Lorge Rogers: I took the liberty of going back over all the presentations to identify research issues that seem to come up repeatedly. Others I thought were particularly important even if they didn't come up often. Some of the issues that were brought up involved technological questions; others involved ecological issues and the physical sustainability of agricultural development—for example, in the use of fertilizers, or the use of more integrated systems approaches to agriculture. It seems that all of those issues, even if they sound technical, affect impoverished people. I'm thinking of the point that one speaker made that wealthy farmers don't avoid use of pesticides but simply pay poor farmers to apply them and to take the risk. In that sense who gets the fragile land? Who gets the land that is most damaged? So when you're talking about trying to preserve the ecological and the environmental security of agricultural practices, it is not just a technical issue that's separate from poverty questions.

I'll start with the technical side first because I know less about it, and I can just signal that the theme I really picked up on was the idea of an integrated and ecologically sustainable agricultural system—production, use of inputs, selection of crops, and so on. And then the long-term damage—the problems Pablo Scolnik talked about—the fear of what might happen with biotechnology, and I think that's an area where research is needed on control of the development of some of these technologies. So that was an area where the theme was sustainability in a physical world. Another area, related to that, is the need to focus specifically on the African situation. It's clear that the details of a particular situation determine the success or failure of policies and of new technologies. One thing that has happened in the field of antihunger work is the recognition that, generally speaking, we aren't going to be able to say, "Here is an answer. Here is the technology," or, "Here is the policy that will work."

The focus of future research ought to be on identifying characteristics that we need to consider in applying different technological advances and different economic policy advances—not to even think of searching for an overall answer but to try to search for the model to use in a particular environment. But can we identify the characteristics of a model that can predict whether something will be effective, whether it will be taken up in the way that we expect? Uma Lele mentioned absorptive capacity, and there are real questions about what determines different countries' capacity to absorb food aid, technological assistance, and economic aid. The question is, how can you structure the absorptive capacity of a country in ways that do not create dependency, but rather use aid in a constructive way leading toward long-term, sustainable, independent development? Anne de Lattre raised the question of how to discipline the transfer of food aid, and I would like to look at the institutional factors that enable countries to be disciplined in accepting food aid.

In terms of ecological sustainability, the view is advanced that research needs to focus on the real-world application of technology, the constraints on the people who we hope will take up the technology, on how new technologies get adopted, and what determines whether a new technology will displace people or benefit them. One evaluation found that average household incomes had increased quite substantially; further research showed that, indeed, incomes had gone up, but in different households. The households that had been on the land originally had been displaced, and new households had come in and benefited from the new technology.

Nevin Scrimshaw made reference to the subject of postharvest losses—an area in which there are both technological and economic questions to be asked. What are the best ways to promote a marketing infrastructure that can help to reduce postharvest losses? There are also the technological questions of food processing and genetic manipulation to reduce the likelihood of spoilage and deterioration of food products. Once again, that's an area where the potential for improving welfare, food availability, and even income certainly rivals the potential from agricultural production increases, if we're looking at 40, 50, or 60 percent postharvest losses.

Among the macroeconomic questions for further research, I'll take the liberty of reiterating a point that I made yesterday. We all have an intuition about what structural adjustment might bring about, but intuitive understandings often turn out to be wrong. The things that we guess will happen are not the things that in fact happen. So I think that research is needed that traces the linkages among those big changes in food prices, in prices of tradables versus nontradables, in employment, in the sectors in which employment is created. We need to learn whether those are the sectors where jobs are accessible to the poor.

Finally, an issue arose on household dynamics, the economics at the household or family level. I was interested when Dr. John Waterlow mentioned that maybe we shouldn't always focus on pregnant and lactating women and infants in relation to food production and food availability. Maybe there's a certain rationale for focusing on the adult male in the household who goes out and earns the income. That set off a real bell in my mind, because we certainly have enough background now to know that the household, any household, has priorities of its own, and that we, the outsiders, may regard pregnant and lactating women and infants under two as our top priorities, but the households themselves are extremely adept at channeling their resources in the directions that they perceive are best for them. So that just confirms that we need to understand more about what determines a household's own priorities, and how these can be most effectively linked to market forces. In other words, it's more productive to find ways to work with the households than against them. It's very difficult to avoid the household's own priorities; it's better to find ways of working with them. I see this as a very important future direction for economic research, that is, to examine who and what determines the household's uses of its own resources.

John Mellor: It is striking that out of perhaps eight or ten issues that I jotted down, five or six of them overlap, but not so obviously. So I have a shorter list of research issues to place before the group.

John Waterlow: I don't want to interrupt the discussion on the issues raised by the last two speakers. However, I would like to respond to Dr. Mellor's points about the poverty line and the role of nutritionists in trying to define a line separating what is acceptable and what is not from a nutrition and health standpoint. At the conclusion of my talk yesterday, I asked this question: Is this kind of enterprise in which many of us have been engaged for many years actually of any importance? And the very clear answer I got from you was, "Yes, it is important," and that's rather encouraging to me. Secondly, I think that it's not quite right to make such a distinction between Western and so-called Third World countries; it's a matter of degree.

As an example, in my country [Great Britain] for many years we've been studying preschool children to discover whether household unemployment and reductions in welfare benefits have any effect on health. Very small differences have been established, which are probably of no biological significance. Even if they are, they would be negligible in a Third World context. Nevertheless, governments have to pay some attention to them. It's all a matter of degree, and I think that we in nutrition do not attempt to draw a line. We can, within a reasonable consensus, provide a kind of sliding scale in very rough terms for children: mild, moderate, and severe malnutrition. We're beginning to be able to do so for adults as well. We do this with great difficulty because after all, the classical end point, death, is a very crude one.

What we're really concerned with is impairment of human faculties and of various aspects of the quality of life, which is, of course, much more difficult to judge. I gave you one small example yesterday of the relationship between body weights in adult men and the amount of time they had off work for illness. We are trying to collect that kind of data, but it's not easy. If this kind of division or scale is important, we desperately need more funds for research on these difficult questions, which verge not only on basic science, physiology, and nutrition, but also on sociological and anthropological characteristics, like impairment of work capacity. I think we're really seriously held up by the difficulty of making a large-scale attack on this particular problem.

Second, obviously policymakers and planners can choose a particular point on the sliding scale. We could at least give them enough information about functional impairments so they could say, "Below this is unacceptable." What is acceptable in India, for example, might be unacceptable in America or Britain. But the question for me is, should policies then be directed toward lifting up those people who are below whatever dividing line you choose, or should they be directed toward lifting up everybody so that, as it were, the bottom lot automatically disappears? This is very important for us in the nutritional field. To what extent should preventive policies be targeted to the worst cases? This is a question that is impossible for us to answer because here we need the economists and the planners to give some ideas about relative costs and cost benefits and all that.

I myself, with a background in medicine and coming from one of the Western democracies where we rely on a social welfare state, am inclined always to emphasize the policy of looking after the worst—those who are obviously in a bad state—and, if we don't have the funds, forget about the others. But that might be a personal moral judgment.

I'm trying very hard to think about whether this is a feasible policy. It involves using the various sectors in a rather different way. So I would very much hope that the discussion could focus a bit on this issue. The targeted policy that I incline to is, of course, a much more health-oriented policy that is rather out-of-date nowadays. I would like to urge that this general distinction is one that ought to be discussed, and I believe that we can provide some guidelines about different levels of nutritional poverty, if you'd like to call it that.

John Mellor: Thank you. If I could just underline two things. I think that I indicated that economists have a reason, because of this absolute poverty question, to think that being able to define such a line is important. Perhaps we should be a little clearer on that and, therefore, more careful in the allocation of research funds. On the other issue, we are very much concerned with what we call human capital and the relationship of investment in people's health and education and economic growth processes. However, economists feel very short of the technical coefficients that we look to nutritionists to provide.

Richard Sabot: I would agree with a theme that seems to be emerging from the comments regarding the need for research to track the interventions that take place and their consequences. The latest issue of the *Journal of Economic Literature* has a long piece by Elizabeth Sawhill reviewing the consequences of the war on poverty in the United States, which makes two points. The first is that poverty measured in absolute terms has not declined in the United States over twenty years, despite an expenditure in excess of $30 billion. As appalling as that may be to social scientists, perhaps even more appalling is the fact that we don't know why, that nothing was put into place for all of these programs to analyze which ones were most effective in cost-benefit terms. Now if this has happened in the United States, what is the prospect in low-income countries? And my plea would be—I think this is a theme that is implicit in all of the comments—that some effort be explicitly made, as programs are put into place, to track their effects from the start, to build in a research capability that tracks every act of intervention and its consequences.

Uma Lele: I want to make a few comments on what we know about poverty programs, following up on Dick Sabot's comments. I have found it interesting that so little is known in many parts of the world about what happens in programs to combat poverty, and their effects. As far as I know, there is a broad consensus regarding programs in India, namely, that the proportion of people below the poverty line has dropped in India, and that there is a very close connection between the amounts that go into production and the number of people below the poverty line.

There is much more information in Southeast Asia, for example, about the kinds of programs that are working and the problems of programs that are not working than is the case in the United States. That is because the problems of poverty are so much greater in Southeast Asia that we find there many types of analyses that track the performance of poverty programs. Poverty issues are taken much more seriously in some parts of the world than in other parts. When I organized not long ago a conference on capital flows to developing countries, I found among Latin American economists much less concern about tracking poverty than the concern existing in Southeast Asia. Among people writing papers in Latin America, or for that matter in Africa, there is much more concern about economic growth issues than about tracking whether programs to combat poverty are working successfully.

Before we talk about undertaking new research, I hope very much that the research that does exist has something to tell us about what is known and what is unknown about the performance of poverty programs and their effects.

Nevin Scrimshaw: I want to reinforce what John Waterlow has said, because I feel it is so important to discuss. If there was some unfair sniping at economists yesterday, the economists have retaliated this morning by suggesting that nutritionists have only recently discovered that there is no absolute cutoff in requirement levels. When we talk about an allowance of 0.85 grams per kilo per day of protein for an adult, all we're saying is that if healthy adults are getting that much, all but 2.5 percent of the population should be getting sufficient amounts to meet their needs. If we say they're getting 0.58, it means that statistically half of them are above the average intake required and half of them are below. This is greatly complicated by the fact that in developing countries, infections increase the requirement for protein—we don't know by how much. But that's the principle.

Now when it comes to energy, there is a range in the amount of energy for the amount of activity that people want to engage in, whether for recreation or for work, and if they can't afford enough food, their activity must be progressively restricted. They must stay in balance or they waste away and die. The socioeconomic consequences of this depend on the energy demands of the society. But you get to a point where adaptation by reduction of physical activity is no longer possible. That is the point at which people can survive in a very sedentary manner, but they can perform no occupational activity and they cannot maintain cardiovascular fitness. They will continue to deteriorate physically. Now, is that the limit that you want to take as a cutoff point? When it comes to iron, the World Health Organization cutoff point for anemia for an adult male is 12.5 percent of hemoglobin in the blood. We know anemia is a highly undesirable occurrence. But anemia is a relatively late development of iron deficiency. That's the issue. We need more research to understand the significance of these different levels, but we're under no illusion that there are absolute cutoffs in requirement levels that separate health and ill health.

John Mellor: Thank you very much. I'd like to open up for discussion the sustainability issue, since it was raised by both Beatrice Rogers and Anne de Lattre. Is there anyone else who would like to weigh in on the issues that have been discussed before we turn to another set of issues?

Eileen Kennedy: This relates to comments that Anne de Lattre and John Waterlow had made. Sometimes people interpret ending hunger as ending malnutrition, but the two can mean very different things. I think the reason the health sector as an exclusive approach to ending hunger and malnutrition went out of vogue is because it didn't seem to work by itself. There's now some evidence that other approaches to improving nutritional status also don't work by themselves, as exclusive approaches, at least in the short run. Short of the large-scale world development initiatives, how do health and nutrition join forces with income-generating, technological changes to have a major impact?

Ronald Duncan: I would like to see IFPRI do more work than it does currently on how consumption patterns change as incomes change. We're trying to look at how consumption and production change over time and how consumption changes with levels of income. It's not always up; it can be down. In Africa we're seeing consumption patterns change though incomes are falling and, therefore, that affects which foods people are able to produce.

John Mellor: IFPRI has done a lot of work examining changes in consumption patterns. For the record, I think there are two things that trouble me about where we are now. First, we don't make an adequate connection with the macro side. I keep arguing that we need the marginal propensities in order to get to the macro; we need to do more there so the world is caught less by surprise by some of these macro effects. My favorite example is Taiwan suddenly going from an exporter of cereals in a very short period of time to importing 60 percent of all the cereals consumed. Taiwan correctly has been identified as a great success story in agricultural growth. We were caught by surprise when its livestock base just took off, and so, too, the increased demand for cereals.

The other area where we don't do very well is the one that a number of you have been commenting on. That's going back from these consumption numbers to the effect on what we're ultimately concerned with, namely health and nutritional status. One thing's clear: as people's incomes rise, they do choose to increase the variety in their diet very rapidly. Is that irrational? What is the effect of that on their nutritional status? Did we acquire that taste for variety completely aside from its effect on our nutritional and health status? As economists we don't have very good guidelines in this area. We still notice that people increase their calories more rapidly than we think they should. But they're doing that by getting variety, and we aren't tracing that well enough.

J. E. Dutra de Oliveira: I'd like to make some general comments on what has been said and on the question of how to use research in this area. One thing we have to do is put together what the economists think with what is known in the field of human nutrition. At least in Brazil, there is much talk about poverty and income distribution, and it's very good for politicians, scientists, political scientists to talk about it, but that doesn't necessarily lead to doing something about it.

What I want to emphasize is the research gap that exists on how to make the food chain work, how to get experts in different areas of knowledge to work together, how to apply what we know—and we know a lot. We don't need more data on the economic situation of the population of this or that country. For the sake of food security, we have to try to apply what we know.

Let me raise one other issue, that of communication between governments and international organizations. For me the questions are: how the international organizations could do better at making food available, and how countries can do more to make food available. If some countries like Thailand, Cuba, and Chile have been able to improve their food and nutrition situations, what can other countries do along these lines? After all, we have the examples of countries with different political structures that are improving their situations. Research has to be done on the failure to make better use of existing resources. We really don't need to go back to acquire more and more data in areas in which we now have information.

Peter Temu: I think what has been emerging since we focused on this subject of the food chain is that there is a need to study every point of the chain in relation to a particular food situation, a particular country, or a particular group that one is interested in. One of the points raised yesterday—the application of on-shelf technology to the situation in Ghana, for example—is one thing that would be worth looking at.

I think in a number of countries there are lots of technologies that could be applied but have not been applied. I think there is a need, for research purposes, to zero in on specific countries and see exactly what are the main problems that need to be addressed along the food chain. In some cases it may be production, while elsewhere it may be the reduction of food losses, or else nutritional education. The various disciplines will come together in studying various aspects of the food chain. Economists probably are the best on the production end, but when we get toward the point of consumption and then begin to look more at the medical, the biological, and the nutritional aspects, that is where medical science can make a greater contribution. And then the economists will try to size up the various costs of the entire package, so that shows a very convenient meeting point. And then it seems to me that there is a need for a kind of conceptual consensus in trying to figure out the research priorities—first, the main elements of the problem, and then ultimately agreeing on an approach that is targeted to a specific situation.

Norman Borlaug: First of all, I would like to point out that I think most of us around this table are strongly biased in favor of research. What's the purpose of the research? It's to produce new technology that has the potential to produce more food. The question of equity we'll leave to one side for the moment because I have some pretty strong feelings about this also. Inequities and inequalities didn't start recently—they existed back in the hunting age, when the strong tribes controlled the best grassland and consequently harvested the big antelopes and the big carnivores, and the weak tribes were pushed into more marginal ecosystems where they had to work more hours each day hunting small animals and picking less favorable plants to supplement their diet.

Going back to research and production: you can do research from now till kingdom come and not necessarily produce any more food. Each of us is biased in favor of our own discipline, and we forget that it's only one little part of all of these pieces that have to be put together in order to promote change. And I say that from forty-four years of experience in working with governments around the world. Any place where I have been able to contribute something of significance, it has involved taking bits and pieces of research that are available and putting the pieces together. It's like trying to be an architect: to take the pieces of brick, too many of which are of one kind when you are missing some of the key pieces, yet you have to build some kind of a structure right now with what's available. Then, later on, you worry about including those other kinds of bricks that would make for a better house. But we have chaos in the brickyard because of the separation of disciplines, and I say this as a researcher.

My first thirty-five years of work were spent developing the pieces of the wheat production jigsaw puzzle. But I saw in the first six or eight years that the program in Mexico was going noplace until someone assumed the responsibility of convincing the government officials, the people who had the authority, after we had demonstrated the potential to increase yields fourfold or fivefold. At that time it was less complicated than I found it to be many years later. We didn't have back then all of these planning committees or the many people who sit there in judgment and advise the political leaders, who are themselves very far removed from the realities of the world such as the small farmer who is producing the food.

The biggest problem is how to develop integrators, those rare individuals who can see the big picture and put together as best as possible those pieces that are available now—and where there seem to be some bricks that just don't fit, get the research moving in that direction to figure out a solution. We're all so proud of our own discipline that we stand behind it and say the rest of the disciplines are of secondary importance. Until we shed all of this silliness, we're going to continue to have problems. At meetings like this one, all too often, and in many of the organizations, there is a lack of representation of the developing nations themselves that could bring into harmony these different points of view. We tend to say, "Do it like we've done in the developed nations of today." I think that's very wrong, and it undermines our training of scientists. Until we build better educational institutions in the developing nations, so that more of their scientists are trained in the environment in which they are going to be working, it will always be one step forward and two backward, or one and one, and not the kind of progress that we should have. But a lot of learned papers and a lot of talk are poor substitutes for action programs that bring all of this knowledge together to produce more food and to equitably distribute the benefits that should be generated by researchers.

John Mellor: I'd like to just make a small response to that. At IFPRI, we're increasingly trying to pull out topics in the frameworks in which the policymakers would deal with them. Here we are, building an arch, and then we have to say, "Let us assume this keystone because we don't happen to have it at the moment." We are trying to fill in the chinks; in the meantime, we assume a keystone and hope it's a sensible assumption, but I agree with you entirely that one has to move ahead, one has to bring in the different disciplines.

I'm going to end with a note about sustainability so that we will then be on that topic. I do think we need to move around a little, and the sustainability issue did come up and clearly does interact with the poverty issue. I'm increasingly struck by the fact that in developed countries environmental degradation largely is a consequence of wealth and industrial development, while in developing countries environmental decline basically is a function of poverty, the movement of increasing numbers of rural people onto marginal and fragile lands for the sake of survival. Development and environmental issues have different causes and characteristics.

Gelia Castillo: One of the most profound statements I have heard was made by a very distinguished Singaporean who said that the trouble with you researchers is you tend to substitute research for wisdom.

John Mellor: Economists are the most reasonable of all researchers.

Gelia Castillo: One of the most intriguing pieces of research that has come out of IFPRI concerns changing consumption patterns in West

Africa. If people there prefer to eat rice and wheat, what are we going to do? We support the efforts to improve the processing of millet and sorghum, because it has been said that it is the desire for greater convenience that is causing the shift from millet and sorghum to rice and wheat. So you have a technological issue, but I think a lot of it is also going to be socioeconomic. So if, in fact, people want to eat rice and wheat, and this is a growing trend, should these countries begin to grow rice and wheat? It's obvious that these are not necessarily the best places to grow rice and wheat. It seems to me these are terribly big issues, and I think IFPRI can work well with the other institutes on these issues. Here you have the issue of sustainability.

The second issue of sustainability is whether we have enough evidence to show that when people have security over land, through land reform, that this leads to better land utilization and greater conservation measures. In some instances when you give the person land, that in itself becomes his security, and sometimes he doesn't even have to cultivate it.

The third issue I have that relates also to sustainability is that every time we look at the factors of production—credit, fertilizers, insecticides, and what have you—the matter of the brainpower of farmers, their ability to manage new technologies, is never mentioned as a factor of production. The technology is simpler, but it requires a great deal to take place in the farmers' minds before they can adopt it. So as we move to the issues of sustainability, there's a great deal more that is required of whoever is managing the resources and technologies in terms of management capability. We have not really made great strides along these lines. I have been pushing this so far, but I hope that somebody else can pick it up; it is very much a research issue. We now have on-the-job projects in integrated pest management in the Philippines that are so fascinating because the concept is completely different from the calendar spraying that farmers have been taught. Now farmers are being told to distinguish between good insects and bad insects and not to spray until they see so many insects. People get so fascinated by it. The first time we held a meeting there were only a very few farmers; the last time I attended a meeting, the room was filled with people, and even the kids were learning about good insects and bad insects. It requires a great deal of decision-making on the part of farmers at every stage, and I don't think we can go on using these insecticides and pesticides.

John Mellor: Thank you, Gelia. Let me make two brief comments. I'm continually tempted to say that IFPRI is doing this research and that research in response to these issues. I think we do provide a lot of leadership in attacking certain types of issues, and one thing we constantly discover, especially as we build on micro data, is that there isn't a yes-or-no answer. It depends on the circumstances. Regarding land tenure and sustainability, I'm probably extrapolating too much as usual. But I think we can show from some of the work that Chris Delgado and my other colleagues are doing that under certain circumstances, a particular land tenure system will result in a more sustainable agriculture, and in very different circumstances it may not. An institute like IFPRI can illustrate some very important areas of research, but then that has to be picked up by large numbers of people who will replicate that kind of research under varying circumstances and give advice according to those circumstances.

The important thing is to expand human capital by the countries themselves, along with the large farm assistance programs. We do a lot of collaborative research; after all, who is supporting the training and the Ph.D. degrees of the people with whom we work in many countries?

I think Dick Sabot is involved with some very out-front research on the education issue in rural areas. One point that's being missed is that the returns to human capital are increasing in so many rural areas because of the increasing complexity of problems that our people are dealing with. You know, nutrition education starts out very simple—that you just need to get more cassava to get your calorie intake up—but it quickly becomes very complex, and you probably need some underlying education.

Alan Berg: What I have to say may be anathema to a policy research institution, but I think it's fundamental to sustainability. The policies and programs that are undertaken actually work, and I contend that our policy understanding of what to do is in most places far ahead of our understanding of how to do it. There are many good policies in place. There are many good programs in place. Billions of dollars have been spent. But implementation is often appalling. You mention nutrition education. Our efforts in behavioral change are meager at best. Our efforts in food stamps, ration shops, and other forms of consumer food subsidies are far less than adequate. Our efforts at human growth monitoring and school feeding and at aspects of rural extension are seriously lacking. Nutrition training for maternal and child health development is lacking. There are exceptions, of course, and we have to learn the reasons for them. I urge that those institutions with research responsibilities think not only of policy research but also of implementation.

John Mellor: I think very strongly that if there is any distinction, it is that implementation involves issues that are much more micro. Yes, we know we need this kind of work: we go out and the implementation doesn't work, partly because we weren't answering some other questions, including the kinds of people and training programs that have to be involved. I would look at that as a criticism of the kinds of research that are being done on the policy process.

Beatrice Lorge Rogers: In response to Alan Berg, I guess I was a little surprised, since you've ringingly defended the fact that we do have successful programs. There's no question that many of our attempts at implementation are appalling, but I think the last bit of discussion has focused an awful lot on not knowing enough about these issues. And there's the risk of sounding too optimistic. In this case I think it's a mistake always to focus on things that didn't work instead of trying to look at the factors that determine what did work. Nutrition education has obviously failed. I can think of two or three specific studies that found that the nutritional practices of mothers were far more dependent on their general education level than on their access to nutritional education. It didn't seem to be those specific maternal and child health nutrition education programs that helped them so much as a general third- or fourth-grade educational level. I'm familiar enough with the U.S. program to know that saying it didn't work and pointing to 1988 statistics on poverty is like putting someone on penicillin for an infection for a day and a half and then saying, "See, penicillin doesn't wipe out infection," and then taking the person off. In fact, there were a number of programs that had documented success and had the rug pulled out from under them, and certainly early child education was one of them.

I think the questions that have been addressed in IFPRI's research about cash cropping versus food or subsistence cropping indicate that the question really is not, "Is it for cash or is it for food," but rather, "Who has access to the benefits from that land? Who controls the land?" There have been success stories when the benefits of the cash cropping went to the owners of the land, the small farmers. What I'm saying is that I would like us to think a little about the fact that we're making progress through agricultural research and policy research. That's not to say there aren't a million questions that still need to be answered. I think we're pointing to some of them, but I find myself reacting almost emotionally to the implication that we're back at the same square where we started.

John Mellor: Just a minor factual point: Studies at IFPRI do show that there are circumstances in which nutrition education has had a positive impact. I think that it's very important that we track down what are the specific circumstances, what are the interactions that make it successful. And we're probably making some progress there.

Richard Harwood: I think it's helpful when talking about sustainability of agriculture to look at sustainability as the evolutionary process that agriculture goes through. One of the key concerns is that the direction should remain relatively constant. If you assume that capital is a major limiting factor in Third World countries, you have to make sure that the capital investments have a long-term, single direction focus. You can't afford to go back and build irrigation systems where you're going to be salting out in ten years. Along with that, you have to really look at the national structure, the macrostructure, the geographical location of the industries. Let me give an example that ties back into poverty and employment. We haven't talked about employment much—we've talked about family incomes—but employment may be something else.

If we look at alternative technology as a production matter in the Bicol region of the Philippines, in Luzon, we face the question: what kinds of technologies are we going to go with? And we have a choice of putting more investment into rice, perhaps into maize, or into peanuts and groundnuts. Groundnuts will return something like twenty pesos a kilo to the farmer. But if those groundnuts are converted into peanut butter or peanut products, you're talking about a fourfold to fivefold net return, and the employment goes up, of the people who are producing the products. You're creating several new jobs now as compared to just increasing maize production to export it to a Manila feed mill. So we have those technology choices. But we're not given the guidelines; we're not given the targets. We don't know our targets for employment. In India this last year I was struck by the projections on the number of people coming into the job market over the next thirty or forty years that agriculture is going to have to absorb—something like 200 to 300 million, a 40 to 60 percent increase in employment, which will be agriculture's burden, considering industrial growth and growth in the service sectors. How is that translated into growth targets for employment that the production people can relate to in making these decisions on technology?

So I guess that macrostructure is certainly important in the Philippines, whether peanut butter is made in the village or in the Manila factory. And that will have a significant impact on who benefits from the peanut butter manufacture—whether it be the poor villagers, for whom this creates jobs in a net cash flow deficit area; or whether the beneficiaries will be urban dwellers in Manila who will benefit from the additional higher-paying factory jobs. Those are very critical decisions that are out of the hands of the production people but should certainly guide our choice of technologies when we go to the farmers. And we are not even measuring how much additional employment that peanut butter has created. We know that we doubled the income of that farmer family just growing a tenth of a hectare of peanuts, but we don't know what additional income was generated by the processing of peanuts. So we have here the macroeconomic structure as it relates to sustainability, to income and employment, and to the distribution of wealth.

A final point is the pesticide problem. We're not providing people with the tools to assess the environmental and personal risks accompanying new technologies. We could tell all sorts of horror stories. The pesticides are applied by hand in all of the Third World, and there are some pesticides like methylperithione that are quite cheap, the most commonly used with a toxicity factor of four milligrams per kilo. It's physically impossible to apply that pesticide material by hand and stay within the bounds of an exposure level that we would consider reasonable. Should we be providing information and guidelines on these technologies to allow the users to assess the risk? I don't want to say we shouldn't use methylperithione out there—that's for the recipient countries to decide. But we're not providing the tools with which they can make an informed decision.

Unfortunately, what will happen is that the decisions on the use or non-use of these materials will be made emotionally and not based on data, the way for the most part they are in the United States. So we're not providing important pieces of information. As we look at our evolving agriculture, there are big gaps in the sustainability area.

Norman Borlaug: I would like to second what a friend has just said about a spillover effect in the Third World resulting from our emotional reactions to pesticides and other environmental issues—reactions in many instances not based on facts. Now, in a broader context let me raise an issue regarding the sustainability of the use of fertilizer in Africa. The fertilizers are imported from beyond their frontiers, from nations such as the United States that are the biggest consumers of energy. Now what kind of inconsistency is this? I think we'd better examine our own house and how we distort all of these issues for the developing nations. First, let me point out that I'm an advocate of using all the organic waste we can, and there's no better example of this than China. And yet, look what China has done because it realized the necessity of using chemical fertilizer. In the last fifteen years it has developed a fertilizer industry to produce a large portion of it domestically. That's made China one of the largest consumers of chemical fertilizers to supplement their many years of experience with organic fertilizer. We always say, "Oh, we can do it organically," but this is a lot of nonsense. We've got to have both organic and chemical fertilizer, and we'd better use some of this wisdom that Dr. Castillo just talked about. Research is a poor substitute for that wisdom.

Robert Chandler: I feel very strongly that in countries such as many African countries, where the per capita food production and per capita income have been going down, and the economies are largely agrarian, we ought to go back to our experience in other areas and continents. If you can develop through experimental work, in research projects, in agricultural stations, that something has worked and go out and do a lot of demonstrations on how things can work, and bring these efforts to the farmers, they will adopt new changes. We did this in the Philippines, we've done it in India, getting the whole community of rural people working at it. It is not a question of certain people being wise and others not. Some people will grasp new technologies faster than others. All these other studies are great, and we can talk and talk, and nothing will happen unless we get out to the farmers and apply what we know on the farms. Then we can get some change in the rural environment. Some of the technologies will succeed. Some may be wrong. But we won't know until we try.

Curtis Farrar: It seems to me that this discussion typifies the state of thinking about development at the present time: we are perceiving complexity and perceiving location specificity as being important and issues that we must be concerned about. In conversation today, there's been one subject mentioned, and then another, and then another on top of that. It seems to me that when one is concerned with policy and its implementation, it's necessary to think about how to handle complexity in situations where the human resources and the financial resources are limited. I recognize that this is a very general point but it is critical. There's a danger in simplification, and there's also a danger in getting too complicated. If fertilizer subsidies are not good for Bangladesh, they're not likely to be good for any country in Africa. If you implement them, you do a lot of damage, to caricature the point that was made earlier.

John Mellor: Can I just comment on that? Gelia Castillo said something to the effect a few minutes ago of "What are you doing about it?" IFPRI has an extremely good study on fertilizer subsidy in Bangladesh, which should be extremely helpful to someone in Malawi or Senegal. They ought to look at it and ask, "Are there any ideas in this with any relevance to us?" Then they've got to have the people who do the analysis applying it to their circumstances, and then see where they should go from that point. The Bangladesh study can be used as a comparative analysis to see whether any lights flash when you look at it. As long as governments and the donor community are putting such grossly inadequate resources into building human capital at all levels, and building institutional capabilities, we're going to end up coming to Malawi with the Bangladesh study and saying, "This is what you should do," rather than, "Is there anything in this study that is relevant to you although it derives from an entirely different experience?" I think we have some real problems there. IFPRI's hands are tied somewhat on this because of the lack of massive investment and a misallocation of resources in the past.

A. S. Clausi: I'm really not the expert that each of you is in this field, but something that was just said struck me as the core of an important issue. I don't think it's sufficient to have a study that says, "This is what we know about fertilizers; now you take it and decide what you're going to do with it." I think that's what I call the separate discipline approach. Really, we're talking about the need for a multidisciplinary approach. It seems to me there's an obligation on the part of the researcher, in this case, IFPRI, to get those who are knowledgeable about Africa or a specific country in Africa, if that's the target, and say, "Let's get together and on the basis of what you know about your country—the issues having to do with what's doable, what's not doable, what's usable, what's not usable—and let's have a dialogue as to what we know about what the experience has been and let it serve as a bridge, if you will." The responsibility of any researcher is the utilization of the research. You cannot stop with the conclusion of the research. You stop when that research is used, and if that means carrying it on to another step, then I think it becomes the responsibility of the researcher to find what else is needed to implement that research. That is the value of research; otherwise it's just a study.

The other thing that I sense very often in the discussion this morning is a blending of what I call applications and the search for new knowledge. Both involve research. I think that the Norman Borlaug, the Robert Chandler approaches involve taking what is known, and fitting, cutting, and applying it in a specific location to the extent of the current knowledge, and staying with it until it is applied. The other approach is to identify the gaps, what we don't know, and then dedicating long-term research to answering those questions. Questions have been raised about what we don't know about nutritional needs. There's nothing you can do with that tomorrow, but there may be something ten years from now.

John Mellor: At IFPRI we do wrestle with that a lot because we are trying to drive through to policy change. The big problem, of course, is that in order to make a policy decision, you need many pieces from many different disciplines. At any given point in time, we have a few of those pieces in very good shape, and we could make some pretty clear factual statements about them, and then some other equally critical pieces are not in very good shape. If we're going to make a judgment now, we have to extrapolate on the basis of those pieces, and that means getting into some very uncertain areas. I think at IFPRI we've been willing to do that extrapolation, but of course people then wonder how much of it is biased by differences in values and opinions. I don't think that extrapolation should be done alone but rather with a partner or partners who have a stake in the outcome.

John Waterlow: I'd just like to respond to an earlier point, because I feel very guilty when you say research is not finished till it's implemented. I mentioned that thirty years ago I found that oral rehydration was far better for diarrhea than any other treatment. But I never publicized it or thought to announce it to the press. I think you have to recognize that people who do research are a different kind of people. As researchers we're all different from the people who promote knowledge and who seek to apply knowledge. I don't think we can be expected to do everything; perhaps what is needed is better machinery for bringing together the people with these different purposes. After all, we only have a limited amount of time. Some people are superb in both ways, and, obviously, Dr. Chandler is one. But you can't find Chandlers everywhere, even in the research field. I think your criticism is a little harsh. Another solution to this problem is to try to get a better meeting of minds of different kinds of people.

John Mellor: I'm going to make a short summarizing statement of my own and then ask Bob Chandler to make some closing remarks. I think it's very important in this context that someone who can do both—the research and apply it as policy—should pull together whatever he can out of this. We've been talking about the food chain. I suppose that if you were to pull a simple point out of Nevin Scrimshaw's presentation yesterday, it would be that the food chain is very complex and has many parts to it, so it's not at all surprising that it's not quite clear what the complete answer to the food chain problems are. I'm sure that we will each carry away something different. I feel quite happy with this discussion personally; I have some notes here that allow me to carry away some thoughts that will be very useful to my work. I want to express my gratitude to all of you for taking the time to do this, but hopefully your compensation was that you also got some useful ideas, which I suspect are quite different from mine, and that this has been a useful interchange for all of us. I hope that this or a very similar group will be together again next year or on some other occasion, and I want to thank you very much for your participation here at IFPRI.

Robert Chandler: I have very strong convictions in certain areas. I know how complex the total development process is—rural and economic development—in a country. We should do all the research we can to get all of the know-how as far as theory and background and future ramifications are concerned. But at the same time, I do know this—that the food chain begins on the land and that the productivity of the land varies a great deal according to how you manage it, and we've got to start with that. I feel strongly that we've got to somehow help these less developed countries that are really poor and that have been spending all their money servicing their loans rather than bringing in new inputs for food production and other things they need such as developing their schools. We should help them in supporting their experiment stations and their applied agricultural research, and to strengthen their extension systems to give them some mobility and understanding of the training involved in increasing productivity on the land. And most of all, we have to influence the farmer. We do have a crisis on our hands with populations increasing tremendously—Africa is the place we look at mostly today because it's in such a serious condition. We have to continue the work of experimental research in the environments where it's going to be used to find out what really works, what is economically profitable, and what really increases crop yields. We have to get a lot of demonstration projects out where farmers can see them, where they talk about them with researchers and where the extension people are involved.

Now, just one last thing on nutrition. When you travel in China, you notice how healthy the people, the children, look. You don't have to run a nutrition center to find that out; you just look at the people. You go to the Philippines or many places of Africa, and you see all kinds of malnutrition. There is something to learn from the Chinese diet, and they have high production, too. I think we have lessons to learn from success stories.

John Mellor: I'll ask Norman Borlaug for the last word.

Norman Borlaug: I think the lesson in Ghana is worth considering. About four and a half years ago, when the food crisis was at its worst in the Sudan and Ethiopia, I got a call from a Japanese philanthropist who doesn't speak English. Through his public relations man he said, "Why isn't something being done in Africa?" I told him, "I don't know anything about Africa." I thought that was the end of it. The next morning he was back on the phone, and he said, "Then you'd better find out something about Africa because I'm going to put up some money, but only if you can organize a good workshop and see what the state of knowledge is, and what might be done." So we had a workshop in Geneva in July 1985. We brought together a small number of people—anthropologists, religious leaders, and other informed people—and this philanthropist came to me in the morning when we were leaving and said, "We'll put up the money for two programs."

I didn't want to get involved in this at my age, but here we are. So we started this program in Ghana. At that time nothing much in terms of significant change was happening on the farms. Several of the international institutes had generated a lot of information that was lying around unused in the experimental stations. When we got involved, we looked at available data, although there were a lot of gaps in knowledge. We had help from scientists in Mexico, in South Korea, and in Senegal. We picked the two crops that are important in Ghana—sorghum and maize. In the first year all we got out was 40 pecks in each of the crops.

One point that I think is important is that researchers do not understand the psychology of change. These were one-acre plots just like the ones used in demonstrations in India and Pakistan. The small farmer knows how many sacks of a product he gets. He may not know, however, how many grams there are, or be familiar with technical terms. The farmer may at first be suspicious about whether you're telling him fact or fiction. But if he knows how many sacks of corn or sorghum he gets off that one acre, it's a different ball game. There was no credit for farmers given by any bank when we started. We bought the fertilizer and seeds from the core program budget and loaned them to the farmer, working this out with the extension program staff, as to what was the best package. We supervised the farmer training; we had bicycles, a couple of motorcycles, and one pickup for our mobility, and that's how it started.

In the first year, the payback was in line with the inputs of fertilizer and seed—100 percent in the first year. In the second year the payback was 98 percent—the only exceptions being a few plots that were drowned out in the low places. In the season just finished we had 16,000 one-acre plots scattered around the country. The results in virtually all cases were three to four times the traditional crop yields; and the enthusiasm on the farms is equivalent to what I saw in Pakistan and India when we introduced the wheat technology there in the mid-1960s.

There are now perhaps 200,000 to 300,000 small farmers in Ghana who know what can be done. They've seen it on their neighbors' farms, or on their own, and they're starting to ask questions. Why don't we have fertilizer? Why don't we have credit? Why don't we have some assurance of reasonable prices at harvest? We've kept a low profile on policy up until now. We had to for political reasons. Timing is important. Let the technology speak for you and then your policy decisions can more easily be applied. That doesn't mean we shouldn't try to have policy decisions adopted at the same time as the technical experiments and demonstrations, but until we have more informed people in the planning commission and in the political offices, we have to keep a low profile. Some officials don't have realistic judgments on what's happening on the land, since there's a reluctance to even visit and look at the farms and the experimental plots.

Now that the grassroots are on fire in Ghana and the farmers are worked up over the new yields, the new potential, just as they were in Pakistan and India, I can say to the head of the planning commission, the prime minister, or the president: "Unless you change your policy, the grassroots are going to erupt." Of course, there are all kinds of problems that exist in this effort. We haven't yet got the policy adopted at the top that we think is needed. But Ghana's leaders now know that the fires are pretty hot under their feet, and I think that the policy changes to support the farmers will be made.

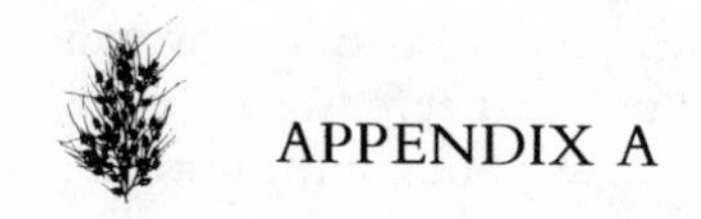

APPENDIX A

Colloquium Program

Tuesday, October 4, 1988
Lecture Hall, S. Dillon Ripley Center, 1100 Jefferson Drive, SW

9:00 AM Opening Remarks

David Challinor, Science Advisor to the Secretary, Smithsonian Institution

A. S. Clausi, Senior Vice President, Retired, General Foods, and Chairman, Council of Advisors, General Foods World Food Prize

Introduction of Speaker

9:15 AM Keynote Remarks: "Completing the Food Chain: From Production to Consumption"

Nevin S. Scrimshaw, Institute Professor Emeritus, Massachusetts Institute of Technology, and Director, Food and Nutrition Programme, United Nations University, Tokyo, Japan

10:15 AM Break

10:30 AM Morning Panel: "Regional Perspectives"

Uma Lele, Chief, Special Studies Division, Country Economics Department, The World Bank, Washington, D.C. [South Asia]

Aree Valyasevi, Resident Coordinator and Founding Director, United Nations University Institute of Nutrition, Mahidol University, Salaya, Thailand [Southeast Asia]

Mohamed A. Nour, Assistant Administrator, United Nations Development Programme, and former Director-General, International Centre for Agricultural Research in the Dry Areas, Aleppo, Syria [The Middle East]

Thomas R. Odhiambo, Director, International Centre of Insect Physiology and Ecology, Nairobi, Kenya [Africa]

J. E. Dutra de Oliveira, Professor of Clinical Nutrition and Internal Medicine, Faculdade de Medicina de Ribeirão Preto, Brazil [Latin America]

Moderator: Anne de Lattre, Special Advisor, Club du Sahel Secretariat, Organisation for Economic Cooperation and Development, Paris, France [Sahel, Africa]

Discussion

12:30 PM Luncheon
Associates Court, National Museum of Natural History

2:00 PM Afternoon Panel: "Disciplinary Perspectives"

John C. Waterlow, Professor Emeritus of Human Nutrition, University of London, Great Britain [Nutrition]

Pablo A. Scolnik, Research Supervisor, Plant Science Section, E. I. du Pont de Nemours & Co., Wilmington, Delaware [Biotechnology]

Ricardo Bressani, Research Coordinator in Food Science and Agriculture, Instituto de Nutrición de Centro América y Panama, Guatemala City, Guatemala [Food Technology]

Richard R. Harwood, Regional Director, Asia, Winrock International, Morrilton, Arkansas [Agroecology]

Sidney W. Mintz, William L. Straus, Jr., Professor of Anthropology, The Johns Hopkins University, Baltimore, Maryland [Anthropology]

Moderator: Beatrice Lorge Rogers, Associate Professor of Food Policy, Tufts University, Medford, Massachusetts [Economics]

Discussion

4:00 PM Break

4:15 PM Summation

Gelia T. Castillo, University Professor, University of the Philippines at Los Baños, The Philippines

Concluding Comments

Robert F. Chandler, Jr., 1988 World Food Prize Laureate

5:00 PM Adjournment

6:30 PM General Foods World Food Prize Award Ceremony
Baird Auditorium, National Museum of Natural History

7:30 PM Reception

APPENDIX B

Biographical Notes on Contributors

Ricardo Bressani

Ricardo Bressani, research coordinator in food science and agriculture, Instituto de Nutrición de Centro América y Panama (INCAP). Educated at the University of Dayton (B.S., 1948), Iowa State University (M.S., 1951), and Purdue University (Ph.D., 1956). Taught food science and nutrition at the Universidad de San Carlos de Guatemala and at INCAP. Served as general editor of the Archivos Latino Americanos de Nutrición, of the Amaranth Newsletter of the National Research Council in the United States, and on the editorial board of the *Journal of Agricultural and Food Chemistry* and the *Journal of Plant Foods for Human Nutrition*. Member of the Task Force of the Post-Harvest Technology Program, United Nations University; the Latin American Nutrition Society; Latin American Society of Animal Production; American Institute of Nutrition; Institute of Food Technologists of the American Chemical Society; National Academy of Sciences; and a founding member of the Third World Academy of Sciences. Recipient of numerous awards, including the Institute of Food Technologists' Babcock Hart Award, American Society for Clinical Nutrition's McCollum Award, the Rodolfo Robles Prize of the Guatemalan Government, and a Guatemalan Ministry of Education award for contributions to school feeding programs. Awarded an honorary degree at Purdue University. Author or coauthor of more than 450 articles and monographs in the fields of human nutrition, animal nutrition, food science and technology. Born in Guatemala City, 1926. Address: Instituto de Nutrición de Centro América y Panama, Carretera Roosevelt zona 11, P.O. Box 1188, 01011 Guatemala City, Guatemala.

Gelia T. Castillo

Gelia T. Castillo, university professor, Department of Agricultural Education and Rural Studies, University of the Philippines at Los Baños. Educated at the University of the Philippines, Pennsylvania State University, and Cornell University (Ph.D., 1960). Taught psychology and rural sociology in the College of Agriculture, University of the Philippines, and at Cornell. Current research includes the study "Understanding the Household and Quality of Life." Author of *How Participatory Is Participatory Development? A Review of the Philippine Experience* (1983, reprinted 1988); *Beyond Manila: Philippine Rural Problems in Perspective* (1979); and *All in a Grain of Rice: A Review of Philippine Studies on the Social and Economic Implications of the New Rice Technology* (1975); as well as more than 75 journal articles. Commissioner, Philippine National Commission on Women. Member, National Research Council of the Philippines; Impact Evaluation Team, WHO Special Programme on Tropical Disease Research; Cabinet Steering Committee on the Philippine Development Plan. Trustee of the Philippine Institute for Development Studies and the Philippine Rice Research Institute. Visiting scientist and member, Task Force on Women in Rice Farming Systems, International Rice Research Institute. Former research fellow at Ford and Rockefeller foundations and at Canada's International Development Research Center. Former president, Philippine Sociological Society. Born in Pagsanjan, Laguna, Philippines, 1928. Address: Department of Agricultural Education and Rural Studies, University of the Philippines at Los Baños, College, Laguna 4031, Philippines.

Robert F. Chandler, Jr.

Robert F. Chandler, Jr., scientist, educator, and administrator; founding director, International Rice Research Institute, the Philippines. Educated at the University of Maine and the University of Maryland (Ph.D., 1934). Held several posts at the Rockefeller Foundation: as associate director for agricultural sciences; assistant director, natural science and agriculture; soil scientist with the Mexican Agricultural Program. Directed the Asian Vegetable Research and Development Center in Taiwan. Served as dean of the College of Agriculture and as president of the

University of New Hampshire. Professor of forest soils at Cornell University; state horticulturist at the Maine State Department of Agriculture. Author of *An Adventure in Applied Research: A History of the International Rice Research Institute* (1982), *Rice in the Tropics: A Guide to Development of National Programs* (1979), and *Forest Soils,* with Harold J. Lutz (1946), along with some 60 articles in professional and trade journals. Recipient, General Foods World Food Prize (1988), United States Presidential End Hunger Award (1986), Special Award of the Republic of China (1975), International Agronomy Award (1972), Golden Heart of the Republic of the Philippines (1972), Star of Merit of the Republic of Indonesia (1972), Star of Distinction Award of the Government of Pakistan (1968), and Gold Medal of the Government of India (1966). Awarded eight honorary degrees from universities throughout the world. Born in Columbus, 1907. Address: 421 East Minnehaha Avenue, Clermont, FL 32711.

Anne de Lattre

Anne de Lattre, special advisor and former director, Club du Sahel Secretariat, Organisation for Economic Cooperation and Development (OECD). Educated at the Université de Paris, Columbia University, and the School of Advanced International Studies at the Johns Hopkins University. Responsible for coordination of research and development projects with the Comité Inter-États pour la Lutte contre la Sécheresse au Sahel, the nations of which include Burkina Faso, Cape Verde, Chad, Gambia, Mali, Mauritania, Niger, Senegal, and Guinea Bissau. Joint projects have covered irrigated agriculture, rainfed agriculture, rural hydraulics, ecology and reforestation, and food security. Has served in a variety of positions at OECD, including as chief, Economic Development Division; as an economist in the Latin American Department at the International Monetary Fund; as economics editor of the journal *Perspectives;* as a parliamentary attaché in the Department of National Defense in Paris; and as a journalist in Iran. Has been visiting professor at Davidson College in North Carolina. Authored two Ford Foundation reports on aid prospects in Africa and on innovations in education in West Africa. Published numerous articles on development assistance in *Perspectives* and *An Experiment in International Cooperation: The Club du Sahel* (1985). Has lectured in many countries of the world. Serves on the boards of the International Food Policy Research Institute and the American Institute for International Education. Born in Paris, 1927. Address: Club du Sahel, Organisation de Coopération et de Développement Économiques, 2 rue André-Pascal, Paris 75775, Cedex 16, France.

J. E. Dutra de Oliveira

J. E. Dutra de Oliveira, professor of clinical nutrition and internal medicine, Faculdade de Medicina de Ribeirão Preto, Brazil. Educated at the Medical School of the University of São Paulo (M.D., 1951) with postdoctoral training at Vanderbilt University, Tulane University, and the University of Cincinnati (1952–54). His principal areas of research and teaching include: clinical and applied nutrition; the uses of soya in infant and child feeding in Brazil; multidisciplinary approaches to nutrition. Former prorector, University of São Paulo, and dean, Medical School of Ribeirão Preto. Previously, professor of internal medicine, Medical School of Botucatu, State University of São Paulo. Has authored more than 200 professional papers and articles, including: "Vitamin E Nutrition of Newborns and Infants in Brazil," with I. D. Desai and F. E. Martinez, in *Vitamins and Minerals in Pregnancy and Lactation* (1988); "Nutritional Needs Assessment of Rural Agricultural Migrants of Southern Brazil," with coauthors, *World Review of Nutrition and Dietetics* (1988); "Case Study: Marginally Malnourished Migrant Adolescent Boy in Latin America," in *Manual of Patient Problems in Clinical Nutrition* (1987); "Vitamin A Status of Young Children in Southern Brazil," with coauthors, *American Journal of Clinical Nutrition* (1986). President-elect, International Union of Nutrition Sciences, and president of the Latin America Nutrition Society. Consultant to Pan American Health Organization, World Health Organization. Recipient of a Rockefeller fellowship and a Pan American Health Organization fellowship. Born in São Paulo, 1927. Address: Faculdade de Medicina de Ribeirão Preto, 14.049-Ribeirão Preto, Brazil.

Richard R. Harwood

Richard R. Harwood, regional director, Asia, Winrock International Institute for Agricultural Development. Educated at Cornell University (B.Sc. in vegetable crops, 1964) and Michigan State University (M.Sc. and Ph.D. in vegetable breeding, 1966, 1967). Fields of specialization include small-farm systems, multiple cropping, low-input farming, and appropriate technologies. Former deputy director of Winrock International's Technical Cooperation Division, coordinating research and technical support for programs in Nepal, Pakistan, and the Philippines. Former director of Rodale Research Center, Rodale Press, Inc. Taught vegetable gardening, plant breeding, and tropical agriculture at Loma Linda University. Directed the Department of Multiple Cropping at the International Rice Research Institute in the Philippines. Served on field staff of Rockefeller University at Kasetsart University in Thailand, operating the sorghum improvement program. Consultant on projects in Indonesia, India, Tanzania, Bangladesh, and Costa Rica. Author of *Small Farm Development: Understanding and Improving Farming Systems in the Humid Tropics* (1979). Author of numerous articles and papers and a forthcoming monograph, *Lessons from Organic Farming,* with W. C. Liebhardt. Has served on a variety of research and scholarly panels at the National Academy of Sciences, International Agricultural Development Service, U.S. Agency for International Development, and the Office of Technology Assessment. Born in Manchester, N.H., 1937. Address: Winrock International Institute for Agricultural Development, Petit Jean Mountain, Morrilton, AR 72110.

Uma Lele

Uma Lele, chief, Special Studies Division, Country Economics Department, The World Bank. Educated at Ferguson College, University of Chicago, and holds M.S. and Ph.D. degrees from Cornell University. Dr. Lele's work at the World Bank since 1971 has spanned research as well as management: as senior economist for country programming in East Asia and Eastern Africa, and as chief of the Development Strategy Division. Currently oversees a research program of studies of aid, capital flows and development, India's agricultural development, the political economy of agricultural pricing, and managing agricultural development in Africa. The latter, a collaborative study of the World Bank, seven donor agencies, and six African nations, already has resulted in 50 working papers that will be issued as country studies and issues-oriented cross-country monographs. Has been visiting professor at Cornell and at Queens University, Ontario. Serves on the editorial board of *Agricultural Economics,* journal of the International Economic Association. Former chairperson of the Program Committee of the International Voluntary Service. Author of *The Design of Rural Development: Lessons from Africa* (1975, French edition in 1977, 1979); *Food Grain Marketing in India: Private Performance and Public Policy* (1971); *Developing Rural India: Plan and Practice,* with John W. Mellor, Sheldon R. Simon, and Thomas F. Weaver (1968); as well as numerous scholarly articles and papers. Address: The World Bank, 1818 H Street NW, Washington, DC 20433.

John W. Mellor

John W. Mellor, director, International Food Policy Research Institute, Washington, D.C. Educated at Cornell University (B.Sc. 1950, M.Sc. 1951, Ph.D. 1954) and Oxford University. Previously chief economist, U.S. Agency for International Development; professor of economics, agricultural economics, and Asian studies, Cornell. Author, *The Economics of Agricultural Development; The New Economics of Growth: A Strategy for India and the Developing World,* a detailed statement of his concept of an agriculture- and employment-led strategy of growth; and numerous other publications. Edited and contributed chapters to *Agricultural Change and Rural Poverty: Variations on a Theme by Dharm Narain* (with G. M. Desai), *Accelerating Food Production Growth in Sub-Saharan Africa* (with C. Delgado and M. Blackie), *Agricultural Price Policy for Developing Countries* (with R. Ahmed). Contributing editor, *Environment.* Fellow, American Academy of Arts and Sciences, American Agricultural Economics Association. Member, board of directors, Overseas Development Council. Recipient of Presidential End Hunger Award (1987), Wihuri Foundation International Prize (1985), the first social scientist so honored, and American Agricultural Economics Association award (1967, 1978, and 1986) for publications and research. Address: International Food Policy Research Institute, 1776 Massachusetts Avenue NW, Washington, DC 20036.

Sidney W. Mintz

Sidney W. Mintz, William L. Straus, Jr., Professor of Anthropology, The Johns Hopkins University. Educated at Brooklyn College and Columbia University (Ph.D., 1951). Teaching experience includes City College of New York, Columbia, Wesleyan University, École Pratique des Hautes Études, Massachusetts Institute of Technology, Princeton University, Yale University, and the Collège de France. Has engaged in field research in Puerto Rico, Jamaica, Haiti, and Iran, and assisted Ruth Benedict in Columbia University's Research Project on Contemporary Cultures. Holder of numerous fellowships, including Wenner-Gren Foundation, Guggenheim, Social Science Research Council (SSRC), Fulbright, Institute for Advanced Study, Woodrow Wilson, Rockefeller Foundation, and Smithsonian Institution Regents, and lectureships, including the Christian Gauss lectureship at Princeton, Harry Hoijer Memorial lectureship at University of California, Los Angeles, Fulbright distinguished lectureship in India, and McCay Memorial lectureship at Cornell University. Has served as consultant to and officer of a number of institutions, including the Ford Foundation, American Council of Learned Societies, Indian Institute of Technology, National Endowment for the Humanities, SSRC, and American Ethnological Society. Author of *Sweetness and Power* (1985); *An Anthropological Approach to the Afro-American Past: A Caribbean Perspective,* with Richard Price (1976); *Caribbean Transformations* (1974); *Worker in the Cane* (1960); *The People of Puerto Rico,* with Julian H. Steward (1956). Editor of *Caribbean Contours,* with Sally Price (1985); *Working Papers in Haitian Society and Culture* (1975); *Slavery, Colonialism, and Racism* (1974); *Papers in Caribbean Anthropology* (1960). Born in Dover, N.J., 1922. Address: Department of Anthropology, The Johns Hopkins University, Baltimore, MD 21218.

Mohamed A. Nour

Mohamed A. Nour, assistant administrator, United Nations Development Programme, and regional director, Bureau for Arab States and European Programmes, United Nations. Former Minister of Agriculture, Sudan. Former director-general, International Centre for Agricultural Research in the Dry Areas, Aleppo, Syria. Former dean and vice-chancellor, University of Khartoum. Holder of B.Sc. and Ph.D. degrees from Exeter University College, London. Served as assistant director-general of the Food and Agriculture Organization. Member of the International Committee on Agricultural Research, Sudan. Chairman, World Conference on Agricultural Training and Education, Copenhagen. Chairman, First Commission of the World Food Congress, the Netherlands. Served as consultant to Ford and Rockefeller foundations on agricultural programs for African nations. Member of the editorial board, *Tropical Science Journal.* Recipient of an honorary degree in science, University of Khartoum; the Nilein Order, Sudan; and the Republic Order, Egypt. Author of 25 scientific papers published in international journals. Born in Omdurman, Sudan, 1925. Address: United Nations Development Programme, One United Nations Plaza, Room 2228, New York, NY 10017.

Thomas R. Odhiambo

Thomas R. Odhiambo, director, The International Centre of Insect Physiology and Ecology; president, African Academy of Sciences. Educated at Makerere College, Kampala, Uganda, and Cambridge University (B.A., M.A., Ph.D.). Research has focused on natural history and insect endocrinology, particularly in relation to insect reproductive biology, on which more than 100 papers have been written. Has taught at the University of Nairobi since 1965; was first professor of entomology, head of the newly established Department of Entomology, and first dean of the Faculty of Agriculture. Was a visiting professor at universities in Africa and India. Founder and editor-in-chief of book series "Current Themes in Tropical Science"; publisher and editor-in-chief, Scientific Editorial Services, of journal *Insect Science and Its Application*. Appointed in 1967 by UNESCO as consultant on entomology and applied biology. Cofounder and member of the board of trustees, International Federation of Institutes for Advanced Study. Founder of East African Academy of Sciences; fellow, Kenya National Academy of Sciences, Third World Academy of Sciences, Indian National Academy of Sciences, Italian National Academy of the 40s, Pontifical Academy of Sciences, and Royal Norwegian Academy of Science and Letters. Member of international jury, UNESCO Science Prize; member of Club of Rome. Recipient, African Hunger Prize (1987) and Albert Einstein Medal (1979). Born in Mombasa, Kenya, 1931. Address: The International Centre of Insect Physiology and Ecology, P.O. Box 30772, Nairobi, Kenya.

Beatrice Lorge Rogers

Beatrice Lorge Rogers, associate professor of food policy, School of Nutrition, Tufts University. Educated at Radcliffe College (B.A., 1968) and the Florence Heller School for Advanced Studies in Social Welfare, Brandeis University (Ph.D., 1978). Principal research areas include: effects of food price policy on household and individual food consumption; and measurement of intrahousehold allocation of resources in developing countries. Conducted research on household consumption in the Dominican Republic and Mali for the USAID Office of Nutrition; conducted research in the International Nutrition Planning Program at Massachusetts Institute of Technology on economic effects of food distribution systems and consumer food price subsidies in Pakistan; and participated in research projects undertaken by the U.S. Department of Agriculture, UN Food and Agriculture Organization, the World Bank, International Food Policy Research Institute, and USAID, in Thailand, the Philippines, India, and Cameroon. Undertook research on U.S. food programs for the President's Commission on World Hunger in 1979. Author of numerous articles and papers, including: "The Role of Women's Earnings in Determining Child Health," *Food and Nutrition Bulletin* (1987); and *Consumer Food Price Subsidies*, volume 4 of *Nutrition Interventions in Developing Countries* (1980). Serves on the Committee on International Nutrition, National Academy of Sciences, the board of directors of the International Nutrition Foundation for Developing Countries, and was a former member of the editorial board, *Nutrition Planning*. Address: School of Nutrition, Tufts University, 126 Curtis Street, Medford, MA 02155.

Pablo A. Scolnik

Pablo A. Scolnik, research supervisor, Plant Science Section, E. I. du Pont de Nemours & Co. Educated with degrees in biology and biochemistry at the University of Buenos Aires and St. Louis University (Ph.D., 1980). Specialist in plant molecular biology, agricultural biotechnology, and genetics. UNESCO lecturer in plant molecular biology, Rosario, Argentina. Consultant for the Agricultural Biotechnology Program of Ducilo S.A., Argentina. Former staff scientist, Cold Spring Harbor Laboratory; research professor and National Institutes of Health postdoctoral fellow at University of Chicago; research associate at St. Louis University; research assistant at the National Institute of Microbiology in Buenos Aires; and fellow, National Institute of Pharmacology, Buenos Aires. Published articles include: "A Genetic-Physical Map of the *Rhodobacter Capsulatus* Carotenoid Biosynthesis Gene Cluster" (1988); "Genetic Research with Photosynthetic Bacteria" (1987); "Somatic Instability of Carotenoid Biosynthesis in the Tomato Ghost Mutant and Its Effect on Plastid Development" (1987). Address: E. I. du Pont de Nemours & Co., Plant Science Section—CR&D, E402/4231, Wilmington, DE 19898.

Nevin S. Scrimshaw

Nevin S. Scrimshaw, Institute Professor Emeritus, Massachusetts Institute of Technology (MIT), and director, Food and Nutrition Programme, United Nations University, Tokyo. Educated at Ohio Wesleyan University (B.A., 1938), Harvard University (M.A. in biology, 1939; Ph.D. in biology, 1941; M.P.H., 1959), and at the University of Rochester (M.D., 1945). Interned at Gorgas Hospital, Panama, and completed residencies at Strong Memorial and Genesee hospitals in Rochester. Editor, *Food and Nutrition Bulletin*. Founding director, Instituto de Nutrición de Centro América y Panama. Chaired the Department of Nutrition and Food Science and headed the Clinical Research Center at MIT. Directed the Development Studies Division and the

Food, Nutrition, Biotechnology, and Poverty Program of the United Nations University in Tokyo. Former chairman, WHO Advisory Committee on Medical Research and Malnutrition Panel of the U.S.-Japan Cooperative Medical Sciences Program. Former visiting professor, Columbia University, and visiting lecturer, Harvard. Past president of the International Union of Nutrition Sciences. Former trustee of the Rockefeller Foundation. Author of more than 600 publications, including: "The Phenomenon of Famine," *Annual Review of Nutrition* (1987); *Diarrhea and Malnutrition: Interactions, Mechanisms, and Interventions,* editor with Lincoln Chen (1983); *Nutrition and Agricultural Development: Significance and Potential for the Tropics,* editor with Moses Behar (1976); *Nutrition, National Development, and Planning,* editor with Alan Berg and David L. Call (1973); *Interactions of Nutrition and Infection,* with Carl E. Taylor and John E. Gordon (1968). Member, National Academy of Sciences Institute of Medicine and American Academy of Arts and Sciences. Born in Milwaukee, 1918. Address: Center for Population Studies, Harvard School of Public Health, 9 Bow Street, Cambridge, MA 02138.

Aree Valyasevi

Aree Valyasevi, resident coordinator and founding director, United Nations University Institute of Nutrition, Mahidol University, Thailand. Educated and trained in medicine at Siriraj Medical College, Bangkok (M.D., 1951), University of Pennsylvania (M.Sc., 1957, and D.Sc., 1959), and in the University of Pennsylvania Hospital in pediatrics (1957). Founded and served as dean of the Faculty of Medicine and professor of pediatrics, Ramathibody Hospital, Bangkok. Member of the University Council, Mahidol University. Served as president, Federation of Asian Nutrition Societies; vice president, International Union of Nutrition Sciences; as a member of the Expert Committee of the World Health Organization; and as a member of the American Institute of Nutrition and American Clinical Nutrition. Author of more than 80 publications, including: "Pellagra, Beri-beri, and Scurvy," in *Tropical and Geographical Medicine* (1983); "Bladder Stone Disease in Children," in *Advances in International Maternal and Child Health* (1982); "Nutritional Disorders in Thailand" (1979); and "Beri-beri," in *Textbook of Children in the Sub-tropics and Tropics* (1978). Recipient of the Distinguished Research Award, Thai National Research Council (1976); the Dushdi Maha Medal for public service (1983); the nutrition award of the Universität Giessen, Federal Republic of Germany (1985); the research award of the National Research Council of Thailand (1986); and the

Ramon Magsaysay Award (1987). Born in 1925. Address: Institute of Nutrition, Mahidol University, c/o Faculty of Medicine, Ramathibody Hospital, Rama VI Road, Bangkok 10400, Thailand.

John C. Waterlow

John C. Waterlow, professor emeritus of human nutrition, London School of Hygiene and Tropical Medicine, University of London. Educated at Eton College, Trinity College, Cambridge, and London Hospital Medical College. Served on the staff of the Human Nutrition Research Unit, Medical Research Council, in the West Indies, Basutoland, and Gambia. Lecturer in physiology, professor in experimental medicine, and director, Tropical Metabolism Research Unit, University College of the West Indies, Jamaica. Served as consultant physician to the University Hospital of the West Indies and to the University College Hospital, London. Consultant on nutrition, Department of Health and Social Security and the Ministry of Overseas Development, U.K. Has chaired a number of research and consultant panels for the Food and Agricultural Organization, World Health Organization, Pan American Health Organization, Caribbean Medical Research Council. Author of numerous books, articles and papers, including: *Nitrogen Metabolism in Man,* with J. M. L. Stephen (1981); "Crisis for Nutrition" (1981); *Protein Turnover in Mammalian Tissues and in the Whole Body,* with P. J. Garlick and D. J. Millward (1978); "Oxidative Phosphorylation in the Livers of Normal and Malnourished Infants" (1961); "Fatty Liver Disease in the British West Indies" (1948). Holder of honorary degrees from the University of the West Indies and the University of Reading. Fellow of the Royal Society. Charles West lecturer of the Royal College of Physicians. Recipient of the Murgatroyd Prize for tropical medicine; the J. B. Chaudhury Medal, Calcutta School of Tropical Medicine; and Bristol-Myers Prize for Nutrition Research. Born in 1916. Address: 15 Hillgate Street, London W8 7SP, Great Britain.

Pattanee Winichagoon

Pattanee Winichagoon, assistant professor, Mahidol University, Thailand. Received B.Sc. in food technology in 1972; M.S. in nutrition in 1976; at present doctoral candidate in international nutrition at Cornell University. Author of four publications.

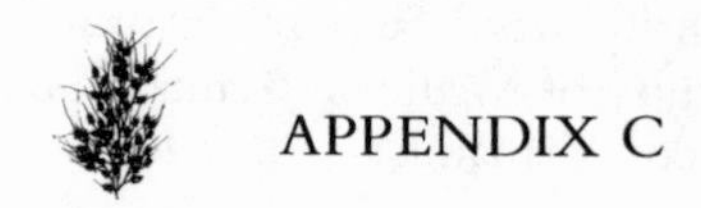

APPENDIX C

List of Colloquium Participants

Alleyne, Dr. George A. O.
Area Director
Health Programs Development
Pan American Health Organization
525 Twenty-third Street, NW
Washington, DC 20037

Ashrey, Dr. Mohamed T.
Vice President for Research & Policy Affairs
World Resources Institute
1735 New York Avenue, NW
Washington, DC 20006

Athwal, Dilbagh S.
Senior Vice President
Winrock International
Route 3, Petit Jean Mountain
Morrilton, AR 72110

Barnett, Joan Burrows
5130 Chevy Chase Parkway, NW
Washington, DC 20008

Bateman, Dr. Durwood
North Carolina State University
Box 7601
Raleigh, NC 27695-7601

Beaton, G. H.
University of Toronto
Faculty of Medicine
Toronto, Ontario, M58 1A8, CANADA

Bell, Rosemaria B.
5046 Silver Hill Court, #2
Suitland, MD 20747

Bender, Filmore
Associate Director
Maryland Agric. Exper. Station
University of Maryland
Symons Hall
College Park, MD 20742

Berg, Dr. Alan
Nutrition Advisor
The World Bank
1818 H Street, NW
Washington, DC 20433

Best, Lorna R.
3311-B Loud Place, SE
Washington, DC 20020

Beyerle, Shaazka M.
Director, Successor Generation Exchange Program
1400 South Joyce Street, #C313
Arlington, VA 22202

Borden, Carla
Senior Program Specialist
Office of Interdisciplinary Studies
SI-T550
Smithsonian Institution
Washington, DC 20560

Borlaug, Dr. Norman E.
Department of Soil & Crop Sciences
Texas A & M University
College Station, TX 77843

Brady, Dr. Nyle C.
Senior Assistant Admin. for Science and Technology
Bureau for Science & Technology
U.S. Agency for International Development
Room 4942, New State Department
Washington, DC 20523

Breth, Steven A.
Program Officer
Winrock International
1611 North Kent Street
Suite 600
Arlington, VA 22209

Brewster, Dr. Allan
Director
World Resources Institute
1750 New York Avenue, NW
Washington, DC 20006

Brush, David M.
General Foods Fund
250 North Street, T12-1
White Plains, NY 10625

Busta, Dr. Frank
Head, Department of Food Science & Nutrition
University of Minnesota
1334 Eckles Avenue
St. Paul, MN 55108

Byerly, Dr. Theodore C.
6-J Ridge Road
Greenbelt, MD 20770

Byrnes, Dr. Frank
Senior Associate
Winrock International
1611 North Kent Street
Arlington, VA 22209

Byrnes, Gregory
Science Magazine
1333 H Street, NW
Washington, DC 20005

Call, David L.
Dean
School of Agriculture & Life Science
122 Roberts Hall
Cornell University
Ithaca, NY 14850-5901

Cante, Dr. Charles J.
Director, Central Research
General Foods Corporation
250 North Street, T12-1
White Plains, NY 10625

Challinor, Dr. David
Science Advisor to the Secretary
National Zoological Park
Education Building
Smithsonian Institution
Washington, DC 20560

Chandler, David C.
6606 West Eighty-first Street
Los Angeles, CA 90045

Chandler, Mrs. David (Nancy)
6606 West Eighty-first Street
Los Angeles, CA 90045

Chandler, Ms. Sara E.
P.O. Box 1369
Westbrook, ME 04092

Chen, Dr. Chia Ting
Senior Industrial Hygienist
U.S. Department of Labor
Room 3718
200 Constitution Avenue, NW
Washington, DC 20210

Chen, Robert
Assistant Professor
World Hunger Program
Brown University
Campus Box 1831
Providence, RI 02912

Chiavarolli, Dr. Eugene
Bureau of Science Adviser
U.S. Agency for International Development
320 Twenty-first Street, NW
Washington, DC 20523

Chicoye, Dr. E.
Director of Research
Miller Brewing
3939 West Highland Boulevard
Milwaukee, WI 53201

Chytil, Dr. Frank
Department of Biochemistry
Tennessee State University
School of Medicine
Light Hall, #535
Nashville, TN 37232

Clausi, Dr. A. S.
Senior Vice President, Retired
General Foods Corporation
250 North Street
White Plains, NY 10625

Coccodrilli, Dr. Gus D. (Bud)
General Foods Corporation
250 North Street
White Plains, NY 10625

Coonrod, Dr. John
Prize Administrator
The Hunger Project
Global Office
One Madison Avenue
New York, NY 10010

Crawford, Dr. Lester
Administrator
Food Safety & Inspection Service
U.S. Department of Agriculture
Room 331 E Administration Building
Washington, DC 20250

Cummings, Dr. Ralph W.
812 Rosemont Avenue
Raleigh, NC 27607

Cylke, Owen
Acting Assistant Administrator
Bureau for Food for Peace and Voluntary Assistance
U.S. Agency for International Development
Washington, DC 20523

Davidson, Frances
Office of Nutrition
Bureau of Science and Technology
U.S. Agency for International Development
320 Twenty-first Street, NW
Washington, DC 20523

Deaton, Dr. Brady
Assistant Dir. for Int'l. Development
Virginia Polytechnic Institute and State University
Blacksburg, VA 24061

de Barros, Barreto Nelson
Universidad Nacional de Paraguay
College of Agronomy
Asuncion, PARAGUAY

Dillon, Dr. Wilton S.
Director
Office of Interdisciplinary Studies
SI-T550
Smithsonian Institution
Washington, DC 20560

Doll, James A.
5826 Dewey Street
Cheverly, MD 20785

Dow, Dr. Michael
National Research Council
2101 Constitution Avenue, NW
Washington, DC 20418

Echave, John
National Geographic
1145 Seventeenth Street, NW
Room 878
Washington, DC 20036

Farrar, Dr. Curtis
Executive Secretary, CGIAR
The World Bank
North Building, Fifth Floor
1818 H Street, NW
Washington, DC 20433

Fontana, Barbara
Director, Agric. & Rural Development
National Governor's Assn.
444 North Capitol Street, NW
Washington, DC 20001

Forristal, Linda
The World and I Magazine
2850 New York Avenue, NE
Washington, DC 20002

Franklin, John W.
Office of Interdisciplinary Studies
Smithsonian Institution
Washington, DC 20560

Gaines, Danee C.
1408 Fourth Street, SW
Washington, DC 20024

Gathright, Vera
Liaison Officer
Int'l. Fund for Agric. Development
1889 F Street, NW
Washington, DC 20006

Gilles, Dr. Kenneth A.
Assistant Secretary
Marketing and Inspection Svcs.
U.S. Department of Agriculture
Room 228-W
Fourteenth Street & Independence Avenue, SW
Washington, DC 20250

Gritzner, Dr. Jefferey
Sr. Assoc., Dir. of Africa Project
World Resources Institute
1735 New York Avenue, NW
Washington, DC 20006

Guardia, Dr. E. J.
General Foods Corporation
250 North Street, T12-1
White Plains, NY 10725

Guthrie, Dr. Helen
Head, Nutrition Program
The Pennsylvania State University
106 Human Development Building
University Park, MD 16802

Hall, Dr. Richard L.
7004 Wellington Court
Baltimore, MD 21212

Hanrahan, Charles
Library of Congress
CRS-ENR
First Street & Independence Avenue, SE
James Madison Bldg., Room 423
Washington, DC 20540

Harris, Renee L.
Director, Information Systems
5526 Volta Avenue
Bladensburg, MD 20710

Havel, Dr. Richard J.
Chairman, Food & Nutrition Board
National Academy of Sciences
Director, Cardio-Vascular Research Inst.
University of Calif. School of Medicine
San Francisco, CA 94143

Havener, Dr. R. D.
President
Winrock International
Route 3, Petit Jean Mountain
Morrilton, AR 72110

Herdt, Dr. Robert
Director
Division for Agricultural Sciences
The Rockefeller Foundation
1133 Avenue of the Americas
New York, NY 20036

Herrera, Mr. Hector
Food Technician Specialist
Organization of American States
1889 F Street, NW
Washington, DC 20006

Higgins, Dr. Brenda C.
Acting Executive Director
League for Int'l. Food Education
915 Fifteenth Street, NW
Washington, DC 20005

Hirschoff, Paula
336 N Street, SW
Washington, DC 20024

Hopper, Dr. Paul
President-Elect
Institute of Food Technology
84 Londonderry Drive
Greenwich, CT 06830

Horwitz, Cecilia de Medici
5504 Dorcett Avenue
Chevy Chase, MD 20815

Hostetler, James C.
Christian Children's Fund, Inc.
1730 North Lynn Street, Suite 403
Arlington, VA 22209

Jimenez, Dr. M. A.
Editor
IFT International Newsletter
1604 Treboy Avenue
Richmond, VA 23226

Johnson, Lynn
National Geographic
1145 Seventeenth Street, NW
Washington, DC 20036

Johnson, Nancy
Miller Meester Advertising
2001 Kilpelrew Drive
Minneapolis, MN 55425

Kates, Dr. Robert W.
Director
World Hunger Program
Brown University, Box 1831
Providence, RI 02910

Kauffman, Dr. Harold E.
Director, Int'l. Soybean Program
College of Agriculture
University of Illinois
113 Mumford Hall
Urbana, IL 61801

Kotler, Dr. Neil
Special Assistant to the Director
Office of Interdisciplinary Studies
Smithsonian Institution
SI-T550
Washington, DC 20560

Koyama, Mr. Kiyosi
Science and Technology Foundation of Japan
Shiseikaikan
1-3 Hibiya-koen
Chiyoda-ku, Tokyo, JAPAN

Kumar, Dr. Surinder
Vice President
Pepsico Research & Tech. Svcs.
100 Stevens Avenue
Valhalla, NY 10595

LaBerge, Cheryl
Acting Director
Office of Conference Services
Smithsonian Institution
Quad 3123
Washington, DC 20560

Landis, Mr. Ronald
Agriculture Br. Chief
NEOB
726 Jackson Place, NW
Washington, DC 20503

Ledford, Dr. Richard A.
Chairman, Department of Food Science
Cornell University
114 Stocking Hall
Ithaca, NY 14853-7201

LeMay, Brian Jacques
International Liaison Officer
International Activities
Smithsonian Institution
Quad 3123
Washington, DC 20560

Lewis, Martha
Director
Women in Development
Partners of the Americas
1424 K Street, NW
Washington, DC 20005

Linko, Prof. Pekka
Dept. of Chemistry
Helsinki University of Technology
SF-02150
Espoo 15, FINLAND

Linowes, Prof. David F.
308 Lincoln Hall
University of Illinois
Urbana, IL 61801

Lopez-Ocana, Carlos
World Resources Institute
1735 New York Avenue, NW
Washington, DC 20006

Marler, Dr. Eric
Director
IBM World Trade Americas
Town of Mount Pleasant
Route 9
North Tarrytown, NY 10591

Mastny, Dr. Catherine L.
6212 Ridge Drive
Bethesda, MD 20816

Mattson, Howard
Executive Director
Institute of Food Technology
221 North LaSalle Street
Chicago, IL 60601

Meier, Albert
Agricultural Division
CIBA-GEIGY
Basel, SWITZERLAND

Miller, Dr. Kenton
Sr. Associate & Program Director
World Resources Institute
1735 New York Avenue, NW
Washington, DC 20006

Milner, Dr. Max
Food and Nutrition Sciences
10401 Grosvenor Place, #721
Rockville, MD 20852

Minners, Dr. Howard A.
Science Advisor
U.S. Agency for International Development
Room 720, SA-18
Washington, DC 20523

Morse, Bradford
411 East Fifty-third Street
New York, NY 10022

Murphy, Hugh T.
Vice President
Finance and Administration
Winrock International
Route 3, Petit Jean Mountain
Morrilton, AR 72110

Nicoilier, Felix
Office of Third World Relations
CIBA-GEIGY
Basel, SWITZERLAND

O'Neill, Peggy
Office of Dr. A. S. Clausi
General Foods Corporation
250 North Street
White Plains, NY 10625

Ordoobadi, Dr. Abbas
International Economic Counsellor
8101 Connecticut Avenue
Chevy Chase, MD 20815

Perry, Dr. Jack
Dean Rusk Program
Davidson College
P.O. Box 1719
Davidson, NC 28036

Pesson, Lynn
Executive Director, BIFAD/S
Room 5314A NS
U.S. Agency for International Development
Washington, DC 20523

Pierson, Merle
Dept. of Food Science & Technology
Virginia Polytechnic Institute and State University
Blacksburg, VA 24061

Pino, Dr. John A.
1515 South Jefferson Highway
Crystal Square Apts., #1203
Arlington, VA 22203

Plucknett, Dr. Donald
The World Bank
1818 H Street, NW
Washington, DC 20433

Rabinowitch, Dr. Victor
National Research Council
2101 Constitution Avenue, NW
Washington, DC 20418

Robarts, Richard C.
Executive Director
Near East Foundation
29 Broadway, Suite 1125
New York, NY 10006

Rodrock, Linda A.
6023 Crocus Court
Alexandria, VA 22310

Ronk, Richard J.
Director
Center for Food Safety & Nutrition
U.S. Department of Health and
Human Services
Federal Building 8, Room 6815
200 C Street, SW
Washington, DC 20204

Rothe, Gail
The World Bank
1818 H Street, NW
Washington, DC 20433

Rumburg, Charles D.
Deputy Administrator
CSRS
U.S. Department of Agriculture
Washington, DC 20250

Sai, Fred
The World Bank
1818 H Street, NW
Washington, DC 20433

Schleidt, Sabine
1901 Columbia Road, NW, #505
Washington, DC 20009

Schmertz, Kennedy
Smithsonian Institution
1100 Jefferson Drive, SW
Washington, DC 20560

Schulz, Bill
Public Affairs Specialist
Office of Public Affairs
Smithsonian Institution
A&I 2410
Washington, DC 20560

Simonelli, Danelle K.
6036 Richmond Highway, #710
Alexandria, VA 22303

Slavik, Mr. Juraj
Program Officer
Meridian House International
1776 Massachusetts Avenue, NW
Washington, DC 20036

Smith, James C.
U.S. Department of Agriculture
Beltsville, MD

Smith, Meredith F.
Dept. of Foods/Nutrition
Kansas State University
Manhattan, KS 66506

Steele, James
Bread for the World
802 Rhode Island Avenue, NE
Washington, DC

Stilkind, Jerry
USIA News Service
301 Fourth Street, SW
Room 456
Washington, DC 20547

Stovall, Dr. John
Chief, Research Division
BIFAD
U.S. Agency for International
Development
Room 5318, New State Department
Washington, DC 20523

Stratford, Suzanne D.
4694B Thirty-sixth Street
Arlington, VA 22206

Strauss, Deborah
Diversity Magazine
727 Eighth Street, SE
Washington, DC 20003

Streit, Peggy
The Hunger Project
World Development Forum
1300 Nineteenth Street, NW, Suite 407
Washington, DC 20036

Stumpf, Samuel E.
Resident Professor
Jurisprudence & Medical Philosophy
Vanderbilt University
Nashville, TN 37240

Sumner, Dan
Senior Economist (Agriculture)
Council of Economic Advisors
Executive Office of the President
Room 317
Washington, DC 20500

Teller, Dr. Charles
Director
Int'l. Nutrition Unit
OIH/DHHS, Suite 205
121 Congressional Lane
Rockville, MD 20852

Temu, Peter E.
Chief
World Food Council
United Nations, Room S-2955
New York, NY 10017

Thacher, Peter
Sr. Counselor
World Resources Institute
1735 New York Avenue, NW
Washington, DC 20006

Timbers, Dr. Gordon E.
Vice Chairman
VIII World Congress of Food Science & Technology
3340 Orlando Drive
Mississauga, Ontario, L4V 1C7, CANADA

Turk, Dr. Kenneth L.
259 Morrison Hall
Cornell University
Ithaca, NY 14853

Turkoz, Ismail Orhan
Counselor, Agricultural Affairs
Embassy of Turkey
2523 Massachusetts Avenue, NW
Washington, DC 20008

Van Orman, Chandler L.
Wheeler & Wheeler
1729 H Street, NW
Washington, DC 20006

von Braun, Dr. Joachim
IFPRI
1776 Massachusetts Avenue, NW
Washington, DC 20036

Wallace, Dr. Ben J.
Professor and Chair
Dept. of Anthropology
Southern Methodist University
Dallas, TX 75275-0336

Wang, Dr. Qing
Beijing Food Research Institute
#3 Hong-tong-xiang
Dong-zong-bu Hutong
Beijing, PEOPLE'S REPUBLIC OF CHINA

White, Heather Little
c/o James Haldeman
P.O. Box 16
Roberts Hall
Cornell University
Ithaca, NY 14853

Wiley, Dr. Robert C.
Chairman, Food Science Program
University of Maryland
Holazpfel Hall, Room 1122A
College Park, MD 20742

Williams, Edward L.
Administrator
General Foods World Food Prize
Winrock International
Route 3, Petit Jean Mountain
Morrilton, AR 72110

Williams, Mollie
Winrock International
1611 North Kent Street, Suite 600
Arlington, VA 22209

Witcher, Renée Michelle
1408 Fourth Street, SW
Washington, DC 20024

Woods, Michael
3524 Highview Place
Falls Church, VA 22044

Yudelman, Dr. Montague
The Conservation Foundation
1250 Twenty-fourth Street, NW
Washington, DC 20037

Zheng Xuan, Madame Zhu
Second Secretary
Embassy of the People's Republic of China
2300 Connecticut Avenue, NW
Washington, DC 20008

About the Editors

Paula M. Hirschoff is an editor-writer specializing in food and development issues. As a newspaper reporter, she received numerous journalistic awards. She also was assistant editor of *Africa Report* magazine and has had articles appear in publications produced by the African Development Foundation and the World Hunger Education Service, among others. She served as a Peace Corps volunteer in Kenya and has traveled extensively in Africa. A former legislative assistant in the U.S. House of Representatives, she was educated at Macalester College in St. Paul, Minnesota.

Neil G. Kotler is special assistant to the director, Office of Interdisciplinary Studies, Smithsonian Institution, and served as program coordinator of the colloquium on which this volume is based. He studied at Brandeis University, the University of Wisconsin, and the University of Chicago, where he received his Ph.D. in political science. He has written and edited articles and books, including *A History of Eritrea*, an outgrowth of his service as a Peace Corps volunteer in Asmara, Ethiopia. He is a former legislative assistant in the U.S. House of Representatives.